Fiction Writers Guidelines

Fiction Writers Guidelines

Over 200 Periodical Editors'
Instructions Reproduced

compiled and edited by
Judy Mandell

McFarland & Company, Inc., Publishers
Jefferson, North Carolina, and London

808.3
M273

Library of Congress Cataloguing-in-Publication Data

Mandell, Judy, 1939–
Fiction writers guidelines.

Includes index.
1. Fiction—Authorship. I. Title.
PN3355.M26 1988   808.3   88-45206

ISBN 0-89950-249-0 (pbk.; 50# acid-free natural paper) ∞

Printed in the United States of America.

McFarland & Company, Inc., Publishers
Box 611, Jefferson, North Carolina 28640

For Jerry, Jim,
Pam, and Scott

Table of Contents

Magazines That Accept Freelance Contributions But Have No Writer's Guidelines   307

Index   311

Preface

Fiction Writers Guidelines includes guidelines prepared by the editors of two hundred and thirty-one magazines that publish fiction as well as comments from the editors of fifteen additional publications that do not provide guidelines but do accept freelance contributions. The book should be a useful tool for novice and professional writers, students, scholars, and teachers of writing. It also provides a behind-the-scenes look at the editorial policies of magazines.

The compilation includes magazines found on large and comprehensive newsstands, periodicals sold on a subscription basis only, and literary magazines. The little literaries may serve as springboards for novice writers, while the larger, more prestigious magazines provide outlets for well-established writers of fiction.

All fiction writers will find this compilation of guidelines extremely useful. This book should help the writer who is uncertain about where to send the work he or she has written as well as the writer who already has the periodical in mind but doesn't quite know the requirements of the publication. Even if the author has thoroughly read the magazine and thinks he's figured out its tone, style, content, and readership, he's better off knowing exactly what the magazine's editors have to say about what they want from freelancers.

I wish to thank the magazine editors who encouraged me in this project and sent me their fiction writer's guidelines for publication in this book.

I'm equally grateful to the editors of magazines that do not provide guidelines but do accept freelance contributions, whose interviews and contributions provided valuable material for the readers of this compilation.

And thanks again, Jerry.

Judy Mandell
Earlysville, Virginia

The Guidelines

ABORIGINAL SF

P.O. Box 2449, Woburn, MA 01888-0849

Writer's guidelines

1. All stories must be in English. Stories submitted from foreign countries should first be translated into English. Stories sent from the Bronx also should be translated before submission.

2. All stories should be typed or printed, double-spaced, on one side of a sheet of white regular-sized paper (8½ by 11 inches). Good dot-matrix printing is acceptable. Computer printouts which haven't been separated into individual sheets will be considered replacements rolls of TP. Good quality photocopies are acceptable. Simultaneous submissions are *not* acceptable.

3. All submissions must be accompanied by a self-addressed envelope large enough for the manuscript's return and with adequate postage for that return. Manuscripts sent without proper return postage will not be returned. *Aboriginal Science Fiction* assumes no responsibility for submissions, lost manuscripts or lost horizons. We respond within 3 to 4 weeks on most submissions. Occasionally we take as long as 8 weeks.

Manuscript requirements

1. *Aboriginal Science Fiction* will only consider original science fiction stories or science fiction poetry. We buy first North American serial rights and do not use reprints. Stories should be between 2,500 and 4,500 words in length, though some exceptions may be made. Poetry should be one to two pages, typed, double-spaced. Payment will be $200 for stories; $15 to $25 for each poem. *Aboriginal Science Fiction* also accepts cartoons and jokes. Jokes should be 50 to 150 words in length and be on a science, or science fiction topic. We pay $5 for jokes and $15 for cartoons. All stories, poems, jokes and/or cartoons *must* be original and previously unpublished.

2. *Aboriginal Science Fiction* is looking for good science fiction stories. While "hard" science fiction will get the most favorable attention, *Aboriginal Science Fiction* also wants good action-adventure stories, *good* space opera and science fantasy. We also use at least one humorous science fiction story in each issue. Stories with the best chance of acceptance will make unique use of the latest scientific theories and discoveries, have lively, convincing characters, an ingenious plot, a powerful and well-integrated theme and use an imaginative setting.

3. Do not submit fantasy, sword & sorcery, horror or Twilight Zone-type stories. They will not be accepted. Queries are unnecessary. We do not serialize novels, but we may consider a *short* excerpt from a novel. Do not send the entire novel; just send the excerpt — which should stand on its own as a separate story.

4. We recommend you read *Aboriginal Science Fiction* to obtain an idea of the type of stories we publish and we also recommend you read other science fiction magazines. Watching science fiction on television or at the movies will not provide adequate background to write a good science fiction story.

5. Sample copies are available for $3.00. Those who wish, may subscribe at the special discounted rate for writers: $10 for 6 issues; $20 for 12 issues; or $28 for 18 issues. (The regular rate is: $12 for 6 issues; $22 for 12 issues; or $30 for 18 issues.) The discounted rate for writers or artists who are not residents of the United States is: $13 for 6 issues, $26 for 12 issues, or $37 for 18 issues. All copies are mailed second class. Likewise, residents of foreign countries should add $0.50 per copy to any sample copy orders. Back issues sell for $3.50.

Good luck,
The Editors

Writer's guide

Action!

for ACTION and EVANGEL
Department of Christian Education
901 College Avenue
Winona Lake IN 46590

Action!

is an 8-page take-home paper for children in grades 4-5-6, and needs stories about children in that age bracket. Because the paper's purpose is to supplement and strengthen the concepts learned in Sunday school, each story must have a Christian frame of reference, and should deal with a moral or ethical choice confronting the hero. Situations at home, in school, or on the playground should provide lots of possibilities for action and dialogue.

THE STORY PROBLEM must have significance (be worth worrying about), and the hero who copes with it must be a believable person, with a few weaknesses to balance his strengths. Fiction is limited to 1,000 words, for which we pay $25.

SHORT FEATURES (300-500 words) are also needed. Craft instructions (with photo or sketch), nature oddities, and interviews with children are highly prized, and rewarded with $15. A photo-interview can be about the child's pet, unusual experience, or some special project.

BRIEF NATURE POEMS are accepted for $5. Cartoons $10.

evangel

is an 8-page take-home paper for young adults, and needs stories about young people involved in family and/or occupational crises. Fiction is expected to show how Christ can help a person make satisfactory decisions in practical, everyday affairs, but these improved judgments cannot come easily. The tension between opposite possibilities must be strong to be believable. Stories need not end "happily." However, the implications of a better solution should be clear. Fiction between 1200-1500 words; payment is $35-$40.

PERSONAL EXPERIENCE articles are the favorite type of non-fiction (1000 words-$25).

Preferred stories are those about God's help in crisis situations, giving hope to readers who may face a similar crisis. Relationships, family budgeting, work problems are likely topics. Remember, anecdotes and dialogue add color.

SHORT, filler-type (300-500 words) devotional items are also welcome. These should be centered around a single idea or incident which leads into a brief, cogent observation about life and/or God. $10-$12.

POEMS may be about nature, the human experience, or about God. They should be tightly focused, and present a single, sharp picture. Concrete words are preferred over abstractions, to appeal to the reader's emotion or thought. Five dollars for a poem.

HOW TO IMPRESS AN EDITOR

THE FIRST CLUE to hit the editor's desk is the stamped, self-addressed return envelope that pops out of your just-opened script. This means the editor is dealing with a professional! (We cannot return scripts without a return envelope.) Next thing noticed is the name and address typed in the upper left corner of page one, and the word count in the upper right. A pro, for sure. Starting the story halfway down page one gives the editor room to mark instructions for the printer.

NO EDITOR can help being impressed by black, clean type on fresh, untattered paper. (Editors know you have to circulate scripts to many magazines in order to stay in business, but when a script becomes yellow with age and crumbles as it comes out of the envelope, it's time for retyping.) Scripts of one to five pages should be folded twice and mailed in a number-10 envelope; 6 to 10 pages should be folded once and mailed in a 6 x 9 envelope. Only larger scripts should be shipped flat. (Proper shipping preserves freshness.)

PAYMENT is made "on publication." Actually, your check should arrive at the time your story goes to press: from three months ahead for EVANGEL to nine months ahead for ACTION.

We hope to find a script from you soon!

Aim Magazine

AIM MAGAZINE (I,II) 7308 S. Eberhart Ave., Chicago IL 60619. (312)874-6184. Editor Ruth Apilado. Fiction Editor Mark Boone. Newspaper: 81/2x11; 48 pages; slick paper; photos and illustrations. "Material of social significance: down-to-earth gut. Personal experience, inspirational." For "high school, college and general public."Quarterly. Published special fiction issue last year; plans another. Estab. 1973. Circ. 10,000

Needs: Open. No "religious " mss. Receives 25 unsolicited mss/month. Buys 15 mss/issue; 60 mss/year. Recently published work by Lynda Jackson. Published new writers within the last year. Length 800-1,000 words average. Publishes short shorts. Sometimes comments on rejected mss.

How To Contact: Send complete ms. SASE. Simultaneous submissions OK. Accepts computer print-out submissions. Sample copy for $2.50 with SAE (8x111/2) and 65 cts postage. Fiction guidelines for regular envelope and 1 first class stamp.

Payment: Pays $15-$25.

Terms: Pays on publication for first rights.

Advice: "Search for those in your community who are making unselfish contributions to their community and write about them. Write from the heart. We encourage writers, and have published new writers within the last year."

Aim Magazine Short Story Contest (I), Box 20554, Chicago, IL 60619. (312) 874-6184. Contact Ruth Apilado and Mark Boone, publisher and fiction editor. Estab. 1984. Contest likely to be offered annually when money is available. "To encourage and reward good writing in the short story form. The contest is particularly for new writers." Unpublished submissions. Award: $100 plus publication in fall issue. "Judged by *Aim's* editorial staff." Contest rules for SASE. "We're looking for compelling, well written stories with lasting social significance."

The Alaska Quarterly Review

CALL FOR MANUSCRIPTS

The Alaska Quarterly Review, a new journal devoted to contemporary literary art, and published biannually by the College of Arts and Sciences, University of Alaska, Anchorage, invites submissions in the following areas:

- fiction and poetry, traditional and experimental styles
- literary criticism and reviews, emphasis on contemporary literature
- literary philosophy, articles on the relation between contemporary philosophy and contemporary literature (structuralist poetics and semiotic)

Send manuscripts SASE to: Editors, *The Alaska Quarterly Review*, Department of English, University of Alaska, 3221 Providence Drive, Anchorage, Alaska 99508

SUBSCRIPTIONS

Price: Individual copies $4.00; Individual yearly, $8.00; Institutional, $10.00

NAME _____ ADDRESS _____

CITY _____ STATE _____ ZIP _____

Single copy_____ Subscription_____ Amount Enclosed_____

Please make checks payable to *Alaska Quarterly Review*.

ALFRED HITCHCOCK's
MYSTERY MAGAZINE ®

Thank you for your request for these Writer's Guidelines. We hope that what follows will be helpful to you in submitting manuscripts to AHMM.

<u>Content.</u> Since this is a mystery magazine, the stories we buy must fall into that genre in some sense or another. We are interested in nearly every kind of mystery, however: stories of detection of the classic kind, police procedurals, private eye tales, suspense, courtroom dramas, stories of espionage, and so on. You should feel free to write in any of these sub-genres; we ask only that the story be about a crime (or perhaps the threat of one). We occasionally accept ghost stories or supernatural tales, but those should also involve crime.

We are not particularly interested in "gothics," though, or science fiction, or horror stories, or those involving such creatures as vampires or werewolves, even though any of the foregoing may include crime or crime-solving.

You might, by the way, find it useful to read one or more issues of AHMM; that should give you an idea of the kind of fiction we buy.

<u>Style.</u> The stories should not be longer than 14,000 words; most of the stories in the magazine are considerably shorter than that. They should, of course, be well-written. We are looking for stories that have not been previously published elsewhere, and among them for those that are fresh, well-told, and absorbing. They should also be entirely fictional: please do not send us stories based on actual crimes, for instance.

<u>Manuscript Preparation.</u> Manuscripts should be typed on plain white paper (not erasable paper, please) and double spaced (not space-and-a-half), with your name and address at the top of the first page. If you use a word processor, we prefer that you do not justify the right-hand margin. All the stories should be mailed to us flat, with the pages bound together by a paper clip only -- not stapled or enclosed in a binder of any sort. A cover letter isn't necessary. If you want to have the manuscript returned in the event we cannot use it, you must include a stamped, self-addressed envelope; contributors outside the U.S.A should send International Reply Coupons (available at the post office) in lieu of stamps. If you have sent us a photocopy and do not want it back, please advise us of that and enclose a smaller SASE for notification of rejection. We would also like to ask that revised versions of a story be submitted only on request.

Finding new authors is a great pleasure for all of us here, and we look forward to reading the fiction you send us. In the meantime, thank you again for your inquiry.

380 LEXINGTON AVENUE • NEW YORK, NY 10017 212•557•9100

Patrick Lucien Price
Editor

P.O. Box 110
Lake Geneva
WI 53147

(414) 248-3625

Dear Author:

AMAZING® Stories is published on a bimonthly basis. Each issue of AMAZING Stories contains a wide variety of materials of interest to the science-fiction and fantasy reader. The magazine covers the range of imaginative fiction, from the hardest science to the purest fantasy. It also includes thematic reviews of important science-fiction and fantasy books and films, science-fact articles, interviews with or essays by contemporary authors, letters from the readers, and portfolios by leading artists.

We seek a variety of science-fiction and fantasy themes: hard, speculative, militaristic, or anthropological science stories; space fantasy or opera; high, heroic, ethnic, or contemporary fantasy. However, we are not interested in straight horror or supernatural tales. We specifically seek those stories that present a fascinating scientific or fantastic premise with a character-oriented focus. Be aware, though, that the ratio of science fiction to fantasy in AMAZING Stories is about 3 to 1.

Submitted fiction should be written for an adult audience. However, extensive use of obscene language or sexually explicit detail is not well received by the editorial staff.

We publish short stories, poetry, and nonfiction. A query should be made on serialized fiction and novel excerpts, since these are rarely published in the magazine. For nonfiction articles, queries should be addressed to Martin H. Greenberg, in care of AMAZING Stories. Seven to ten fiction submissions are published per issue; for poetry, five to seven poems, and for nonfiction, one or two articles.

Fiction submissions should run between 500 and 25,000 words in length, although we will consider longer pieces if a query is made prior to submission. Poems should not exceed 30 lines in length. Payment rates for fiction are 5 to 8 cents per word; for poetry, $1 per line. Payment is made upon acceptance for first North American serial rights. Two complimentary copies will be sent to the author upon publication of the work. Notice of acceptance or rejection is made within 60 days.

All submissions and query letters must include a self-addressed, stamped envelope. In no instance can AMAZING Stories assume responsibility for manuscripts or letters not specifically solicited.

Thank you for your interest in AMAZING Stories. Please, address all fiction and poetry submissions to my attention.

All the very best,

AMELIA

329 "E" Street
Bakersfield, California 93304

Frederick A. Raborg, Jr., Editor

WRITERS' GUIDELINES

The best guideline to any magazine's very particular needs is, of course, a copy of the magazine itself. Single copies of AMELIA are available for $5.95 ppd. Single copies of Cicada or SPSM&H are $3.50 ppd. Annual subscriptions to AMELIA are $20 one year, $38 two years, $56 three years. Annual subscriptions to Cicada or SPSM&H are $12 one year, $20 two years. Foreign subscribers to AMELIA should add $12 per year airmail postage; subscribers to Cicada or SPSM&H for foreign delivery should add $3 per year.

AMELIA uses perhaps more traditional fiction and poetry than any other small press magazine published today, but we also look for the fresh and innovative as well. Many of our writers appear regularly in such top magazines as The New Yorker, Atlantic, Redbook and the finer university and small press journals, but we introduce new writers in every issue.

FICTION: We look for depth of plot and strong characterization in stories of any type to 4,500 words. A piece would have to be exceptional to exceed that length. We use science fiction, romance and Gothic horror as well as mainstream. We like to have the feeling of "the whole world" in storylines. Read the works of Ben Brooks, Florri McMillan and Lawrence P. Spingarn, perhaps, to get a strong feeling for the kinds of in-depth writing we like. Payment: $35 plus two copies for First North American Serial Rights only. You may also be interested in our three annual short fiction awards and our annual book-length fiction award. See Cicada & SPSM&H under poetry.

POETRY: We look for a strong sense of kinship with the reader, even a "storyline," a feeling of importance and worth, stance and control in our poetry, any form to 100 lines. We use perhaps 12 haiku in every issue--often the best of those submitted routinely for Cicada. We use all of the traditional forms, and the experimental within those forms. As with Cicada, often we will select the finest sonnets received for SPSM&H to be included in AMELIA. Cicada uses only haiku, and other Japanese forms of poetry, plus fiction and essays relating to Japan or its poetry. SPSM&H uses only sonnets, single or in sequence, plus fiction or essays related to the form. Please indicate on your envelopes to which magazine you are submitting. Payment: In AMELIA, $2-$25 plus two contributor copies; in Cicada, three "best of issue" poets each receive $10 on publication; in SPSM&H, two "best of issue" poets each receive $14 on publication. We are unable to offer free copies to Cicada and SPSM&H, due to their specialized nature.

BELLES LETTRES: We like to use one belle lettre in each issue, any topic including fictional vignettes, to 2,000 words. See the work of Ruth Shigezawa as a good example. Payment: $10 per 1,000 words for First North American Serial Rights only, plus two copies.

TRANSLATIONS: We use translations of excellent quality of both fiction and poetry in above lengths. Copies or photocopies of the original work must accompany each piece, along with a biographical sketch for both the author and translator. Payment: In most cases, the same as for similar categories above, plus two contributor copies.

CRITICISM: We use one critical essay in every issue, approximately
    2,500 words. Essays may evolve from any discipline but must
    be related to literature, and preferably to literature as it
    affects small press. Submissions may be included in theses
    or dissertations not yet completed for degree consideration,
    but none may have been previously published. We use only
    First North American Serial Rights. Payment: $25, plus two
    contributor copies.

BOOK REVIEWS: We welcome review copies of small press books and,
    if we are unable to give extensive review space to a particular
    title, mention each with an informative comment. We do consider
    tightly written reviews of important works from the small press
    on a speculative basis. If the subject book is published by a
    major house, it ought to relate in some way to the small press
    scene. Payment: $10 for First North American Serial Rights,
    plus two contributor copies. Assigned books bring slightly more,
    plus the edition reviewed.

OTHER: We like to be surprised. Give me something excellent which
    I haven't touched on above and I'll take it too. We frequently
    use prose poems, for instance. We also use avant-garde and
    esoterica when quite good. Though we do not wish to see the
    pornographic, we do use well-made erotica. We do not shy away
    from strong language, but we are not a gutter either. We use
    ethnic work, the work of inmates and gay/lesbian material which
    approach subjects with degrees of subtlety and conviction. Do
    not try to shock us for shock's sake: in all likelihood it has
    already been done.

    Illustrations: Because some of you are also artists, bear in mind
    that we also use many b/w spot drawings, more fully realized b/w
    illustrations--fine pen & ink or line--, sophisticated cartoons
    and b/w photos with or without captions. We pay $5-$25 on assign-
    ment to a particular issue, depending on use, size and relationship
    to editorial content. We do consider color for the covers, but
    they have been assigned four issues ahead. See The Artist's Market
    1986 for a more complete description of our needs and rates.

PLEASE NOTE: We are very proud of our record to date: Pattiann Rogers'
    fine poem, "The Objects of Immortality," published in our premiere
    issue, was selected for Pushcart Prizes X. Several of our poets
    were reprinted in Anthology of Magazine Verse & Yearbook of American
    Poetry; and H. E. Knickerbocker's illustration from our April 1985
    issue was reprinted in The Artists Market 1986. We introduce new
    writers in every issue and are proud of their progress. G. Y.
    Jennings' first story sale appeared in our April 1985 issue, and he
    has since published in Westways, Yachting and Sail.

    It is important that you read at least one issue of any magazine
    for which you would like to write. When you succeed with us, we
    are as delighted as you are. Now, let us see some of your work.

                                    Frederick A. Raborg, Jr.
                                    Editor, AMELIA Magazine

RECOMMEND US TO YOUR UNIVERSITY OR CITY LIBRARIES. SUPPORT SMALL PRESS.

The Danish Brotherhood in America
NATIONAL HEADQUARTERS · 3717 HARNEY STREET · OMAHA, NEBRASKA 68131

GUIDELINES FOR CONTRIBUTORS

TO

"THE AMERICAN DANE" MAGAZINE

The American Dane magazine is the official monthly publication of the Danish Brotherhood in America, a nationwide fraternal benefit organization of approximately 10,000 members.

The American Dane seeks ethnic poetry, prose, puzzles, children's stories and photographs geared toward a conservative, family-oriented Danish-American audience. Material submitted without a Danish ethnic interest will be rejected, as will material the editor feels is in poor taste morally, politically, religiously, or literarily.

a) Word length - no minimum, maximum of 1,500 words.

b) All submissions must be typewritten, double-spaced, and can only be returned if accompanied by a self-addressed, stamped envelope.

c) Submissions should be received by August of the current year for scheduling publication in issues for the following year.

d) Payment will be made upon publication in a lump sum to be determined by the editor.

   Payment rates -- Prose -   maximum $50.00
                    Poetry - maximum $35.00
                    Photos - maximum $20.00
                    Puzzles - maximum $15.00

   (Payment to contributors is limited to a total amount per issue.)

e) Manuscripts with strong visuals (photos, art, etc.) are preferred. No additional fee above the maximum rate will be paid.

f) The American Dane magazine purchases first rights only. All rights to the material revert to the contributor following publication.

   Copyrighted material will be accepted only with signed permission of the contributor.

g) Photographs should reflect the magazine's editorial policies - black and white preferred.

We appreciate your interest in contributing to The American Dane and hope we will be able to publish your material to your and our mutual satisfaction.

CGAD-86

AMERICAN SQUARE DANCE

"THE NATIONAL MAGAZINE WITH THE SWINGING LINES"

**P.O. Box 488
HURON, OHIO
44839**

Phone: 419-433-2188
or 433-5043

**UPS & DELIVERIES:
216 WILLIAMS ST.
HURON, OHIO 44839**

Stan & Cathie Burdick

Editors, Publishers

CC–2

Media Code 8 195 0400 2.00

Published monthly by Burdick Enterprises, P.O. Box 488,
Huron, Ohio. Phone: 419-433-2188.

Publisher's Editorial Profile

American Squaredance Magazine is designed for the modern square
dancer. Special features cover a wide range of topics of
interest to dancers, teachers, callers and leaders in the square
dance movement. National coverage of conventions, interviews
with square dance personalities and a choreography workshop
section are included. Regular features include reviews of new
square and round dance records, news of new products available
on the square dance market, profiles of square dance festivals
and vacations, and articles devoted to round dancing.

Words: 600 to 900 preferable.

Style: Serious or light; fact or fiction features; prose or
poetry; informative features about program, personalities, and
places where dancing flourishes anywhere are especially sought.
Photos accompanying stories are very welcome.

Format for submission: Double spaced, typewritten copy.

Compensation: $1.00 per column inch of printed copy (magazine
is 5½"x 8½") or minimum of $10.00 per printed page when photos,
art, titles, or white space is used for special effects.

Write: Stan and Cathie Burdick
Co-editors

PHOTOS WELCOME Square Dance subject matter only. Rates: $5.
$10. $25.   Black and white glossy preferred.

ART WORK AND CARTOONS Square dance subject matter only. $10.
for cartoons; range of $35. – $50. for cover art.

THE AMERICAN VOICE

THE AMERICAN VOICE, The Kentucky Foundation for Women, Inc., Suite 1215, Heyburn Building, at 4th Ave., Louisville KY 40202. (502)562-0045. Editor: Frederick Smock. A quarterly literary magazine "for readers of varying backgrounds and educational levels, though usually college-educated. We aim to be an eclectic reader—to define the American voice in all its diversity, including writers from Canada, the U.S., and South America." Estab. 1985. Circ. 1,500. Pays on publication. Publishes ms an average of 3 months after acceptance. Byline given. Offers 50% kill fee. Buys first North American rights. Photocopied submissions OK. Computer printout submissions acceptable; prefers letter-quality to dot-matrix. Reports in 1 month on queries; 2 months on mss. Sample copy $3.50; writer's guidelines for SASE.

Nonfiction: Essays, opinion, photo feature, and criticism. Buys 10 mss/year. Send complete ms. Length: 10,000 words maximum. Pays $400/essay; $150 to translator. Sometimes pays the expenses of writers on assignment.

Fiction: Buys 30 mss/year. Send complete mss. Pays $400/story; $150 to translator.

Poetry: Avant-garde and free verse. Buys 40 poems/year. Submit maximum 10 poems. Pays $150/poem; $75 to translator.

Tips: "We are looking only for vigorously original fiction, poetry, and essays, from new and established writers, and will consider nothing that is in any way sexist, racist or homophobic."

Broadway at 4th Avenue, Heyburn Suite 1215
Louisville, KY 40202

GUIDELINES FOR THE PRESENTATION OF MANUSCRIPTS TO AMERICAS

Américas magazine and the OAS

Américas is a bimonthly publication of the Organization of American States issued in separate language editions of English and Spanish. As an organ of the OAS, it is not a commercial enterprise and does not carry advertising. Américas is apolitical in content and seeks to advance mutual understanding among the peoples of the Western Hemisphere. It is a general interest magazine focusing on OAS member nations that contains the work of writers from all parts of the Hemisphere. Its articles are abundantly illustrated with black and white as well as color photographs.

Type of Articles Desired
The articles in each issue cover a wide variety of topics including anthropology and archaeology, history, literature, the visual arts (pre-Columbian, colonial, modern) and the performing arts, architecture, travel, wildlife, science and technology, socioeconomic development and interviews. A short story contest and a photography contest are annual features.

Américas is especially interested in articles that emphasize what is happening in the Hemisphere today, and those people who are making it happen. OAS member countries include: Antigua and Barbuda, Argentina, Barbados, Bolivia, Brazil, Chile, Colombia, Commonwealth of Dominica, Commonwealth of the Bahamas, Costa Rica, Cuba, the Dominican Republic, Ecuador, El Salvador, Grenada, Guatemala, Haiti, Honduras, Jamaica, Mexico, Nicaragua, Panama, Paraguay, Peru, Saint Kitts and Nevis, Saint Lucia, Saint Vincent and the Grenadines, Suriname, Trinidad and Tobago, the United States, Uruguay and Venezuela. Articles focus heavily on Latin American and Caribbean members and very rarely cover U.S. topics unless they have some Latin American or Caribbean tie-in.

Américas is not a news magazine; articles should not report on events as news, but rather focus on their broader implications. Highly technical articles and articles of limited and local interest are not used.

Readers of Américas are of diverse cultural backgrounds--writers should keep in mind that what is common knowledge in one country is not necessarily so in others. For example, a figure who might be well-known in his own country may be little-known even in a neighboring country. For this reason, brief identifications, including full name, occupation and nationality, should be provided or included in the text for each person or reference mentioned.

Submitting Manuscripts
Articles may be submitted in English, Spanish, Portuguese or French. (Américas provides translations.) Manuscripts must be unpublished and should be approximately 8-10 typewritten, letter-sized pages in length, double spaced (2,500 words maximum). We do not accept multiple submissions. The focus of Américas is unique, and articles written for other publications generally will not work for us.

Américas relies heavily on freelance contributors. Authors are requested to query the editors regarding specific topic suggestions before submitting manuscripts. All articles are received only on speculation, and decisions on publication are made by the editors. Américas reserves the right to edit articles for style and length.

- 2 -

If a manuscript is accepted, a modest honorarium will be paid upon publication, necessarily limited by Américas' character as a nonprofit enterprise. A minimum of $200 is paid for a full-length article. Checks are issued in U.S. dollars for authors residing in or possessing bank accounts in the United States, or in the national currencies of the countries where authors live abroad.

Américas is copyrighted, and no part of the magazine may be reproduced without prior written permission. In special cases we make material available for reprint at no cost to nonprofit cultural and educational institutions.

A selection of professional-quality 8x10 black and white photos or color transparencies should accompany the text. If illustrations are unavailable, suggestions for possible sources of photos, engravings and so on are requested. Preference will be given to manuscripts received with excellent illustrations. Payment for the use of graphic materials is usually made separately from the article payment and also is made upon publication.

Quotations that have been translated must be accompanied by the text in the original language, and the source must be noted. Américas does not use footnotes, so explanatory material should be incorporated into the text. To facilitate translation, Américas requests that authors provide titles of published works in the original language and of any published translations; names in the original language of places, buildings, private and government organizations; and Latin names of flora and fauna, along with their local names.

Authors should provide a brief biographical paragraph to serve as the basis for an author's note.

Manuscripts should be sent to:

    Américas Editors
    Organization of American States
    Washington, D.C.   20006

Manuscripts are acknowledged upon receipt. (Self-addressed stamped envelopes are not required.) Photographs and other illustrative material are returned after publication when requested.

                                        November 1986

380 LEXINGTON AVENUE • NEW YORK, N.Y. 10017 • 212-557-9100

Analog will consider material submitted by any writer, and consider it solely on the basis of merit. We are definitely anxious to find and develop new, capable writers.

We have no hard-and-fast editorial guidelines, because science fiction is such a broad field that I don't want to inhibit a new writer's thinking by imposing Thou Shalt Nots. Besides, a really good story can make an editor swallow his preconceived taboos.

Basically, we publish <u>science</u> fiction stories. That is, stories in which some aspect of future science or technology is so integral to the plot that, if that aspect were removed, the story would collapse. Try to picture Mary Shelley's <u>Frankenstein</u> without the science and you'll see what I mean. No story!

The science can be physical, sociological, psychological. The technology can be anything from electronic engineering to biogenetic engineering. But the stories must be strong and realistic, with believable people (who needn't be human) doing believable things-- no matter how fantastic the background might be.

Manuscripts must be typed, double-spaced, on white typewriter paper, one side of the sheet only. <u>Good</u> quality computer printout with these characteristics is fine, but please separate the sheets. Author's name and address should be on the first page of the manuscript. No material submitted can be returned unless accompanied by sufficient postage, stamped addressed envelope, or International Reply Coupons.

Analog pays 5.75-7.0 cents per word for short stories up to 7,500 words, $430-525 for stories between 7,500 and 12,500 words, and 3.5-4.6 cents per word for longer material. We prefer lengths between 2,000 and 7,000 words for shorts, 10,000-20,000 words for novelettes, and 40,000-80,000 for serials.

Please query first on serials <u>only</u>. A complete manuscript is strongly preferred for all shorter lengths.

The entire contents of each issue is copyrighted at the time of publication. Payment is on acceptance.

Good luck!

Stanley Schmidt
Editor

Another Chicago Magazine
Box 11223
Chicago IL 60611

312/524-1289
312/248-7665

GUIDELINES FOR WRITERS

- All manuscripts should be typed. Fiction manuscripts should be double-spaced.

- Manuscripts will not be returned unless accompanied by a self-addressed, stamped envelope.

- Name and address of author should appear on each work. Name and page number (and sometimes title) should appear on each page of multi-paged works.

- We attempt to read and decide on all work within six (6) weeks. If we keep your manuscript longer, it's generally a sign that we are tempted by it. We do not read manuscripts during August nor during December. Manuscripts received during those months will be held and read in the following month. If we've held your work longer than six weeks, feel free to write us; it's always possible that a manuscript has been lost in the mail.

- If we accept your work for publication, we understand that you have given first serial rights to ACM. All future rights to the work are yours. A copy of ACM will be on file with the Copyright Office, Library of Congress, for your future reference.

- We accept the fact that publication is crucial to an author's success. To help authors, we encourage simultaneous submissions to various magazines. However, we expect to be notified at once if you are withdrawing a submission from us, and we insist that if we accept a work for publication, unless notified within a week of receipt of acceptance notice, that work will not be withdrawn, and will not be published in another periodical prior to its appearance in ACM. If we publish your work, we expect that ACM will receive acknowledgement in any subsequent publication of the work.

- We pay a small (barely token) honorarium upon acceptance.

We are interested in work which goes beyond the purely personal and engages the world in both subject and form. We are interested in work which tries to do something new; which is ambitious rather than safely "crafted."

Buy a copy and find out.

ANTAEUS · THE ECCO PRESS

Dear Writer:

Thank you for your letter requesting
guideline information.

When submitting a manuscript to Antaeus, it
is a good idea to enclose a selection of
five to eight poems or one short story.
Please include a self-addressed, stamped
envelope with each submission. Our usual
reporting time is six to eight weeks. If
you would like to be notified of the arrival
of your manuscript, please enclose a
self-addressed, stamped postcard.

ALWAYS ENCLOSE A SELF-ADDRESSED STAMPED
ENVELOPE (make sure that it is large enough
to contain your manuscript) FOR THE RETURN
OF YOUR MANUSCRIPT.

We appreciate your interest in Antaeus and
hope to read some of your work soon.

Sincerely,

The Editors

Antietam Review

A Journal of Creative Writing and Photography
Published by the Washington County, Maryland, Arts Council

33 West Washington Street, Hagerstown, Maryland 21740

Telephone (301) 791-3125

GUIDELINES FOR WRITERS AND PHOTOGRAPHERS

ANTIETAM REVIEW is a regional literary and photography journal published twice a year by the Washington County Arts Council. We use short fiction, poems, and black and white photographs that have not been published previously..

To submit you must live in, or be a native of, our region--Maryland, Virginia, Pennsylvania, West Virginia and Washington, D.C.

We consider materials from October 1 to March 1 each year.

FICTION

We are looking for high-quality literary fiction under 5,000 words. We prefer short stories, but will consider anovel excerpt if it works as an independent piece. It is a good idea to study past issues before submitting, copies are available for $3.50 from the above address. Each year we present the $200 ANTIETAM REVIEW Literary Award for the author of our lead fiction piece. Otherwise the payment is $100 and two copies.

POETRY

We publish ten to twelve poems each issue. Again, we look for well-crafted literary pieces. Submit up to five poems at a time. We pay $25 apiece for poems.

PHOTOGRAPHS

We use about ten photographs per issue. Photographers may submit up to three black and white prints along with a brief biography. All subject matter will be considered. If people appear recognizable in your photogrpahs, please include a copy of the signed model release. A fee of $25 is paid for each photogrpah used and a prize of $100 is paid for one photo chosen at the editor's discretion. If you wish to study a back issue, send $3.00. Please write for the 1987 photo submission form.

Please include a short biography with submissions, of course, a self addressed stamped envelope.

P. O. Box 148
Yellow Springs
Ohio 45387

SUGGESTIONS FOR PROSPECTIVE CONTRIBUTORS

The best answer we can give on inquiries relating to what kind of material the ANTIOCH REVIEW uses is, "read the magazine." Look through a few representative issues for an idea of subjects, treatment, lengths of articles, and stories we have used; it will be far more rewarding than any general theories we might try to formulate.

Unfortunately, we cannot honor requests for free sample copies. The REVIEW is expensive to produce and operates on a precarious financial margin. If copies are not available at your local newsstand or library, we will be happy to send you a back issue for $3.00, or the current issue for the regular price of $4.75.

ARTICLES

Our audience is the educated citizen, often a professional person, who is interested in matters beyond his field of special activity. With a few exceptions, our subjects cover most of the range of the social sciences and humanities. Our approach tries to steer a middle course between the scholar speaking exclusively to other scholars in his field, and the workaday journalist appealing to a broad popular audience; both these approaches have their own journals and audiences. We try for the interpretative essay on a topic of current importance, drawing on scholarly material for its substance and appealing to the intellectual and social concerns of our readers. We are also interested in reviving the moribund art of literary journalism.

FICTION

We seldom publish more than three short stories in each issue. Although the new writer as well as the previously published author is welcome, it is the story that counts, a story worthy of the serious attention of an intelligent reader, a story that is compelling, written with distinction. Only rarely do we publish translations of well known or new foreign writers; a chapter of a novel is welcome only if it can be read complete in itself as a short story.

POETRY

Like fiction, we get far more poetry than we can possibly accept, and the competition is keen. Here, where form and content are so inseparable and reaction is so personal, it is difficult to state requirements or limitations. Studying recent issues of the REVIEW should be helpful. No "light" or inspirational verse. We usually don't read poetry mss. in the summer.

REVIEWS

We do not publish unsolicited book reviews and very seldom do we publish essays on literary problems or on the canons of significant contemporary writers. The editors and their associates regularly prepare a section of short book evaluations, selectively treating recent publications.

STYLE, LENGTHS, PAYMENT, ETC.

Our literary standards are as high as we can enforce them; we do not have the staff to engage in major editorial rewriting, except on rare occasions when the content justifies the effort. We do, however, often return manuscripts with suggestions for rewriting when the subject seems to warrant another look.

Actually, we have no rigid expectations of length, preferring the content and treatment to determine size. Rarely, however, do we use articles or stories over 5,000 words-- 8,000 at the outside limit.

An independent quarterly journal associated with Antioch College

SUGGESTIONS FOR PROSPECTIVE CONTRIBUTORS, cont'd.

In order to be returned to you, <u>all</u> <u>manuscripts</u> <u>must</u> <u>be</u> <u>accompanied</u> <u>by</u> <u>a self-addressed</u> <u>stamped</u> <u>envelope</u>. We cannot be responsible for the return of manuscripts for which postage has not been provided. If you want the ms. discarded, say so and enclose a postcard or stamped envelope which we can use if we do not accept your submission.

Manuscripts should be typed, double-spaced, on one side of white, 8.5 X 11 paper. Please spare the editors the task of reading carbons or dirty Xerox copies or pages with excessive inter-linear corrections and revisions. We also prefer manuscripts to be mailed flat, fastened by paper clip only, and one at a time. Do not mix prose and poetry in the same envelope, please.

We try to report on manuscripts within three weeks, but because material that interests us is occasionally read by several members of our staff, the process can sometimes take up to a month or six weeks. We acknowledge receipt of a manuscript only if accompanied by a return post card for that purpose.

Payment is upon publication at the rate of $10 per printed page (about 425 words) plus two copies of the issue. Authors may buy additional copies at authors' discount ($2.85 each).

All material sent to the ANTIOCH REVIEW is read and considered, although we cannot comment on each rejection. However, we do not read multiple submissions.

APALACHEE QUARTERLY
WRITERS GUIDELINES

AQ publishes four numbers a year, two single issues (Fall and Winter) and a double issue (Spring and Summer). Generally the double issue is devoted to special topics which in the past have included teeth, red shoes and revenge.

The current topic is _____.

Manuscripts must be in by _____.

When sending a manuscript, please remember how busy we are. We try to send a reply in 8 - 12 weeks, but sometimes we get bogged down. This is especially true when we're going to press. Your manuscript is one of hundreds, and we try to read every one.

We don't mind double submissions. Just drop us a line if you've sent us a story or poem that has been taken elsewhere.

Always send a self-addressed stamped envelope with your submission and make sure the envelope is large enough to hold the manuscript.

If you choose to write a cover letter, mention a few of your previous publications. However, we **do** print work by new writers.

Fiction:
- Send only one story (more are acceptable if the stories are very short).
- Stories should be typed, double-spaced, and proofread.

Poetry:
- Send 3 - 5 poems.
- Double or single spaced.

A good way to find out about the kinds of work we like is to order a sample issue. They are $3.50, (postpaid).

Apalachee Quarterly
P.O. Box 20106
Tallahassee, FL 32304

The Arctophile

Bear-In-Mind, Inc.

20 BEHARRELL ST. - CONCORD, MASSACHUSETTS 01742 - (617) 369-5987

The ARCTOPHILE, Bear-in-Mind, Inc., 20 Beharrell St., Concord MA 01742. (617)369-1167. Editor: Fran Lewis. Judy Knoll, Managing Editor. 25% freelance written.

Works with a small number of new/unpublished writers each year. Quarterly newsletter on Teddy Bears and Teddy Collecting. For adult Teddy Bear collectors who are interested in heartwarming or poignant tales about what Teddys mean to them or how they have helped to share feelings or comfort them in times of need. Circ. 10,000. Pays on publication. Publishes ms an average of 3 months after acceptance. Byline given. Buys first North American serial rights. Submit seasonal/holiday material 6 months in advance. Simultaneous, photocopied and previously published submissions OK. Computer printout submissions acceptable; no dot-matrix. Reports in 2 months. Sample copy for SAE and 1 first class stamp.

Nonfiction: Book excerpts, historical/nostalgic, humor, inspirational, interview/profile, personal experience and photo feature. Buys 12-24 mss/year. Send complete ms. Length: 300-500 words. Pays 4-6¢/word.

Fiction: Fantasy and humorous. Buys 12-24 mss/year. Send complete ms. Length 300-500

Poetry: Avant-garde, free verse, haiku, light verse and traditional. Buys 4 poems/year. Submit maximum 2 poems. Length 6-10 lines. Pays $10-15.

Bear-In-Mind, Inc.

20 BEHARRELL ST. - CONCORD, MASSACHUSETTS 01742 - (617) 369-5987

-2-

Fillers: Jokes, gags, anecdotes, short humor and newsbreaks -- all Teddy related. Buys 8-10/year. Length: 15-30 words. Pays $5-10.

Tips: Articles, and fiction and poetry submissions must be Teddy Bear related. Writing should be "direct and crisp."

ART TIMES

CULTURAL AND CREATIVE NEWS OF THE CATSKILL AND MID-HUDSON REGION

P.O. Box 730   Mt. Marion, N.Y. 12456
(914) 246-5170

Cornelia Seckel - Publisher
Raymond J. Steiner - Editor

WRITER'S GUIDELINES

FICTION: Short Stories up to 1500 words. No excessive sex, violence
or racist themes. High literary quality sought. Pays $15
on publication, six (6) extra copies of issue in which work
appears and one (1) year's subscription to ART TIMES.

POETRY: Up to 20 lines. All topics; all forms. High literary quality
sought. Pays in six (6) extra copies of issue in which work
appears and one (1) year's subscription to ART TIMES.

Readers of ART TIMES are generally over 40, affluent and art con-
scious. Distributed over three upstate NY counties and Manhattan.
Points of distribution include galleries, theatres, music halls, and
select restaurants. Subscription mailings: across US to individuals,
museums, universitites, art schools and organizations. ARTICLES in ART
TIMES are general pieces on the arts written by staff AND ARE NOT SOLICITED.
General tone of paper governed by literary essays on arts - no journalistic
writing, press releases or reviews. ALWAYS INCLUDE SASE. Sample copy:
SASE, 3 first class stamps. Guidelines: Business size envelope , 1 first
class stamp.

The
Associate Reformed
Presbyterian

BEN JOHNSTON, *Editor*

Dear Christian Friend:

Here are your guidelines for writing for The Associate Reformed Presbyterian.

This is the official publication of the Associate Reformed Presbyterian Church, a 32,000-member denomination with congregations chiefly in the Southeast. Our readers have a diversity of ages, vocations, interests and backgrounds.

We publish monthly, 32 to 48 pages, circulation 6,000-plus. Most space goes for denominational activities, but we use one or two free-lanced pieces per month.

Theologically the articles we use are from a Reformed and evangelical perspective. We are looking for Christ-centered material, not merely moral-value articles. We want material which is evangelistic, conducive to spiritual growth, can strengthen our readers in their daily walk -- and which is interesting, well written, and perhaps looks at a familiar topic from a fresh viewpoint.

We have discontinued our children's fiction contest. We buy some children's fiction, but we are more interested in articles of practical help for young readers, with illustrations and anecdotes and Scripture documentation.

When you submit a manuscript for consideration, include a self-addressed envelope with adequate return postage. We encourage query letters. We try to reply within three weeks, and we pay on acceptance. Payment for first-time rights is $20 to $50, depending chiefly on length. We also buy one-times and reprints.

We provide authors three copies of issues in which their work appears. You can buy a sample copy of our magazine for $1.

Include with your manuscript a biographical sketch, 50 words maximum, so we can identify you to our readers.

We reserve the right to make editorial changes, to contact the author and ask for a rewrite if major changes are needed for a usable article, and to reject any manuscript. We assume no responsibility for lost manuscripts.

It is implicit that each submission is the author's own work, entirely original except for quotations, paraphrases and statistics, the sources of which will be indicated. We do not use footnotes; attribution should be given within the article. If another published work is quoted extensively, include with your submission a copy of the publisher's permission for this usage.

We anticipate the possibility of a working relationship that will be beneficial to you, to our readers, to us and to the advancement of the Lord's work.

Sincerely,

Ben Johnston

Ben Johnston

ATLANTIC SALMON JOURNAL GUIDELINES

THE ATLANTIC SALMON JOURNAL, 1435 St-Alexandre St., Suite
1030, Montreal, Quebec, Canada H3A 2G4. (514) 842-8059.
Editor: Joanne Eidinger; Editorial Assistant: Diane Edwards

Quarterly magazine. Circulation 20,000. Readers are
anglers and conservationists interested in enhancement,
resource management, new scientific discoveries and unique
places to fish. Free sample copy on request.

Editorial needs:
Informative, lively features (1800-2000 words): foreign or
domestic travel, cuisine, management, salmon biology,
literature, history. Short features (1000-1500 words): Flies
and Fly-Tying, Political Commentary, Anecdote.

Photo needs:
Good action shots of Atlantic salmon fishing, aquaculture, or
salmon rivers in any season. All material held on spec.
unless otherwise stated. Model release preferred; captions
and credits required.
Cover: vertical format preferred; 2¼x2¼ colour transparency or
35 mm slide. $150-$250.
B & W: 5x7 or 8x10 prints, glossy or matte. $20 per photo.
Color: 35mm or superior quality prints. $50-$100

SAE and International Reply Coupons: reply within 4 to 6
weeks. Byline given. Payment upon publication (first-time
rights only); previously published work accepted, but not
encouraged.

Payment:
First rights: text/photo package (1500-2500 wds) $150-$250
Recipes: $25-$50
Columns: $250
Cartoons: $25
Illustrations: $75-$150

BIKECENTENNIAL

The Bicycle Travel Association

BikeReport

A Bikecentennial Publication
P.O. Box 8308
Missoula, Montana 59807
(406) 721-1776

GUIDELINES FOR CONTRIBUTORS

BikeReport is a magazine published nine times yearly by Bikecentennial, a nonprofit service organization for touring bicyclists. Although it has evolved in format and content beyond its origins as a newsletter, the BikeReport remains a publication intended for the Bikecentennial member, whose main interest is bicycle touring.

Accordingly, every article in the BikeReport is about bicycling. Every article does not, however, restrict itself exclusively to that topic. We like imaginative pieces that use cycling as a starting point to investigate or reveal other topics.

The possibilities are endless. We would never presume to supply you with a list, but it would run from "Apple-picking in Washington state-- how I had a great time in an orchard during my tour" to "Zaire's dog problem-- dealing with the roving wild bands." The key is to focus your thoughts. Be specific. Don't tell our readers you had a "wonderful time" on your tour. Tell them what you did.

BikeReport does not print only glowing stories of bicycle touring. We know there can be unpleasant times and we often will print such stories, particularly if something useful is relayed to our readers in the telling.

These are some specific types of stories we use:

TOUR ACCOUNT-U.S.: This is what we're all about. Share your bicycle trip with our readers. They joined Bikecentennial to support and/or to participate in bicycle touring. They may decide to take the trip you describe or simply to experience it vicariously through your writing. Before you let loose with your imaginative angle, make sure you have covered the basics: Where and when did you go? What did you take? Where did you stay overnight? What did you see? What roads did you use? How long did it take? Why did you go? Did you have any particular problems? Would you do anything differently next time?

TOUR ACCOUNT- FOREIGN: Foreign tour accounts should include the same basics as U.S. tour accounts with an important addition-- tell our readers what's different about the country(s) you traveled through. Was it that they didn't have ice for your Coke? Or was it something more? It is important in foreign tour accounts to relate those differences to cycling. Did you find it more or less rewarding to cycle in France as compared to the United States? What should our readers know if they intend to cycle in France?

SPECIAL FOCUS: Tell our readers where you went on tour if you wish, but the real substance of this article will be a specific experience you had as a cyclist. Your experience may have occurred on or off the bike. As long as you keep it tightly focused, almost anything goes. You might take our readers on a tour of a Civil War museum you happened upon in West Virginia. There is one other prerequisite: keep cycling in the story. Maybe you caused an uproar in the museum because your Bata Bikers squeaked terribly on the newly waxed floor. However you do it, let us know you're a cyclist.

ESSAY: We hold a special place here for a well-written essay. The last one we got was about Peg, "a little whisper of a woman," who always leads the pack on club tours, much to the astonishment of the male author. The essay is a genuine and engaging salute to Peg and other women of advanced years and riding skills. Topics are unlimited in this category.

INTERVIEW: There are lots of interesting people out there riding bicycles.
Talk to one of them. If they have done something significant in the world
of cycling, so much the better. If they´re famous in bicycling circles,
that´s even better.

FICTION: To be honest, we´ve yet to receive a fictional story that we´ve
wanted to publish, but we hold out the hope.

HUMOR: All of the categories of manuscripts we have mentioned thus far,
Tour Account, Special Focus, Essay, Interview, and Fiction could be handled
in a humorous way, something we welcome.

These seven categories cover most of the material we use. We rarely use
poetry. An obvious suggestion, which everyone makes, is to read the
magazine. We concur. Consider joining Bikecentennial if you haven´t
already, or contact us for back issues.

BikeReport also runs regular columns. If you have an idea for a
column, let us know. If we like the idea, and we´re not already doing it,
you may become an instant BikeReport columnist.

We are always glad to see manuscripts accompanied by good photos.
While we prefer black and white prints, we can also use color
transparencies. If you didn´t take any photos yourself to go with your
story, consider contacting state agencies such as tourism bureaus or
chambers of commerce. They often have very nice selections of photos. We
almost never use photos without a manuscript to go along with them.

We will tell you within four weeks whether or not we can use your
submission. We cannot, however, guarantee when it will be published.
Another good approach is to send us a query letter, outlining your story and
the approximate number of words it will be. We´ll answer your query letter
immediately.

BikeReport generally uses stories that are between 800-2500 words in
length. We pay three cents per word, on publication, and send a copy of the
issue along with your check. We buy first rights and will consider
simultaneous submissions as long as we are informed of the other
publications considering the manuscript.

Your manuscript should be typed, double-spaced, on 8 1/2" X 11" white
paper, with 1 1/2" margins. Your name, address and phone number should
appear at the top of the first manuscript page.

CAT FANCY
DOG FANCY
BIRD TALK
HORSE ILLUSTRATED
magazines

Editorial Offices
P.O. Box 6050
Mission Viejo, California 92690
Telephone (714) 240-6001

Bird Talk

WRITER'S GUIDELINES

Thank you for your interest in our publications. We would be pleased to see your material. Below we have listed some of the publication requirements of CAT FANCY, DOG FANCY, BIRD TALK and HORSE ILLUSTRATED to assist you in preparing submissions.

ARTICLES

CAT FANCY, DOG FANCY and BIRD TALK are directed at the general pet owning population and written for the adult audience. HORSE ILLUSTRATED is directed at the amateur competitor and pleasure horse owner. We suggest that you read past issues of the magazines to acquaint yourself with the types of material we use. Past issues may be obtained by sending $3.00 to the above address. We need informative articles, limited to 3,000 words, on the care of training of cats, dogs, birds, and horses (health nutrition, training, etc.); photo essays on historical and current events dealing with cats, dogs, birds and horses; how-to articles; human interest stories; and good fiction, with the animal as the primary focus of interest. We rarely use stories in which the animal speaks as if it were human. We use a breed article in each issue, but these articles are assigned. Please query if you have a breed article in mind.

Manuscripts should be typewritten, double-spaced with wide margins. We prefer that articles be accompanied with appropriate art in the form of professional quality color transparencies or black and white photographs (NOT SNAP SHOTS) or professional illustrations. Additional guidelines are available for artists and photographers.

We are always happy to review material on speculation, but with the exception of fiction, the best working procedure is to query before preparing an article. Our usual rate of payment is three to five cents per printed word, five cents if accompanied by good quality photographs. Payment is made in the latter part of the cover month in which your article appears, (i.e., if your piece was in the November issue you would be paid in the latter part of November). We buy first American rights only; all other rights revert back to the author.

We cannot assume responsibility for material submitted, but we assure you that reasonable care will be taken in handling your work. YOU MUST INCLUDE A SELF-ADDRESSED, STAMPED ENVELOPE WITH EACH SUBMISSION.

BLACK & WHITE Magazine
P.O. Box 478318
Chicago, Illinois 60647
(312)278-1778

Dear Artist/Writer,

    Thanks for your interest in <u>Black & White</u>. To submit work please
send the following materials to us:

    Visual artist: slides or black & white print of your work
                    cover letter
                    SASE

    Writer: copies of work to be considered
             cover letter
             SASE

    Please put your name and address on each page or piece of work
submitted. We will give prompt consideration to your submission.

                        Sincerely,

                        Charles R. Seminara
                        Editor/Publisher

LEXINGTON LIBRARY, INC.

355 LEXINGTON AVE., NEW YORK. NEW YORK 10017   (212) 391-1400

Black Confessions

STORY GUIDELINES FOR ROMANTIC MAGAZINES JIVE & INTIMACY

(also BLACK CONFESSIONS, BLACK ROMANCE, and BRONZE THRILLS)

Dear Writer:

For JIVE and INTIMACY magazines, we strive for the stories to lean toward romantic lines. This does not mean that the stories should not have true-to-life experience plots. We simply want to project romance, love and togetherness, rather than to overwhelm our readers with violence or anything too depressing.

Make the stories believable. We do not want to deviate from reality. All endings cannot be happy ones, but we want to try, whenever possible, to cast an optimistic outlook as much as possible.

Hopefully, you can follow these guidelines and will soon be sending in your manuscripts. There is no limit as to how many you can submit at one time. It is good to submit material as frequently as you can, so that outlines for upcoming months can be made. Here are the guidelines:

1. Stories must be written from a young, black female perspective with romance in mind (this is not to discourage male writers, you may use a pen name).

2. Stories must be true-to-life confessions with interesting plots.

3. Stories need to exude an aura of romance.

4. Stories should have at least two descriptive love scenes.

5. Stories must be written in the first person.

6. Stories must be typed and double-spaced, with each page numbered and identified either with your name or the title of your work.

7. Stories should be 3,000 - 4,000 words (between 12 to 15 typed pages).

Allow at least 90 days for confirmation of acceptance or rejection. If we do accept the story, you will receive a release form in the mail. If we do not accept it, your story will be returned if you enclose a self-addressed stamped envelope with it.

Thank you for your interest in our publications.

Sincerely,

Nathasha Brooks

The Editor

LEXINGTON LIBRARY, INC.

355 LEXINGTON AVE., NEW YORK, NEW YORK 10017   (212) 391-1400

Dear Writer:

For our magazines, we strive for the stories to lean towards romantic lines. As well as following the original guidelines, we would like you to know that we welcome black male writers to send us stories from their perspectives also. All writers are entitled to write special feature articles too.

Black women like to know what black men are thinking, in terms of romance and relationships in the '80's. Therefore, your stories, ideas, and articles would be graciously appreciated and accepted.

Dear men, please don't hesitate to let JIVE & INTIMACY know what you are thinking, feeling, doing, or wanting concerning romance.

We welcome your response, and wish you success in your endeavors.

                              Sincerely,

                              The Editors

LEXINGTON LIBRARY, INC.

355 LEXINGTON AVE., NEW YORK, NEW YORK 10017   (212) 391-1400

Dear Writers and Photographers:

Here are the payment rates for JIVE and INTIMACY. Where variance (range) in payment rate appears, it gives the editor leeway to evaluate (Length, quality, etc.) the material in question. Any exceptions to the indicated rate structure must be pre-approved by the publisher, John J. Plunkett.

EDITORIAL	PAYMENT RATE
Standard Confession Stories	$ 75-60
Special Features	100-75
Service Articles	100-75
Horoscope	100
Advice	75
Reprint Fee (Story/Service Article)	50

PHOTOGRAPHY	
Cover Photo (Color)	$ 250
B/W Confession Story Photos	80 ea.
B/W Service Article Photos	40 ea.
B/W Reprint	25

Most assignments are given on speculation. However, we do request that photographers present samples of their work, as well as 35 mm slides of models whom they feel are cover material. Photographers should supply their models with model releases.

LEXINGTON LIBRARY, INC.
355 LEXINGTON AVE., NEW YORK, NEW YORK 10017   (212) 391-1400

POETRY GUIDELINES

Dear Poet:

We welcome poetry that deals with romance, love, and normal sex between a heterosexual couple. Poems should not be derogatory or stereotypical towards Black people in any way, form or fashion. Our people should be seen in as positive a light as possible in any poems submitted.
Poems should be written in free verse, blank verse or Haiku. If you are writing poems in Haiku, please say so somewhere on your work. Cute, rhyming poems are NOT acceptable. Poems dealing with cultural issues are also acceptable.

All poems should be typewritten, preferably double spaced on white bond paper. Please edit your work before sending it in, use a dictionary, thesaurus, style book or any helpful writer's aids to familiarize yourself with any problem areas.

Poems should be at least five lines long, but never over twenty-five lines.

Payment for poems upon publication is ten dollars per poem. All unused poems will be returned to the poet.

Yours truly,

Nathasha Brooks

Nathasha Brooks
Editor

Black Family Magazine

Shaping Positive Lifestyles

WRITER'S GUIDELINES

BLACK FAMILY Magazine is a national publication for today's black family. Our goal is to improve the family structure through informative, how-to articles and by providing positive role models. Therefore, we seek articles that fall into the following categories:

Family Profiles: Black families, not necessarily famous, but who are excelling in business, politics, religion or entertainment.

Articles with a Black Slant: Articles addressing or explaining a problem or concern common to black families-whether it be in education, politics, health, finance, or society in general.

How to Articles: "Do-it-yourself" articles or articles that explain points to consider when going about a purchase, choice, or decision. These stories may fall under several departments, for example: "How to Install Tile" (Home). "How to Deal with Unemployment" (Family Focus). "How to Choose a Fur" (Consumer Corner) or "How to Prepare a Will" (Legal).

Leisure: Articles on travel to interesting and existing places are welcome.

Senior Citizen Profiles: Features on blacks who are 65 and older and still making valuable contributions to society through their tireless efforts.

Fine Arts: Profiles of black artists in the various arts (opera, dance, theatre, sculpture, etc.)

We also accept poetry and short stories for consideration. Remember, stories must be positive and uplifting "slice of life" type.

It is advisable to send a query letter, before composing the article, outlining its main points. This will save you time and effort, as you will be less likely to submit a piece that does not fit our editorial needs. A response to your query will follow in approximately four weeks. When submitting a manuscript for consideration, please enclose a self-addressed stamped envelope, or it will not be returned.

Payment: BLACK FAMILY pays from $50.00 to $300.00 for articles selected for publication. Payment is made only after the article appears in the magazine. If your article or manuscript is accepted a letter of agreement will be sent to you for your approval with the amount to be paid indicated.

All inquiries should be mailed to: **BLACK FAMILY Magazine**
11800 Sunrise Valley Drive, Suite 320
Reston, VA. 22091
(703) 860-3411

LEXINGTON L LIBRARY, INC.

355 LEXINGTON AVE., NEW YORK, NEW YORK 10017   (212) 391-1400

Black Romance

STORY GUIDELINES FOR ROMANTIC MAGAZINES JIVE & INTIMACY

(also BLACK CONFESSIONS, BLACK ROMANCE and BRONZE THRILLS)

Dear Writer:

For JIVE and INTIMACY magazines, we strive for the stories to lean toward romantic lines. This does not mean that the stories should not have true-to-life experience plots. We simply want to project romance, love and togetherness, rather than to overwhelm our readers with violence or anything too depressing.

Make the stories believable. We do not want to deviate from reality. All endings cannot be happy ones, but we want to try, whenever possible, to cast an optimistic outlook as much as possible.

Hopefully, you can follow these guidelines and will soon be sending in your manuscripts. There is no limit as to how many you can submit at one time. It is good to submit material as frequently as you can, so that outlines for upcoming months can be made. Here are the guidelines:

1. Stories must be written from a young, black female perspective with romance in mind (this is not to discourage male writers, you may use a pen name).

2. Stories must be true-to-life confessions with interesting plots.

3. Stories need to exude an aura of romance.

4. Stories should have at least two descriptive love scenes.

5. Stories must be written in the first person.

6. Stories must be typed and double-spaced, with each page numbered and identified either with your name or the title of your work.

7. Stories should be 3,000 - 4,000 words (between 12 to 15 typed pages).

Allow at least 90 days for confirmation of acceptance or rejection. If we do accept the story, you will receive a release form in the mail. If we do not accept it, your story will be returned if you enclose a self-addressed stamped envelope with it.

Thank you for your interest in our publications.

Sincerely,

Nathasha Brooks

The Editor

LEXINGTON LIBRARY, INC.
355 LEXINGTON AVE., NEW YORK, NEW YORK 10017   (212) 391-1400

Dear Writer:

    For our magazines, we strive for the stories to lean towards romantic lines. As well as following the original guidelines, we would like you to know that we welcome black male writers to send us stories from their perspectives also. All writers are entitled to write special feature articles too.

    Black women like to know what black men are thinking, in terms of romance and relationships in the '80's. Therefore, your stories, ideas, and articles would be graciously appreciated and accepted.

    Dear men, please don't hesitate to let <u>JIVE</u> & <u>INTIMACY</u> know what you are thinking, feeling, doing, or wanting concerning romance.

    We welcome your response, and wish you success in your endeavors.

                Sincerely,

                The Editors

LEXINGTON ⬛ LIBRARY, INC.
355 LEXINGTON AVE., NEW YORK, NEW YORK 10017   (212) 391-1400

Dear Writers and Photographers:

Here are the payment rates for JIVE and INTIMACY. Where variance (range) in payment rate appears, it gives the editor leeway to evaluate (Length, quality, etc.) the material in question. Any exceptions to the indicated rate structure must be pre-approved by the publisher, John J. Plunkett.

EDITORIAL	PAYMENT RATE
Standard Confession Stories	$ 75-60
Special Features	100-75
Service Articles	100-75
Horoscope	100
Advice	75
Reprint Fee (Story/Service Article)	50

PHOTOGRAPHY	
Cover Photo (Color)	$ 250
B/W Confession Story Photos	80 ea.
B/W Service Article Photos	40 ea.
B/W Reprint	25

Most assignments are given on speculation. However, we do request that photographers present samples of their work, as well as 35 mm slides of models whom they feel are cover material. Photographers should supply their models with model releases.

LEXINGTON LIBRARY, INC.
355 LEXINGTON AVE., NEW YORK, NEW YORK 10017   (212) 391-1400

<u>POETRY GUIDELINES</u>

Dear Poet:

We welcome poetry that deals with romance, love, and normal sex between a heterosexual couple. Poems should not be derogatory or stereotypical towards Black people in any way, form or fashion. Our people should be seen in as positive a light as possible in any poems submitted.
Poems should be written in free verse, blank verse or Haiku. If you are writing poems in Haiku, please say so somewhere on your work. Cute, rhyming poems are NOT acceptable. Poems dealing with cultural issues are also acceptable.

All poems should be typewritten, preferably double spaced on white bond paper. Please edit your work before sending it in, use a dictionary, thesaurus, style book or any helpful writer's aids to familiarize yourself with any problem areas.

Poems should be at least five lines long, but never over twenty-five lines.

Payment for poems upon publication is ten dollars per poem. All unused poems will be returned to the poet.

Yours truly,

Nathasha Brooks

Nathasha Brooks
Editor

The Boston Review

33 Harrison Avenue, Boston, Massachusetts 02111   (617) 350-5353

Writers' Guidelines

The Boston Review, a bimonthly magazine of arts and culture since 1975, publishes in depth reviews and essays on literature, public policy, music, painting, film, photography, dance, and theater.

Brief reviews (up to 800 words), essays, reviews (up to 1500 words), interviews (up to 2000 words), and longer pieces (up to 5000 words) are welcome. Manuscripts must be typed and double spaced. Each submission must be accompanied by a self-addressed stamped envelope, or it will not be returned.

A writer with an idea for an article or a review can check the idea with us by submitting a brief description. If we are not familiar with the writer's work, but the idea sounds appealing, we may suggest that the writer proceed on speculation.

The Boston Review considers all types of fiction (up to 5000 words), poetry, novel excerpts, and humor pieces.

For non-fiction, fiction, and poetry, the Boston Review pays from $20 to $200 per piece.

Thank you for your interest in the Boston Review.

BOTTOMFISH

Bottomfish accepts lyric poems and short fiction of less than 5000 words, including portions of novels, and experimental fiction. Upon acceptance of a manuscript, *Bottomfish* acquires first North American serial rights. Copyright returns to the author upon publication. Payment to the author will be two copies of the magazine. Normally, we take about six weeks to reply to submissions. We take longer with manuscripts received between June 1 and September 15, since we read manuscripts sporadically during that period.

We are interested in carefully crafted, artful work. In fiction we look for a narrative voice that is consistent and credible; the writer's obvious command of the English language; a pattern of image, action, and feeling that is fresh and worth rereading. In poems we look for the same qualities, with special attention to sharp, fresh imagery, economy, form, rhythm, and sound. When a poem attempts a traditional form, we look for mastery of that form. When the poem seeks its own form, we look for the speaker's invention of his own "game": a pattern of sound, image, action, feeling, meaning, and visual layout that is consistent, unified, and worth rereading. We return poems that become less coherent and more puzzling with each rereading.

We are now accepting submissions for consideration in our eleventh edition, to be published in spring, 1989. Please include a self-addressed, stamped envelope, if you wish us to return your manuscript in the event we decide not to use it.

You can purchase a copy of the 1987 *Bottomfish* for $3.50 , which includes postage. Mail check to *Bottomfish*, De Anza College, 21250 Stevens Creek Blvd., Cupertino, CA 95014.

De Anza College   •   *21250 Stevens Creek Blvd., Cupertino, CA 95014*   •   *[408] 996-4545, 996-4547*

SCOUTING/USA

A program for Cub Scouts, Boy Scouts and Explorers

Magazine Division
BOY SCOUTS OF AMERICA

1325 Walnut Hill Lane
P.O. Box 152079, Irving, Texas 75015-2079
214-580-2000

FICTION WRITER'S GUIDELINES

Boys' Life

BOYS' LIFE FACTS. Published monthly since 1911 by the Boy Scouts of America. Readers are mostly boys 8 to 18. Sold by subscription only. Paid circulation: 1.3 million. Total boy/girl readership: 6.5 million. Editorial content covers practically every interest of all boys.

FICTION REQUIREMENTS. Length: 750-2500 words. All short stories feature a boy or boys. Humor, mysteries, science-fiction, adventure.

For original material, we buy first magazine rights only. Copyright returned to author 90 days after publication. Payment--$750 and up--on acceptance.

A FINAL NOTE. No set of guidelines can substitute for careful reading of as many back-issues as possible. Boys' Life can be found in the children's section of most libraries.

LEXINGTON LIBRARY, INC.

355 LEXINGTON AVE., NEW YORK, NEW YORK 10017   (212) 391-1400

Bronze Thrills

STORY GUIDELINES FOR ROMANTIC MAGAZINES JIVE & INTIMACY

(also BLACK CONFESSIONS, BLACK ROMANCE and BRONZE THRILLS)

Dear Writer:

For JIVE and INTIMACY magazines, we strive for the stories to lean toward romantic lines. This does not mean that the stories should not have true-to-life experience plots. We simply want to project romance, love and togetherness, rather than to overwhelm our readers with violence or anything too depressing.

Make the stories believable. We do not want to deviate from reality. All endings cannot be happy ones, but we want to try, whenever possible, to cast an optimistic outlook as much as possible.

Hopefully, you can follow these guidelines and will soon be sending in your manuscripts. There is no limit as to how many you can submit at one time. It is good to submit material as frequently as you can, so that outlines for upcoming months can be made. Here are the guidelines:

1. Stories must be written from a young, black female perspective with romance in mind (this is not to discourage male writers, you may use a pen name).

2. Stories must be true-to-life confessions with interesting plots.

3. Stories need to exude an aura of romance.

4. Stories should have at least two descriptive love scenes.

5. Stories must be written in the first person.

6. Stories must be typed and double-spaced, with each page numbered and identified either with your name or the title of your work.

7. Stories should be 3,000 - 4,000 words (between 12 to 15 typed pages).

Allow at least 90 days for confirmation of acceptance or rejection. If we do accept the story, you will receive a release form in the mail. If we do not accept it, your story will be returned if you enclose a self-addressed stamped envelope with it.

Thank you for your interest in our publications.

Sincerely,

Nathasha Brooks

The Editor

LEXINGTON LIBRARY, INC.
355 LEXINGTON AVE., NEW YORK, NEW YORK 10017   (212) 391-1400

Dear Writer:

For our magazines, we strive for the stories to lean
towards romantic lines. As well as following the original
guidelines, we would like you to know that we welcome black
male writers to send us stories from their perspectives also.
All writers are entitled to write special feature articles too.

Black women like to know what black men are thinking,
in terms of romance and relationships in the '80's. Therefore,
your stories, ideas, and articles would be graciously appreciated and accepted.

Dear men, please don't hesitate to let JIVE & INTIMACY
know what you are thinking, feeling, doing, or wanting concerning romance.

We welcome your response, and wish you success in your
endeavors.

                              Sincerely,

                              The Editors

LEXINGTON LIBRARY, INC.

355 LEXINGTON AVE., NEW YORK, NEW YORK 10017   (212) 391-1400

Dear Writers and Photographers:

Here are the payment rates for JIVE and INTIMACY. Where variance (range) in payment rate appears, it gives the editor leeway to evaluate (Length, quality, etc.) the material in question. Any exceptions to the indicated rate structure must be pre-approved by the publisher, John J. Plunkett.

EDITORIAL	PAYMENT RATE
Standard Confession Stories	$ 75-60
Special Features	100-75
Service Articles	100-75
Horoscope	100
Advice	75
Reprint Fee (Story/Service Article)	50

PHOTOGRAPHY	
Cover Photo (Color)	$ 250
B/W Confession Story Photos	80 ea.
B/W Service Article Photos	40 ea.
B/W Reprint	25

Most assignments are given on speculation. However, we do request that photographers present samples of their work, as well as 35 mm slides of models whom they feel are cover material. Photographers should supply their models with model releases.

LEXINGTON ▨ LIBRARY, INC.
355 LEXINGTON AVE., NEW YORK, NEW YORK 10017   (212) 391-1400

POETRY GUIDELINES

Dear Poet:

We welcome poetry that deals with romance, love, and normal sex between a heterosexual couple. Poems should not be derogatory or stereotypical towards Black people in any way, form or fashion. Our people should be seen in as positive a light as possible in any poems submitted.
Poems should be written in free verse, blank verse or Haiku. If you are writing poems in Haiku, please say so somewhere on your work. Cute, rhyming poems are NOT acceptable. Poems dealing with cultural issues are also acceptable.
All poems should be typewritten, preferably double spaced on white bond paper. Please edit your work before sending it in, use a dictionary, thesaurus, style book or any helpful writer's aids to familiarize yourself with any problem areas.
Poems should be at least five lines long, but never over twenty-five lines.
Payment for poems upon publication is ten dollars per poem. All unused poems will be returned to the poet.

Yours truly,

Nathasha Brooks

Nathasha Brooks
Editor

BROOMSTICK

RECENT TITLES

- Just Among Us Superwomen
- Hair
- Bootstrap Health
- Politics of Disability
- Of Time and Arthritis
- On The Road Without A Man
- Fifty and Loving It
- Gathering Power
- Old Is a 4-Letter Word
- Sassy and Mean
- The Crones
- A Sense of Control
- Change and Creativity at Midlife

A unique,

reader-participation magazine by, for, and about women over forty.

A national network printing the work, experience, and thoughts of midlife and older women.

THE BROOM

We reposses the Broomstick as a symbol of our strength and unity. It stands for many aspects of our lives and interest.

SKILLS
Homemaking and paid jobs.

HEALING
Witches were ancient healers.

CHANGE
The new broom sweeps clean.

POWER
The witch flies on the broom.

CONFRONTATION
Exposing what society calls ugliness.

Can you use a *Broomstick?* It makes a great gift,too!

SOME VOICES

Two years ago I discovered I was Ms. ME, a person in my own right, not simply So-and-so's wife or Junior's mother. After three marriages I am now happily free at last. I became a Pagan and a feminist simultaneously.

— *Brigid*

Teeth. You had better have some. Medi-Cal will only pay for one bridge of six teeth. You had better figure on getting along with only your five remaining lower front teeth. How you chew with no lower molars is a secret of the government. Again, would that those of us with no molars understood the secret. Still, we could endure these monstrosities better if they were even doled out to us with a modicum of courtesy and thought.

— *Wilma Elizabeth McDaniel*

Please send gift subscriptions of *BROOMSTICK* to my mother and my grandmother, in thanks for their strength and spirit. Your (younger) sister, Kate.

— *Kate*

I had to cook while he fished off the dock. While he played golf, I had to cook some more. When he grew ill, I nursed him by the clock. And when he died, he left me very poor.

But, woman-like, I'm living the good life.
It's easier as person than as wife.   — *Charlotte St. John*

I also began exploring myths. One of the most important ones for me was the generation gap myth that says that in order to "grow up" we must escape from our mothers' "negative influence." By exploring my relationship to my own mother, I came to see the many positive aspects to our relationship which I had been denying. I also realized that the bad things in my life which I had blamed on my mother's personal failure or ill will were in fact due to societal oppression we both suffered as women.

— *Mickey Spencer*

I also acknowledge that some of what I am feeling could be associated with menopause. However, I resent it tremendously when people assume that I am distressed because I am approaching menopause. My hormones may be affected by this time of my life; I do not believe they are the cause of the difficulties of that time.

— *Scottie Daugherty*

I am like the canaries that miners carried into the mines to test for toxic gasses. I react more severely than most people, but the toxins I react to are largely those that are not good for anybody. Telling me to clean up my emotional act is futile as well as insulting. What needs cleaning up is our increasingly poisonous air, water, food and our failure to evaluate our culture by its impact on people.

— *Polly Taylor*

In *The Power of the Old Woman* I said that I didn't have any special wisdom that comes with age to give to those who are younger. But in writing this afterword, I begin to see that I may have, and if I have, so have all the other old women. For us to pass that knowledge on, we have to break yet one more barrier of silence, the silence of the old. We have to hear that silence as political, and know that just beneath all imposed silences lies power.

— *Barbara Macdonald*

BROOMSTICK Writers' Packet

In addition to this (free) style brochure, we offer an extensive collection of ideas about feminist writing and editing, developed by BROOMSTICK authors and editors. These ideas form the basis for our editorial decisions.

Along with "how-to" material, our packet discusses content, style, and our editing and selection process. It gives ways we and our authors have found to get ideas across—how to achieve greater clarity without sacrificing our personal approaches and styles.

The packet explains in detail what we mean by "political," how we avoid jargon and sexist language, and our thoughts about checking out words and ideas that might be read as racist, classist, derogatory to fat or disabled women, and so forth.

We have included excerpts from a wide range of BROOMSTICK editorials—on humor, language, ethics, poetry, romance, and many other topics related to writing.

We are delighted to find that this packet has been used by other periodicals as a guide to feminist writing as well as by our own writers. We know you too will find it useful, encouraging, and interesting in its own right. To order, send your check with the attached coupon.

A treasure trove for ANY feminist writer!

ORDER FORM ON BACK

We want the material we print in BROOMSTICK to be relevant to our age group, to be clear and understandable, and to support our feminist position as stated in our editorial policy (see p. 2 of any issue).

Please write directly from your own experience, using "I" rather than "they" or "you" helps the reader understand that we are sharing our own points of view. We do not accept material written in an academic, abstract, or "objective" style.

We prefer prose to poetry because the political meaning is often clearer.

We don't have a page or word limit for material sent to BROOMSTICK. A piece should be as long as it needs to be to say what it has to say. This may be a few lines or many pages. It is easier for us to read a manuscript which is typed and double-spaced with wide margins; sending two copies saves us photo-copy expense. Please send 2 self addressed stamped envelopes (SASEs) as well—one so we can let you know we received your submission and a second one large enough and with enough postage so we can return your work with our comments. While we occasionally accept work exactly as written and send a postcard, more often we write a letter to suggest small changes or ask for revisions, or to explain why we cannot use a piece. A second copy and stamped envelopes save us time and money.

Don't be discouraged! The rigid rules of some publications can be intimidating and costly. We don't want to scare away older women; you have lots to say to us. If you don't have access to a typewriter and/or copier, send us a clearly written copy with plenty of space between lines and in the margins. Or just write us a letter and we will help you get your message across to our network of women over forty.

We send each author and artist two copies of any issue in which her work appears. Please subscribe to BROOMSTICK and support the magazine that supports you as an author or artist.

Please print/type/rubber stamp/sticker your name, pseudonyms, name changes, and your full address, including zip, on everything you send us. It is the only way your work and your requests will survive our filing system. Say how you want your "by-line"—generally your name and city. Be sure to tell us that you are over 40. Sign drawings legibly so we can give you credit for your work.

Address material to:
BROOMSTICK
3543 18th St. #3
San Francisco, CA 94110

Editors:
Mickey Spencer and Polly Taylor

You Can Write For BROOMSTICK

BROOMSTICK is a reader participation magazine. Our purpose is to give women over forty who have an interest in feminism space to share experiences, ideas, insights, feelings, and needs. We invite you to join our conversation.

BROOMSTICK welcomes submissions of articles, stories, poems, and drawings from women subscribers who are over 40. Your experiences and insights are important to other older women. Graphics must be black and white (we cannot process grays), and can either illustrate writing or stand alone. For ideas, topics, and themes, see the "Wanted: Articles" section of Broomstick Bazaar in a current issue.

3543 18th St., #3,   (415)552-7460
San Francisco, CA 94110

TAKE AN ACTIVE PART IN THE BROOMSTICK NETWORK OF OLDER WOMEN — BE A BROOMSTICK AUTHOR

Writers' Packet Order Form

BROOMSTICK
A Feminist Magazine By, For, & About Women Over Forty

[   ] WRITERS' PACKETS at $2.50 (including postage). Enclosed: $_____ (U.S. funds) We keep the price of this Writers' Packet below cost to make it available to all older women. Please send more if you are able to. Low income? Send us what you can afford.

NAME _____

ADDRESS _____ CITY _____ STATE ___ ZIP _____

BROOMSTICK 3543 18th St., #3, San Francisco, California 94110 (415)552-7460

SB-7

CALYX

A Journal of Art and Literature by Women

Dear

Thank you for your interest in *CALYX*. *CALYX* accepts submissions of essays, reviews, interviews, short fiction, poetry and visual art. The writer's/artist's guidelines are as follows:

> <u>Reviews</u> should not exceed 1,000 words. Please write for additional review guidelines.
>
> <u>Prose</u> (includes essays) should be double-spaced and should not exceed 5,000 words.
>
> <u>Poetry</u> submissions are limited to 6 poems.
>
> <u>Interviews</u> should be limited to 3,000 words.
>
> <u>Visual Art</u> should be submitted on 35 mm slides or 8"x10" black and white glossy photographs (limit 6 slides or photos). Please write for additional visual art guidelines.

All submissions should include author's name on each page and be accompanied by a brief biographical resume or statement, a self-addressed, stamped envelope (separate SASE's for each submission category), and a phone number. Please indicate if it is unnecessary to return submission(s).

CALYX assumes no responsibility for submissions received without adequate return postage, packaging, or proper identification labels. CALYX can only respond to submission queries accompanied by a stamped, self-addressed envelope.

CALYX will be accepting submissions from _____ through _____ for the _____ issue.

Sample copies of *CALYX* are available for $6.50 plus $1 postage and handling. Send to: CALYX, P.O. BOX B, CORVALLIS, OR. 97339.

Again, thank you for your interest in *CALYX*. We look forward to reviewing your work.

Sincerely,

for *CALYX*

P.O. Box B, Corvallis, OR 97339   (503) 753-9384

CANADIAN
FICTION MAGAZINE

Canada's Finest
Literary Quarterly

Box 946, Station "F"
Toronto, Ontario
Canada
M4Y 2N9

Consider:

• CFM has published over 500 stories by the best new and established writers and artists resident in Canada and Canadians residing abroad, and has established new standards for traditional and innovative fiction.

• CFM Interviews are the most important introduction to the creative minds behind Canadian short and long fiction. The writers talk about their narrative strategies, dealing with the possibilities of the blank pages, and the demands the contemporary world often makes upon their art and craft.

• CFM Fiction in Translation from the Quebecois and from the unofficial languages of Canada. CFM has done several book length anthologies that stand as milestones in contemporary Canadian translation, including Metis, Inuit, and Native writers of Canada, and Latin American writers in Canada.

Consider:

• CFM Forum on the future of fiction. CFM examines the possibilities of genre fiction, magic realism, modernism, the future of literary magazines, innovation and change in the "new" short story, tactics in the novella, parody, metafiction, postmodernism, and the avantgarde.

• CFM Literary Portraiture. CFM has been a pioneer in the field of contemporary Canadian literary portraiture, featuring prize winning portfolios by Paul Orenstein, John Reeves, Sam Tata, Kero, Helena Wilson, V. Tony Hauser, and Arnaud Maggs.

• Each issue of CFM averages 148 book pages, includes a dozen or more short stories, portfolio of art or photography, interview with a leading author, and selected literary criticism. Each issue speaks for itself; together they form the history of the contemporary Canadian short story.

Consider:

• CFM is the only literary magazine in Canada devoted exclusively to the developing art of short fiction. Contributors are frequently reprinted in *Best Canadian Stories,* *Coming Attractions,* major anthologies, and prize winning single author collections. CFM contributors include Governor General's Award winners David Donnell, Suzanne Jacob, Mavis Gallant, Leon Rooke, Guy Vanderhaeghe, Josef Skvorecky, George Bowering, Nicole Brossard, Gwendolyn MacEwen, and Jack Hodgins. Other contributors include Susan Musgrave, Michael Bullock, Keath Fraser, John Metcalf, Jane Urquhart, Susan Kerslake, Matt Cohen, Aritha Van Herk, Ray Smith, Veronica Ross, W.D. Valgardson, and dozens of other new and established writers.

• CFM Special Issues on Robert Harlow, Jane Rule, Mavis Gallant, Leon Rooke, Martin Vaughn-James, Homage to Michel Tremblay, and 45 Below: The ten best fiction writers in Canada.

To all writers:

There is no need to query fiction. CFM has no restriction on length, style, or subject matter. Work published in CFM has been as short as a one paragraph prose-poem and as long as a 100 manuscript page novella. However, prospective contributors should familiarize themselves with several recent back copies of the magazine. CFM is a professional literary quarterly interested in all aspects of contemporary creative writing. Well-written traditional fictions are as welcome as metafictions, anti-fictions, and fictions of the marvellous. Writers must include SASE. Works submitted without return postage (in Canadian stamps, loose U.S. postage, or International reply coupon) will not be returned. Writers should query reviews, criticism, manifestoes, interviews, artwork, and photography. CFM usually responds to submissions within six weeks.

* CFM has an Annual Contributor's Prize of $500 for the most outstanding story published in French or English in each year's previous four issues. Previous winners include Leon Rooke, W.P. Kinsella, Mavis Gallant, John Metcalf, Guy Vanderhaeghe, Keath Fraser, David Sharpe, Douglas Glover, Patrick Roscoe, Matt Cohen, Ann Copeland, and Rohinton Mistry.

* CFM is edited by Geoffrey Hancock, first winner of the Fiona Mee Award from *Quill & Quire* for outstanding literary journalism.

The CFM Writers' Kit and Guidelines! a $50 value for $25

Selected back issues of CFM that highlight the major achievements in Canadian short fiction. This kit is essential reading for Canadian writers of short fiction.

Each kit includes:

*An interview with Alice Munro, and prize winning fiction by Matt Cohen

*Interviews and fiction by Jack Hodgins, Rudy Wiebe, George Bowering, W.D. Valgardson, W.P. Kinsella, and more

*Trans2: Fiction in Translation from the Unofficial Languages of Canada

*A special issue on Leon Rooke winner of the 1983 Governor-General's Award

*Martin Vaughn-James' theory of visual fiction and fiction without words

*Two volumes on 'The Art of the Novella'

As an extra bonus, each kit includes CFM's writer's guidelines, and a short fiction reading list.

INCLUDING MARTHA'S VINEYARD & NANTUCKET

May, 1987

GUIDELINES FOR WRITERS

RATES:

ASSIGNED: $400-$750 for extensively researched articles.
$250-$400 for single-subject profiles or for
"casual" articles.

Publisher reserves right to pay a kill fee for
sub-standard assigned articles.

NON-ASSIGNED: $250-$500 for feature articles, depending
on subject matter.
$200-$350 for fiction and essays.

$25-$50 per poem, for poetry.

RIGHTS: All fees are for first-time rights, one-year
exclusivity guarantee by writer.

TRAVEL POLICY: No travel expenses paid except for ferry fare
to Martha's Vineyard or Nantucket for assigned
articles, and for lodging if extended stay is
necessary.

SPECS: Payment upon acceptance. All blind submissions
and queries received will be answered by publisher
in two to six weeks. Articles will not be returned
unless accompanied by SASE. Idea queries from
established writers only will be considered.

CQ | Carolina Quarterly

GREENLAW HALL 066A • UNIVERSITY OF NORTH CAROLINA • CHAPEL HILL, NC 27514

CAROLINA QUARTERLY is a literary journal published three times yearly. Circulation: 1000. We pay on acceptance. Byline is given. We buy first North American serial rights. Clean photocopied submissions are permissible, as are legible computer printouts. No proportionally-spaced or photo-typeset submissions. No simultaneous submissions. Self-addressed, stamped envelope required. Reports in 2-4 months. Address: Greenlaw Hall 066A, University of North Carolina, Chapel Hill, NC 27514. Phone: (919) 962-0244.

Guidelines for Writers

FICTION

We are interested in mature writing: control over language; command of structure and technique; understanding of the possibilities and demands of prose narrative with respect to style, characterization, and point of view. We publish many unsolicited stories; CQ is a market for newcomer and professional alike.

We buy 12-18 MSS each year. Send complete MS. Length: maximum, 7000 words without prior arrangement. We pay $3.00 per printed page.

POETRY

CQ places no restrictions on the length, form or substance of poems considered for publication, though limited space makes inclusion of works of more than 300 lines impractical.

We buy 40-60 MSS each year. Please submit 2-6 poems, no more. We pay $5.00 per printed poem.

PRIZES

Poets and fiction writers without substantial publication credits whose work appears in the *Quarterly* are eligible for the Charles G. Wood Award for Distinguished Writing, a $500 prize awarded annually by the editors.

NON-FICTION

Non-fiction articles are not commissioned; used at Editor's discretion. We may buy 1-2 MSS each year. Send complete MS. Length: maximum, 6000 words. We pay $3.00 per printed page.

PHOTOGRAPHY

We are interested in several high-quality photographs per issue. No restrictions on content. We pay $5.00 per photograph.

CAT FANCY
DOG FANCY
BIRD TALK
HORSE ILLUSTRATED
magazines

Editorial Offices
P.O. Box 6050
Mission Viejo, California 92690
Telephone (714) 240-6001

Cat Fancy

WRITER'S GUIDELINES

Thank you for your interest in our publications. We would be pleased to see your
material. Below we have listed some of the publication requirements of CAT FANCY,
DOG FANCY, BIRD TALK and HORSE ILLUSTRATED to assist you in preparing submissions.

ARTICLES

CAT FANCY, DOG FANCY and BIRD TALK are directed at the general pet owning population
and written for the adult audience. HORSE ILLUSTRATED is directed at the amateur
competitor and pleasure horse owner. We suggest that you read past issues of the
magazines to acquaint yourself with the types of material we use. Past issues may
be obtained by sending $3.00 to the above address. We need informative articles,
limited to 3,000 words, on the care of training of cats, dogs, birds, and horses
(health nutrition, training, etc.); photo essays on historical and current
events dealing with cats, dogs, birds and horses; how-to articles; human interest
stories; and good fiction, with the animal as the primary focus of interest. We
rarely use stories in which the animal speaks as if it were human. We use a breed
article in each issue, but these articles are assigned. Please query if you have
a breed article in mind.

Manuscripts should be typewritten, double-spaced with wide margins. We prefer that
articles be accompanied with appropriate art in the form of professional quality
color transparencies or black and white photographs (NOT SNAP SHOTS) or professional
illustrations. Additional guidelines are available for artists and photographers.

We are always happy to review material on speculation, but with the exception of
fiction, the best working procedure is to query before preparing an article. Our
usual rate of payment is three to five cents per printed word, five cents if accompanied by good quality photographs. Payment is made in the latter part of the
cover month in which your article appears, (i.e., if your piece was in the November
issue you would be paid in the latter part of November). We buy first American
rights only; all other rights revert back to the author.

We cannot assume responsibility for material submitted, but we assure you that
reasonable care will be taken in handling your work. YOU MUST INCLUDE A SELF-
ADDRESSED, STAMPED ENVELOPE WITH EACH SUBMISSION.

Cavalier

DUGENT PUBLISHING CORP.
2355 Salzedo St., Coral Gables, Florida 33134/(305) 443-2378

GUIDELINES FOR WRITERS

DUGENT PUBLISHING CORP. publishes three magazines, Cavalier, Gent and Nugget. We buy all fiction and articles from freelance writers. Each magazine has its own editorial slant and a description of each magazine's special needs follows:

CAVALIER is a sophisticated men's magazine aimed at the 18 to 35 year old male. We feature beautiful girls and entertaining fiction and articles. Stories must be professionally written and presented (first-timers welcome) and articles must be carefully researched and documented, if necessary. Subject matter for both stories and articles can vary from serious to sex to humor, keeping our readership in mind.

FICTION: We buy all types of fiction -- all kinds of plots, but they must be well-plotted and exceptionally well written. We are looking for good, solid stories...no intellectual or obtuse exercises and no poetry. We prefer at least one very graphic and erotic sexual encounter in each story and we are also interested in scenes of girl/girl fighting, or boy/girl fighting within the context of a story whether it is murder, science fiction, sex, horror or whatever. Length: 1,500 to 3,500 words. Pay from $200 to $300.

ARTICLES: Also cover a wide range but within the restriction that it must be a subject of interest to our readers, not dated material (since we have a four month lead time) and, preferably, that it be on a subject that is somewhat off-beat and not something that will be extensively covered by the media nationally. Please query first with a brief but comprehensive outline. First time writers may be asked to submit the finished article on speculation, but we give firm assignments to regular contributors. Where necessary, material must be carefully researched and documented. We are not interested in expose type articles, politics, historical figures or current events unless different and off-beat. Pay is similar to fiction but we pay additional for photos if submitted with article (and if professional and appropriate) and length is the same as for fiction. Our most urgent need is for non-fiction and we welcome beginners.

GENT: Specializes pictorially in large D-cup cheesecake and prefers both fiction and non-fiction articles gauged to the subject of breasts, bras, fat women, lactation, etc. Fictional female characters should be described as extremely large busted with detailed descriptions of breasts. Fiction length can vary from 2,500 to 3,500 words. Articles from 1,500 to 3,000 words. Payment is from $125 to $150 (with more for specialized material and articles with photos) upon publication. Query first on non-fiction articles, with brief comprehensive outline.

NUGGET: This magazine is primarily concerned with offbeat, fetish oriented material (sado-masochism, TV, TS, B&D,WS, amputees, fetishism, etc) and we prefer both fiction and articles slanted to this variety of subjects. Payment, length, etc., same as GENT magazine. Query first on articles.

WE DO NOT PUBLISH material on minors, religious subjects or on characters or subjects that might be considered libelous. Interviews (query first) must be accompanied by permission of the interviewee and supporting documentation. ALWAYS enclose self addressed stamped envelope for returns.

LARRY FLYNT PUBLICATIONS

CHIC FICTION/ARTICLE SPECIFICATIONS

All submissions should be written in a simple, straight-
forward style which is intelligent, yet easily readable.
PLEASE: All manuscripts <u>must</u> include a return envelope,
STAMPED AND SELF-ADDRESSED. All others will be destroyed.
Allow six weeks for response.

FICTION

Maximum length: 4000 words   Fee: $500.00

At present we are buying stories with emphasis on erotic
themes. These may be adventure, action, speculative fiction,
mystery or horror stories, but the tone and theme must involve
sex and eroticism. The main sex scene should be a minimum
of one-and-half pages of length. However, the erotic nature
of the story must not subordinate to the characterizations and
plot; the sex must grow logically from the people and the
plot, not be contrived or forced.

Stories should start fast and continue to move forward,
with a minimum of flashbacks, preferably none at all. The
dialogue should sound authentic and carry the story forward
as well as reveal the story's characters.

We do <u>not</u> buy poetry. Please refrain from stories with
themes about sex with minors, incest, homosexual activity
or blasphemy.

ARTICLES

Maximum length: 4000 words   Fee: $750.00

a. Satirical, light-hearted pieces on mainstream and adult
    entertainment industry - e.g. Stars, filmmakers, etc.
b. Hard-hitting, documented exposes.
c. Highly readable, well-researched material on all
    contemporary, social, political and sexual topics.

NOTE: All information, statistics and quotations used in
articles must be verifiable. (Every article is thoroughly
checked by our Research Department.) Please refrain from
using the first-person singular. Query first.

2029 CENTURY PARK EAST, SUITE 3800, LOS ANGELES, CALIFORNIA 90067 (213) 556-9200

PROFILE

Maximum length: 4000 words   Fee: $500.00

Up-close and personal looks at well-known or trend-setting individuals. Absolutely no promotional copy. Please refrain from using the first person singular. Query first.

SEX LIFE

Maximum length: 1500 words   Fee: $350.00

Informative pieces, written from a well-researched reportorial stand-point, on sexual mores around the world. Material can cover cultural pressures, rites of passage, bedroom technique, new trends in sexual medicine, surgery, therapy, etc.

THIRD DEGREE

Maximum lingth: 1000 words   Fee: $300.00

Interesting and unusual interviews with personalities in and out of the news who have something to say. Most often, people from off-beat walks of life are featured. Past examples include prostitutes, heavy-metal females, rock artists, transsexuals, ex-Moonie, and New York vice cop. The format is question/answer. Tape of conversation is required for back-up. An accompanying color photo of the interviewee pays an extra $50. The questions should be hard-hitting uncensored and provocative.

EDITORIAL GUIDELINES

INDIVIDUAL MAGAZINE NEEDS

MUCH OF THE MATERIAL USED IN ALL OF OUR MAGAZINES IS HEALTH-RELATED. THIS INCLUDES STORIES, POETRY, ARTICLES, AND ACTIVITIES.

TURTLE MAGAZINE FOR PRESCHOOL KIDS (ages 2 to 5)
HUMPTY DUMPTY'S MAGAZINE (ages 4 to 6)
CHILDREN'S PLAYMATE MAGAZINE (ages 5 to 7)

TURTLE uses bedtime or naptime stories (approximately 200 to 600 words) that can be read to the child. HUMPTY DUMPTY'S MAGAZINE and CHILDREN'S PLAYMATE use easy-to-read stories for the beginning reader. Fiction can be 500 to 800 words. All of these magazines use short, simple poems or stories in rhyme. Games and crafts should involve a minimum of adult guidance and have clear, brief instructions. Humorous stories and poems are especially needed. In HUMPTY DUMPTY and CHILDREN'S PLAYMATE, healthful recipes requiring little or no need for the stove are used.

JACK AND JILL (ages 6 to 8)
CHILD LIFE (ages 7 to 9)
CHILDREN'S DIGEST (ages 8 to 10)

Stories may run from 500 to 1800 words. Articles may run from 500 to 1200 words. When appropriate, articles should be accompanied by photographs or transparencies. Nonfiction material should list sources of information. We may use factual features dealing with nature, science, and sports—also some historical and biographical articles. Preferred fiction includes realistic stories, adventure, mysteries, and science fiction. Humorous stories are highly desirable. Also needed are healthful recipes (see page 2).

SAMPLE COPIES

We regret that we are unable to provide free sample copies of the magazines. Individual copies may be obtained for seventy-five cents each by writing to Children's Better Health Institute, P.O. Box 567, Indianapolis, IN 46206.

GENERAL INFORMATION

Children's Better Health Institute
Benjamin Franklin Literary & Medical Society, Inc.
1100 Waterway Boulevard
P.O. Box 567
Indianapolis, Indiana 46206

TURTLE MAGAZINE FOR PRESCHOOL KIDS

HUMPTY DUMPTY'S MAGAZINE

CHILDREN'S PLAYMATE MAGAZINE

JACK AND JILL • CHILD LIFE • CHILDREN'S DIGEST

Our goal at the Children's Better Health Institute is to provide children with good reading that not only entertains but also educates, primarily about good health. We have a constant need for high-quality stories, articles, and activities with an exercise, nutrition, safety, hygiene, or other health-related theme. Our emphasis is preventive medicine, and we are seeking material that will encourage young readers to practice better health habits.

Health information may be presented in a variety of formats. We are looking for fresh, creative ways to encourage children to develop and maintain good health. Fiction stories that deal with a health theme need not have health as the primary subject but should include it in some way in the course of events. Main characters in fiction stories should adhere to good health practices, unless failure to do so is necessary to a story's plot. Word and math puzzles, games, and other activities can also successfully convey health messages if they are enjoyable to youngsters and age-appropriate. We also use factual articles that teach scientific facts about the body or nutrition. Writers should avoid an encyclopedic or "preachy" approach. We try to present our health material in a positive manner, incorporating humor and a light approach wherever possible without minimizing the seriousness of what we are saying.

In all material, please avoid references to eating sugary foods, such as candy, cakes, cookies, and soft drinks. In recipes submitted for publication, ingredients should be healthful. Avoid sugar, salt, chocolate, red meat, and fats.

We are also interested in material with more general themes. We are especially in need of holiday material—stories, articles, and activities. Send seasonal material at least eight months in advance. Also remember that characters in realistic stories should be up-to-date. Many of our readers have working mothers and/or come from single-parent homes. We need more stories that reflect these changing times but at the same time communicate good, wholesome values.

MANUSCRIPT FORMAT

Manuscripts must be typewritten and double- or triple-spaced. The author's name, address, telephone number, Social Security number, and an approximate word count must appear on the first page of the manuscript. KEEP A COPY OF YOUR WORK. We'll handle your manuscript with care, but we cannot assume responsibility for its return. Please send the entire manuscript; queries are not necessary. The editors cannot criticize, offer suggestions, or enter into correspondence concerning unsolicited manuscripts that are not accepted, nor can they suggest other markets for material that is not published. MATERIAL CANNOT BE RETURNED unless it is accompanied by a self-addressed envelope and SUFFICIENT return postage.

PHOTOS

WE DO NOT PURCHASE SINGLE PHOTOGRAPHS. We do purchase short photo features (up to 6 or 8 pictures) or photos that accompany and help illustrate editorial matter. (Please include captions.)

REVIEW TIME REQUIRED

Time required to review manuscripts properly is about eight to ten weeks. Each manuscript is carefully considered for possible use in *all* the magazines, not only that one to which it was originally addressed; therefore, if a manuscript is returned, it should not be resubmitted to a different youth publication at this address.

RATES AND PAYMENT POLICIES

Fiction and articles: approximately six cents a word. Poetry: $7.00 and up. Photos: $7.00 minimum. Puzzles and games: no fixed rate. Payment is made upon publication. Each author will be sent two complimentary copies of the issue in which his or her material is published. Additional copies may be purchased for seventy-five cents each.

RIGHTS

We prefer to purchase all rights. Simultaneous submissions are not accepted.

CHILDREN'S CONTRIBUTIONS

Except for items that may be used in the children's columns that appear each month, the editors do not encourage submissions from children. Even highly talented young people are not usually experienced enough to compete on a professional level with adult authors.

CHIMERA CONNECTIONS, INC.
3712 NW 16th Blvd
Gainesville, FL 32605

Dear Potential Contributor:

Thank you for your interest in CHIMERA CONNECTIONS. The other enclosed
sheet describes some of our current projects, as well as subscription
rates. We urge you to purchase a sample copy, which will at least give
you a general idea as to what we look for.

As to specifics, we look for most of the same things other publications
look for. In good poetry, we look for use of language/poetic conventions,
imagery, emotion, and originality. In good prose, we look for clarity
of expression, strong plot lines or strong characterization (or both).
We are not biased against any particular "group" or "school of thought."
We prefer to look at works rather than the person behind the writing.
For example, our Fall/Winter 1987 issue will feature a fantasy story
by Harlan Ellison, a piece on the Beat Generation by A.D. Winans, and
a novel excerpt set in Appalachia (non-fiction) by Jane Stuart. Interviews with NEA Fellows Carol Muske and Yvonne Sapia are also included.

In all works, we look for strong verbs and nouns. We don't like lots
of adjectives or prepositions. All rules are made to be broken, however,
and we are willing to look at everything.

One last note: we write comments ON all rejected manuscripts. If you
do not want pencil marks on your work or do not want comments at all,
please let us know when you submit.

Sincerely,

Jeff VanderMeer   Duane Bray
Editors

PS--As mailing costs form our largest overhead, we appreciate extra loose
22¢ stamps. We also appreciate informative cover letters, whether telling
about yourself or about new markets which we can include in our market
section. Also, all writers accepted for our biannual issues are elligible
to enter our yearly chapbook contest free of charge. Only contributors
are allowed to enter a manuscript in this contest.

Chimera Connections

SUBSCRIPTIONS

Sample Copy
$3.50 postpaid
(Overseas add $2.00)

Subscriber
$12.00 (3 issues, 6 newsletters)

Colleague
$20.00 (3 issues, 6 newsletters, 9 indepth poetry critiques or 4 prose critiques, reduced contest entry fee of $1.00 per poem)

Associate
$30.00 (same as subscriber plus all cassettes and chapbooks produced during the subscription period)

Associate+
$40.00 (Colleague and Associate benefits)

Overseas subscribers add $10.00 to each rate. All amounts in U.S. funds only. No foreign money orders.

GENERAL GUIDELINES

CC accepts all forms of literature, including essays, nonfiction, novel excerpts, one-act plays, poetry, reviews, and short stories. No style restrictions. Submissions longer than 30 pages will have to be exceptional for publication. Other than length, there are no limitations. Anything is eligible, though many erotic and religious themes (as received through submissions) are overdone.

Response time: Maximum of 2 weeks. Payment: 2 copies, small amounts of cash for frequent contributors.

SASE with appropriate postage for return of manuscripts is required. No SASE, no response.

POETRY CONTEST

Entry fee: $2.00 per poem
Prizes: $50.00 + $30.00 **CC** products
$25.00 + $20.00 **CC** products
$15.00 + $10.00 **CC** products
Honorable Mentions receive a subscription to the magazine

1--No style/length restrictions
2--Typed, name/address on each page
3--SASE for return

DEADLINE: SEPTEMBER 26, 1987.

Winners plus honorable mentions are published in the magazine; poets receive 2 copies each. HMs are awarded as quality permits, though no more than 30 will be given out. The decisions of the judges are final. Comments will be written on all rejected manuscripts unless the poet objects prior to judging.

▬FUTURE ISSUES▬

A SPECIAL edition newsletter (~~June~~) will feature an interview with Pulitzer Prize-winner Richard Eberhart.

The Fall/Winter 1987 issue of the magazine, scheduled for ~~October~~ December distribution, will feature work from and interviews with NEA Fellows Carol Muske and Yvonne Sapia. Muske's latest book is **Wyndemere**. Sapia's **The Rooms of Ruined Light**, winner of the Morse Award and finalist for The Walt Whitman Award, will be published this fall. A short story by the master of dangerous visions, Harlan Ellison, and a novel excerpt from Jane Stuart's latest effort, **Why We Couldn't Keep Our Children**, are additional high-lights so far. Poetry contributions to the fourth issue include work by David J. Feela, Edward Lynsky, and A.J. Wright. Chimera Connections is still open to all forms of literature for the Fall/Winter issue.

The Spring/Summer 1988 issue will include interviews with Pulitzer Prize-winner Richard Wilbur and the author of the critically acclaimed **The Golden Gate**, Vikram Seth. Personal CC contact with overseas universities in Egypt, Taiwan, England, and Australia should bring in more foreign submissions to the magazine. Spread the word.

OF SPECIAL INTEREST: Sam Bruno's **Caught in a Revolving Door** and Janet McCann's **The Ghosts of Christmas**, co-winners of CC's first annual chapbook competition, are forthcoming from **Chimera Connections Press**. A poetry reading scheduled for the Fall will feature Yvonne Sapia and possibly Sam Bruno and Lola Haskins. For more information on these or any **CC activities**, send an SASE to 3712 NW 16th Blvd, Gainesville, FL 32605 (USA).

CLUBHOUSE MAGAZINE
Box 15
Berrien Springs, MI 49103

CLUBHOUSE is a Christian magazine for children between the ages of 9 and 14. It is designed to help young people feel good about themselves.

Our staff supplies a central Bible story with its accompanying puzzles and games for each issue of CLUBHOUSE Other stories, puzzles, games and recipes are usually supplied by freelance writers and are not religiously oriented in an overt way. However, they do represent Christian principles of behavior in action.

CLUBHOUSE needs:

Stories which demonstrate the good qualities and capabilities of young people. The best CLUBHOUSE stories are those which relate clever, selfless, kind, brave, heroic, etc. adventures in the lives of children who are 9 to 16 years of age.

Stories written in the first person. Often first-person stories are best, because the honest emotions (love, joy, hope, jealousy, annoyance, fear) on the part of the protagonist can be accepted by the reader without the tension of feeling preached at by adults. Stories written in the third person are also accepted.

Dynamic, entertaining stories. Humor, suspense, drama, clever storytelling, human interest, etc. are positive elements. Stories written to hammer a moral home are not the ones which are selected to appear.

Historical, health-related, inspirational stories. Each issue of CLUBHOUSE usually contains one story of an historical nature, one which is health-oriented (anti-drugs, pro good nutrition, etc.) and one which inspires faith that God is there to help kids.

Poetry: Most poems which we accept are from 4 to 24 lines in length, are humor or mood pieces and are on themes especially of interest to children.

Puzzles: We accept word-searches, mind-benders, deduction puzzles, secret codes, drawings with hidden objects, etc. Puzzles on Biblical themes are not accepted from freelance authors.

Crafts: Crafts should be suitable for 12-year-olds. Remember that boys read the magazines as well as girls, and crafts should be of interest of both.

Recipes: We try to stay away from recipes requiring sugar and artificial colorings and flavorings. Nutritious snacks, easy entrees and seasonal beverages are the most popular.

AGE APPEAL: Program your items for the 12- to 13-year-old child.

SPECIAL CONSIDERATIONS: Some of the denominations using CLUBHOUSE as supplementary material for their young people are conservative. Therefore, we cannot accept material dealing with certain topics including: Santa Claus, elves, reindeer, etc.; Halloween, witches, ghosts, magic; etc.; space fantasy, science fiction, and supernatural happenings not involving God.

FORMAT: Stories should be approximately 1000 to 1200 words long, typewritten or computer generated and double-spaced.

SUBMISSION TIME: Think spring! Please send your material during March and April. During the month of May, final selections will be made. Notifications of acceptance or rejection will be made in mid-June. Items submitted at times other than March-April will be read, evaluated and sent back. Authors will be notified to return items of interest during the next April for possible acceptance. Any suggestions given for improvement should not be considered as an assignment, but rather as a way to make the material more likely to be accepted.

RIGHTS: CLUBHOUSE is copyrighted. We buy one-time rights—first, second or reprint rights—and accept simultaneous submissions.

PAYMENT: Stories—$25 to $35—most are $30 Poetry—usually $10 to $20; Puzzles—$10-$12; Crafts—$10-$12; Recipes—$10-$12. Notification of acceptance will be made in mid-June, and checks will clear the accounting office about mid-August.

Writers' Guidelines and Theme List

Editor-in-Chief: Carolyn P. Yoder
Assistant Editor: Lisa L. Elsemore
Admin. Assistant: Holly S. Blanchette

General Information: Historical accuracy and lively, original approaches to the subject are the primary concerns of the editors in choosing material. All material must relate to the theme of a specific issue in order to be considered (write for themes of upcoming issues). COBBLESTONE purchases all rights to materials. Previously published material is sometimes accepted (one-time rights purchased).

Sample issue is available at $3.95. Allow several weeks for delivery. Writers are encouraged to study recent back issues for content and style.

Procedure: A query must consist of all of the following to be considered: a brief cover letter stating the subject and length of the proposed article; a one-page outline explaining the information to be presented in the article; a bibliography of materials the author intends to use in preparing the article; a self-addressed stamped envelope. (Writers new to COBBLESTONE should send a writing sample to be kept on file.)

A writer may send as many queries for one issue as he or she wishes, but each query must have a separate cover letter, outline, bibliography, and SASE. Telephone queries are not accepted. Handwritten queries will not be considered.

Guidelines: Feature articles, 800-1,200 words. Includes in-depth nonfiction, plays, and biographies. Pays 13¢-15¢ per printed word.

Supplemental nonfiction, 200-800 words. Includes subjects directly and indirectly related to the theme. Editors like little-known information but encourage writers not to overlook the obvious. Pays 10¢-12¢ per printed word.

Fiction, up to 1,500 words. Authentic historical and biographical fiction, adventure, retold legends, etc., relating to the theme. Pays 10¢-15¢ per printed word.

Activities, up to 1,000 words. Includes crafts, recipes, woodworking projects, etc., that can be done either by children alone or with adult supervision. Query should be accompanied by sketches and description of how activity relates to theme. Pays on an individual basis.

Poetry, up to 100 lines. Clear, objective imagery. Serious and light verse considered. Pays on an individual basis. Must relate to theme.

Puzzles and Games (no word finds). Crosswords and other word puzzles using the vocabulary of the issue's theme. Mazes and picture puzzles that relate to the theme. Pays on an individual basis.

On the following page are some themes and deadlines for previous issues.

COBBLESTONE (continued)

Month	Theme	Query Deadline
Sep/87	The American Revolution: British Loyalists Living Here	1/15/87
Oct/87	Albert Einstein	2/15/87
Nov/87	The Amish--by assignment*	3/15/87
Dec/87	Theater	3/15/87
Jan/88	War of 1812	6/29/87
Feb/88	The South as Perceived by Its Artists	8/3/87
Mar/88	U.S. and Canada	8/31/87
Apr/88	Mystic/Life in a Nineteenth-Century Sea Town-- by assignment	9/28/87
May/88	Five Great Lakes	11/2/87
Jun/88	Battle of Gettysburg	11/30/87
Jul/88	Daniel Boone: Exploring the U.S. Frontier	1/1/88
Aug/88	American Architecture	2/1/88
Sep/88	Thomas Jefferson and Andrew Jackson: Birth of the Two-Party System	2/29/88

Note: Queries may be submitted at any time, but queries sent well in advance of deadline MAY NOT BE ANSWERED FOR SEVERAL MONTHS. Answers to queries are usually sent approximately 5-6 months before the publication date.

*By-assignment writers have been published at least three times in COBBLESTONE.

hsb/10-86

Cobblestone Publishing, Inc. • 20 Grove Street • Peterborough, N.H. 03458 • (603) 924-7209

Colorado Review

The Colorado Review prefers fiction submitted in the following format: first and foremost--clean copy; double-spaced typescript (no dot matrix please); we will consider xeroxed copies, though we hope that does not mean the author is multi-submitting. Name of author should appear on each page. We copyright first North American serial rights; permission to reprint carries with it an agreement to acknowledge Colorado Review in subsequent publications. We are looking for contemporary stories that are keenly observant, psychologically insightful, important thematically, and carried off with a language that is detailed, textured, and convincing. Payment in free subscription unless grants make cash possible. COLORADO REVIEW, Fiction Ed., c/o English Department, Colorado State University, Ft. Collins, CO 80523.

conditions

Submissions

Submissions will be accepted for the upcoming edition of *conditions: 15* from September 1987 to April 1988. The collective welcomes writing by women from all over the world who feel that a commitment to women is an integral part of their lives.

We are interested in manuscripts of poetry, fiction, drama, novel and correspondence excerpts, interviews, journal entries, translations, book reviews, and critical articles. The issues of race, class, age and women's/lesbian movements, relationships and institutions are of particular concern. We are also accepting photographs and other visuals for inclusion in our publication.

conditions magazine is especially committed to publicizing and reviewing women's press publications, and welcomes review copies.

Manuscripts

- Only writings previously unpublished in the United States will be considered.
- Manuscripts must be typed and double-spaced.
- Submissions four pages or less may be submitted in any language if accompanied by an English translation.
- Submissions over four pages must be translated into English.
- Enclose a self-addressed envelope with sufficient United States postage or International Certificate for return of manuscripts or further correspondence.
- Include a fifty word biographical statement which includes your date and place of birth, current residence and phone number.
- Be sure to retain a copy of your submission.
- If you wish to have receipt of your material acknowledged, please enclose a self-addressed stamped postcard.

Visuals

- Photographs, graphic designs, line drawings and visuals in any media should be suitable for reproduction in black and white 8½"x5" format.
- Photographs must be labeled with information regarding the subject matter, date and place of shooting.
- Other visuals should indicate media used, and original size.
- Enclose biographical information and sufficient U.S. postage or International Certificate for return of material.

Send all manuscripts and artwork to *conditions*, P.O. Box 150056, Van Brunt Station, Brooklyn, New York 11215-0001, U.S.A.

The *conditions* collective is comprised of editors whose diverse cultural background, racial and regional backgrounds reflect the magazines continuing concern for recording the experiences and viewpoints of women of color, lesbians, working class, older and disabled women.

Corvette Fever Magazine

Contributor Guidelines

a publication of
PROSPECT PUBLISHING CO., Inc.
P.O. Box 44620
Ft. Washington, MD 20744

(301) 839-2221

Corvette Fever Magazine is actively developing a world-wide network of writers, photographers and artists to contribute to the magazine. We want your talent and we're willing to pay for it. If you're anxious to team up with the fastest growing Corvette publication in the field, read the rest of this. You can turn your Corvette knowledge, experience and enthusiasm into gold. And become (almost) famous between the covers of Corvette Fever.

Major Features

Cover Feature Stories: We run a full length cover feature article every issue. Recent features have included the Z06, the ZL-1, and the Grand Sports. The car is used on the cover in four color, given a two-page, four-color spread inside, and normally another color page plus two or three additional black and white pages. These are *not* run-of-the-mill Vettes — our cover features are all special cars in one way or another. Plenty of color slides and 1,200 plus words of text are used.

Feature Length Technical Articles: Each issue we publish at least one and usually two detailed technical articles on some mechanical aspect of the Corvette. We've recently done full length treatment of transmissions, clutches, water injection, manifolds, carburetors, etc.

Major Event Coverage: These are the large national or regional events that all of our readers are interested in, whether they attend or not. In past issues we've covered Bloomington, the NCCC and WSCC conventions, the NCRS Florida Winter Meet, the McDorman swap meet, Carlisle, Knoxville, and others.

Regular Departments

Shop Profile: We need detailed stories on the major manufacturers, distributors, designers, modifiers and repairers of Corvettes.

Personality Profile Interview: This is the department where we talk at length with the people who have made, are making, or will make an impression of some kind on the Corvette community, whether it's in design and engineering, modifying, manufacturing, racing, restoring, collecting, or whatever.

Readers' Cars: Want your Vette to be seen and envied by thousands of other owners? Send us a clear color print along with the year of the car and a complete name and address. (These are not returned unless accompanied by a SASE.)

Restoration: Spent a lot (or a little) time and money reconstructing a venerable basket case? We want our readers to know about it. You *must* have before, during and after photo sequences detailing exactly what you did and how you did it, along with a similarly detailed description.

Club News: Put us on your mailing list for your club newsletter. We want our readers to know about your club, and it's a good way for you to tell readers in your area about your organization, its people and events.

Literature Reviews: If you're publishing a new book, catalog, poster, calendar, etc., send us a copy and we'll let our readers know about it.

Humor: Had a funny thing happen to you and your Vette? Write it up and send it in. Sometimes a good sense of humor is the only thing that keeps many of us from trading the plastic beast in on a nice Chevette!

Letters to the Editor: How are we doing? Do you like what you see in the pages of Corvette Fever? Have we been ignoring your favorite subject, model year, etc.? Spending too much time on something? Do you agree with us — disagree? Did we do something wrong (or right)? Make a mistake? Let us and the readers know!

Tech Q & A: Have a technical question about your Vette? Not getting straight answers from Mr. Goodwrench? Send it in. Our Technical Editor is one of the best Corvette restoration experts in the country.

Vanity Plates: Does your Vette have a license plate that expresses your feelings about your car, your life, yourself? Send us a good photo.

Competition: Cover racing/rallying/drag events for Vettes and send the story to us.

New Products: If you're manufacturing or distributing something of interest to other owners, send us news releases and good black and white photos (5'' x 7'' or 3'' x 5'').

Performance: Found a way to make your Vette go faster, handle better, get improved gas mileage, etc.? Share it with our readers.

Vettevents: Want to increase the attendance at your next swap meet, concours, race or speed event or charitable function? A lot of our readers will attend — but first you have to tell us so we can tell them. Send in your flyer or brochure and we'll let the Corvette world know about it.

Wheelin' & Dealin': If you're buying and selling Corvettes for a living and want to tell our readers about the sales activity in your part of the country, send us a letter to that effect and wait for our call. Every issue we talk with dealers and publish the interviews.

Vettemates: Photograph your favorite beauty and plastic car in color. They may grace the only 4-color centerfold in the Corvette world. This section requires 35mm slides or 2-1/4'' x 2-1/4'' transparencies.

Did We Miss Anything? Probably. Corvette owners are among the best educated, highest income people in the country, and their interests are wide-ranging. If you have an idea for a regular department, let us know. There's always room for more information of interest to our readers in Corvette Fever.

Need Some Article Ideas?

Here are just a few we haven't had time to work on:

● Special interest Vettes: LT-1, L-88, L-89, LS-6, all the big blocks
● Fuel injection: the concept, the hardware, the cars, the people
● Custom Vettes and customizing parts
● Indy Vette and Silver Anniversary retrospective — the how, why, when and where
● Basic emissions controls: do we need them, why do we have them, what do they do, is there any (legal) way around them?
● Survey of female and over 55 Vette owners — who are they?

►►

- Basic bolt-ons — carbs, manifolds, heads, tires, shocks,etc.
- Soft tires and racing — good or bad?
- Production figures by year, option and option combination
- How to set up a speed event
- Basic fiberglass: the what, how and why
- Basic articles on electrical fuel, suspension, steering systems
- Why didn't the T-Bird stay in pursuit of the Vette?
- How good is Corvette customer service?
- Spectators at events — who are they, why are they there?
- Where does the Vette fit into GM's future?
- Zora: where is he now, his thoughts on Vettes of the future
- Different types of paints and how they're used
- How things are made: plugs, shocks, engines, transmissions, tires, etc.
- How to install articles: tops, seat covers, mufflers, etc.,etc.,etc.

How and Where to Send Material

Manuscripts

Policy: All manuscripts must be directly or indirectly related to the Corvette. Feature articles may cover a variety of Corvette-related topics including historical or futuristic pieces, technical or mechanical how-to articles or pictorials, Corvette personality profiles, event coverage, customized or unusual (rare) Corvettes, the Corvette division of General Motors or personal experiences with a Corvette. Articles may be humorous, serious, satirical, informative or controversial.

Preparation: A query letter with an outline is recommended but not essential.

Length of manuscripts should be between 500 and 1,800 words. Copy is to be typed and double-spaced with wide margins. Any manuscripts received must be free of libel and plagiarism and must be original.

We prefer a minimum of three photographs for every 500 words.

Payment: 10¢ per published word. Payment is made within 60 days of publication.

Photography

Policy: Photographs are used only with copy or as assigned. If you would like to be considered for future assignments, send samples of your work to be kept on file.

Preparation: Clear black and white or color prints can be reproduced, however, transparencies and slides are requested.

Covers should be vertical color transparencies or slides allowing adequate space for printing. They must relate to an article within the issue. Potential cover photos should be accompanied with articles. Cover photos may also be done by assignment.

Centerspreads are to be horizontal 35mm or larger slides or transparencies. They should include a model, a Corvette and a complimentary setting, composed to create an attractive photograph. A minimum of four photographs should be submitted for Vettemate. A signed model release *must* be included. Supply information about the model such as name, interests, age, occupation and Corvette involvement. Name car owner if credit is desired. Complete details on the car should also be included.

Payment: B&W: $5 to $25
Color: $10 - $40
Cover: $150
Centerspread: $150
Payment is made within 60 days of publication.

Artwork

Policy: Corvette Fever is mainly a photographer's magazine. Artwork is accepted when accompanied by an article or by assignment. If you would like to be considered for future assignments, send samples of your work to be kept on file.

Payment:
Cartoons: $5 - $50
Other artwork: Payment negotiable
Payment within 60 days of publication

Mailing Procedure

Corvette Fever will handle your work with care, however, we assume no responsibility for loss or damage. If you would like materials returned, enclose a self-addressed encelope with sufficient postage. When mailing, consider the advantages of insured, first class mail. Materials which are published become the property of Corvette Fever Magazine, and will not be returned. Send all materials to:

Corvette Fever Magazine
Editorial Department
P.O. Box 44620
Ft. Washington, MD 20744

Telephone: (301) 839-2221

Editorial Profile

Corvette Fever encompasses the complete story of the Corvette, from its early history as a prototype to its emergence as one of today's most lucrative investments. It is aimed at the enthusiast and owner alike who have interests in restoration techniques, performance tips, new product developments plus insights into the total Corvette market.

Corvette Fever publishes technical how-to articles, historical features and Corvette personality profiles to provide the reader with a comprehensive view of the Corvette world. Every issue Corvette Fever reaches across the nation reporting on a variety of Corvette related products to more readers than any other Corvette magazine on the market today.

Corvette Fever is unique in its viewpoint and therefore reaches an audience of professional people as well as those eager to mold their own fender flares. Corvette Fever appeals to all sectors involved with the marque and will very soon become known as the *only* Corvette magazine.

COSMOPOLITAN

224 West 57th Street, New York, New York 10019

COSMOPOLITAN, 224 West 57th Street, N.Y., N.Y. 10019

Helen Gurley Brown, Editor. Issued monthly, $~~1.95~~ 2.50 a copy, ~~$24.00~~ $24.97 a year.

Non-Fiction: Roberta Ashley, Executive Editor. Magazine aims at young career women. All non-fiction should tell these readers 1) how they can improve their lives, 2) better enjoy their lives, and 3) live better lives. Within this sphere, articles can be of the widest range, from celebrity profiles to psychological/ sociological pieces of humor. Crisp, incisive, entertaining writing is a must, with a heavy emphasis on reader involvement. Full-length articles should be about 5,000 words, features 1,000 to 3,000 words. Payment for full-lengthers usually varies from $750 to $1500, but this is open to negotiation. Payment for features is proportionately less.

Fiction: Betty Kelly, Fiction and Books Editor.
Stories must have solid upbeat plots, and sharp characterization. They should focus on contemporary man-woman relationships. Sophisticated handling and sensitive approach is a must, and female protagonists are preferred since our readers most easily identify with them. Short-shorts range from 1,500 words to 3,000 words; Short-stories from 4,000 to 6,000 words. Payment is $1,000 andup for short stories, from $300 to $600 for short- shorts. Previously published serious novels and mystery and suspense novels are sought for condensing and excerpting; payment here is open to negotiation, with the author's agent or hard cover publisher.

PLEASE ENCLOSE A SELF-ADDRESSED STAMPED ENVELOPE OR YOUR

SUBMISSION CANNOT BE RETURNED

COTTONWOOD MAGAZINE AND PRESS

Box J, Kansas Union   Editor: George F. Wedge
University of Kansas   Fiction Editor: Tamara Dubin Brown
Lawrence, Kansas 66045   Poetry Editor: Philip Wedge

Publishes: 3/yr
established: 1965
circulation: 500
copyrighted

COTTONWOOD is a literary magazine publishing new and well-known writers. We
publish a wide variety of styles of poetry and fiction but tend not to accept
academic writing, workshop produce, or rhymed couplets. We generally prefer
work that comes from experience and are particularly interested in work from
or about the Kansas midwest. Poetry submissions should be limited to the five
best, fiction to one story. In fiction we are not interested in stories which
are contrived or slick. We also tend not to accept highly experimental work.
Past issues have included interviews with William Stafford, Galway Kinnell,
and Seamus Heaney. We have published recent work by Harley Elliott, William
Kloefkorn, Ted Kooser, William Stafford, Jared Carter, Victor Contoski, Robert
Day and Rod Kessler. We welcome submissions of photos, graphics, short
fiction, poetry, and reviews of books from authors or presses in the midwest.
We critique rejected mss. when there is time and if they show promise. All
correspondence should include an SASE with correct postage. We acquire one-
time rights.

fiction length: 500-8000 words
poetry length: 10-75 lines
acceptance: 3-5 stories/issue, 20-25 poems/issue
reporting time: 1-3 months
payment: 1 copy
samply copy: $3, $2 for back issues
subscription price: $12/year

Country Woman

5400 South 60th Street ● Greendale, WI 53129 (414) 423-0100

GUIDE FOR FREE-LANCERS

Country Woman (formerly Farm Woman) is a 68-page, full-color bimonthly magazine for rural women. It is a positive, upbeat, entertaining publication that reflects the many interests and roles of its readers through short, photo-illustrated personality profiles of rural women and features about parenting and grandparenting, church and community involvement, decorating and crafts, cooking, health and fitness, and partnership in farm, ranch or rural businesses.

Free-lance material to be considered for publication no longer needs to be limited to coverage of farm women, but should have a rural theme and be of specific interest to women who live on a farm or ranch, or women who live in a small town or country home, and/or simply have an interest in country-oriented topics.

Contributors are strongly urged to study the magazine carefully before querying or submitting. (CW is not available on newsstands--sample copies can be obtained for $2.00 and a 9x12 self-addressed, stamped envelope. Subscriptions are $12.98/year. Since we sell no advertising and support Country Woman solely with subscriptions, we have no "comp" list.)

Many of the stories, columns, anecdotes and photos in CW come directly from its readers. But we count on free-lancers such as you for the balance of each issue. Here are some of our regular features that free-lancers help us with:

Profiles of Country Women...told in a light, conversational style with plenty of direct quotes and illustrated with bright, clear, candid color photos (see photo tips at end of guidelines). Should have a strong, readily identifiable "angle" and point and clearly explain the "why" behind what the woman is doing. Recent issues have included: A California farm woman who promotes agriculture through helium balloons that she fills on her ranch...a farm woman who helped her husband regain his health after a fall from a silo...a farm woman who has made a hobby of collecting antique clothing. Again, these profiles are no longer limited solely to farm women; feaues on women who live on a country place or in a small town are welcomed. Payment for text-and-photos package, on acceptance: $100-$225.

Country Commerce...features about country women who have started their own cottage industries or assumed management of a farm, ranch or rural business. Maximum length: 1,000 words. Rate: $85-$225.

Service Features...A good approach is to focus on a country woman who has first-hand experience in health, safety, fitness and/or self-improvement. Provide specific "how to" information and indicate sources of further information readers may seek out. Maximum length: 1,000 words. Rate: $85-$200.

Country Crafts, Sewing, Needlework...emphasizing crafts with a country theme. Photos should show the item in the making as well as in completed form. Include

-over-patterns and directions. If no photos are available, please enclose actual item.

We can always use features on contemporary sewing methods and ideas and practical wardrobe planning also. Rate: $50-$150.

Decorating...Focusing especially on country kitchens, which are featured in each issue. In addition, we're always looking for features on home improvements--along with before and after photos--short tips on decorating and exciting features on how-to accomplish that "country look". Again, good quality color transparencies are a must. Rate: $40-$225.

Nostalgia...We're looking for well-written nostalgic pieces that fall into three categories: "I Remember When..." is a country woman's recollection of a past event that the vast majority of readers can identify with; "I'll Never Forget..." is a more personal recollection describing an event unique to the writer; general nostalgia captured in fiction and poetry. Length: 500 words. Rate: $60-$90.

Inspirational...Rather than running an inspirational column by the same writer each issue, we use the thoughts and reflections of various authors and rural women. We don't want material to be denominational but rather focus on faith as it relates to the daily life of country families. Many of these pieces appear as "thoughts from the country" on the back cover. Length: 500 words. Rate: $60-$120.

Poetry...Must have a rural theme; we prefer traditional poetic styles. Please no more than 6 poems per 1 submission per month. Poems should be 4 to 20 lines in length, with some exceptions. Rate: $40-$65.

Fiction...Well-written short fiction is a continuing need. The subjects should center on life in the country, its problems and joys, as experienced by women, and contain a positive, upbeat message. Length: 750 words. Rate: $90-$125.

Country Almanac...This regular feature is a page of short, seasonal pieces ranging from poetry, inspiration, tips, how-to's and reflections that fit together for an "almanac look". We are eager to receive short pieces that would work on this page. Rate: $25-$75.

Free-lance Photography (and photography included to illustrate an article)... Country Woman is always looking for high-quality color photography. For reproduction purposes, we prefer 35 mm or 4 x 5 transparencies.

Our rates for front-cover color range from $100-$300 per shot depending on quality. (Please request our special cover guidelines if interested.) Generally, a back page photo is either a mood-setting shot or a nice scenic. $75-$125 is our standard rate.

Rates for inside photos or photo essays in color and black-and-white vary... depending on use.

Again, covers are planned in advance. As a result, submissions should be in our hands at least 6 months before the issue's date. Please send photography via certified or registered mail and include return postage. If registered, please indicate the value of the material so we may insure it for the proper amount.

Unless a specific assignment is made, all free-lance material will be considered

--3

on a speculative basis. CW is published 6 times a year. The ideal deadline
for free-lance material is 5 months before the date of the issue. Manuscripts
should be typed and double spaced. Please enclose a stamped, self-addressed
return envelope. A decision on free-lance material is generally made within
a month after receipt of the article. Payment is upon acceptance. If querying,
please enclose a stamped, self-addressed envelope.

If you are notified that your manuscript is being held for future publication
and later on you have an inquiry about its status, please enclose a self-addressed
return envelope. Be sure to remind us of the subject matter of the article in
your letter--don't just give the title. This will help us locate it in our files.
Of course, articles we hold are not available for resale until we've notified
you of publication.

Please send your material to Eleanor Jacobs, Managing Editor, Country Woman,
P.O. Box 643, Milwaukee, WI 53201. (For a sample copy, send $2.00 to the above
address.)

<u>Cream City Review</u> Submission Guidelines

All submissions must be typed. The author's name and address should appear on the first page of the manuscript. Photocopies are acceptable, and we do consider simultaneous submissions.

Please include a few lines about your publication history and other personal information you think of interest. Address your envelope to the appropriate department. Enclose a SASE (stamped self-addressed envelope) with each submission. Be sure to keep a copy of your work--<u>CCR</u> cannot be responsible for lost manuscripts.

Reporting time is from three to eight weeks, though we will try to respond as quickly as possible. Payment varies with funding. Contributors also get two free copies. Copyright reverts to author after publication.

The stories we publish are usually shorter than thirty pages, but we will consider longer material. We seek experimental as well as traditional work and strive for a balance of the two in every issue. No anecdotes, sexism, erotica, or "formulas" please.

Send all submissions to:
<u>Cream City Review</u>
Department of English
PO Box 413
University of Wisconsin--Milwaukee
Milwaukee, WI 53201

Please send
$2.00 for
sample copy.

In September 1973, the Open Court Publishing Company started publication of CRICKET, a literary magazine for children ages 6 to 12.

CRICKET publishes original stories, poems, and articles written by the world's best children's authors. In some cases, CRICKET purchases first North American serial rights for excerpts from books yet to be published. Each issue also includes several reprints of high quality selections.

CRICKET measures 7" x 9", contains 64 pages, has a full-color cover, and is staple-bound. Black-and-white illustrations of the highest quality appear throughout the magazine with selective use of one additional color.

We hope that the following information will be useful to prospective contributors:

Editor-in-Chief: Marianne Carus

Art Director: Maryann Leffingwell

Published: 12 months a year

Price: $22.50 for 1-yr. subscription (12 issues)

Categories

Fiction: realistic, historic, fantasy, science fiction, folk tale, fairy tale, legend, myth, picture stories

Non-Fiction: biography, history, science, technology, natural history, social science, geography, foreign culture, travel, adventure, sports

Poetry: serious, humorous, nonsense rhymes, limericks

Other: puzzles, jokes and riddles, plays, music, art, crafts, recipes

Length: stories - 200 to 1500 words
articles - 200 to 1200 words
poems - not longer than 100 lines

- 2 -

Rates: stories and articles - up to 25¢ per word
(1500 words maximum)
poems - up to $3.00 per line
payment on publication

Art: CRICKET commissions all art separately. Any
review samples of artwork will be considered.

Comments: We would like to reach as many children's
authors and artists as possible for original
contributions, but our standards are very high,
and we will accept only top quality material.
Please do not query first. We will consider
any manuscripts or art samples sent on speculation and accompanied by a self-addressed stamped
envelope. If you are sending an original art
portfolio, package it carefully and insure the
package.

CRICKET normally purchases the following rights for works
appearing in the magazine:

1. For stories and poems previously unpublished, CRICKET
purchases first North American serial rights. Payment is
made on publication.

2. For stories and poems previously published, CRICKET purchases
second North American serial rights. Fees vary, but are
generally less than fees for first serial rights. Payment
is made on publication. Same applies to accompanying art.

3. For re-occurring features, CRICKET purchases the material
outright. The work becomes the property of CRICKET, and
it is copyrighted in the name of Open Court. A flat fee
per feature is usually negotiated. Payment is made on
publication.

4. For commissioned art, assigned by CRICKET's art director,
CRICKET normally purchases all reproduction rights subject
to the terms outlined below:

(a) Physical art remains the property of the illustrator.

(b) Payment is made on acceptance.

Address any inquiries regarding these policies to:

Permissions Department   Telephone: 815/223-2520
CRICKET
P.O. Box 300
Peru, IL 61354

THE MAGAZINE

The *Crusader* is a Christian-oriented magazine for boys aged 9-14. It circulates among 13,000 boys in the United States and Canada who are members of a Christian youth organization known as the Calvinist Cadet Corps. Boys from several Protestant denominations make up *Crusader's* audience.

Although the *Crusader* is the official publication of the Cadet Corps, it publishes material designed to appeal to every pre-adolescent boy.

Generally speaking, *Crusader* boys are active, inquisitive, and imaginative. They imitate "heroes" they see in the world around them, and they love adventure. They are sociable and form gangs easily. Many of them make decisions for Christ that affect them the rest of their lives.

CRAFTS & HOBBY ARTICLES: Stimulating with clear, accurate instructions. Made with easily accessible materials. Our artists can illustrate.

SPORT ARTICLES: Coaching tips, articles about athletes, articles about developing Christian character through sports — up to 1,500 words. Black and white photos appreciated. Be original.

CAMPING & NATURE: Camping skills, nature study, survival exercises. Practical "how to do it" approach works best. "God in nature" themes also appreciated, if done without "preachiness."

FICTION: Fast moving stories that appeal to a boy's sense of adventure or sense of humor are always welcome. Avoid "preachiness." Avoid simplistic answers to complicated problems. Avoid long dialog and little action.

CARTOONS: Boy oriented, of course.

MISC: Nothing is too strange to be read and considered.

SUBMISSIONS

COPY: Typed, double-spaced, on a good grade of white paper. Name and address in upper left corner, along with number of words, statement regarding terms of sale (all rights, first right, or second rights.)

Enclose a stamped, self-addressed envelope for return.

Address correspondence and submissions to:

Managing Editor
***CRUSADER* Magazine**
Box 7259
Grand Rapids, MI 49510

SECOND RIGHTS: We have no qualms about purchasing rights to articles that have been printed elsewhere, providing the audiences do not overlap.

CARTOONS: Single gags, panels, and full-page cartoons. Send finished cartoons and self-addressed, stamped envelop for return.

EDITING & REJECTIONS: The *Crusader* staff reserves the right to edit any accepted manuscript or cartoon. Rejected submissions will be put in the mail within one week of the final decision.

RATE OF PAYMENT: Payment is made upon final acceptance of the material, occasionally varying according to the amount of editing required. The current rates:

WRITTEN MATERIAL: 3¢ per word and up (first rights with no major editing)

CARTOONS: $5.00 and up for single gags — $15.00 and up for full page panels.

PUZZLES: rates vary

PHOTOS: $5.00 for each photo used with an article.

Guidelines

for Writers
Photographers
Cartoonists
Illustrators
Clipping Services
and other Freelancers.

Voice of the National Organization for River Sports

Address all material to:
NORS/CURRENTS Editor
314 No. 20th Street
Colorado Springs, CO 80904
(303) 473-2466

Follow These Steps:

1. If you haven't seen a recent issue, ask at your local river-equipment shop. (If there isn't one near you, send us 75 cents in postage stamps and we'll send one.) Examine the issue, and see how your article or art might fit in. All too often we get material that is not about kayaking, rafting, or river canoeing, or that treats river running at a very introductory level such as would be found in a Sunday newspaper supplement. Don't waste your and our time with materials that don't belong in a river magazine!

2. Send a query letter and sample of your previous work. (If your article, photo, or art is already done, just send it.) Include a self-addressed, stamped envelope, with sufficient postage on it to cover the weight of your materials.

3. After we have examined your materials, or your query, we'll send a reply. If we have decided to buy rights to your material, the reply will include payment. If not, it will include your materials.

4. If we buy rights to your material, we will publish it then send you a couple of copies and your originals.

Note: Normally you should only send photos and manuscripts that have never been published elsewhere, and you should not send duplicates to other magazines at the same time. If you have a truly unique piece that you think should appear in several publications, mark it clearly: "Simultaneous Submission—also sent to _____," or "Previously Published Submission—appeared in _____."

We usually buy first rights, for one-time publication. When you get your originals back from us after publication, you can re-sell rights to another editor, marking the materials clearly: "Previously Published Submission—appeared in CURRENTS."

Know Your Audience

In rough figures, about 60% of the readers are kayakers, 25% are rafters, and 15% are river canoeists. We usually lump the three together as "river runners." Material should strive to **appeal to all three.**

Readers are generally well-educated. Average age is around thirty. Readers are in all parts of the U.S. and several foreign countries. Manuscripts must appeal to this national audience, and must not contain unclear references to local landmarks.

Most readers are at least moderately experienced paddlers. They turn to CURRENTS for expertise and authority. We therefore don't publish materials about "my first raft trip" or "my experiences while learning to kayak." (You may be able to sell such articles and photos to the lifestyle section of your local newspaper.)

Organization of *CURRENTS*:

The first half of the magazine contains several different "Sections," which are articles about the river scene and its evolution. The second half of the magazine is "**Departments**," which contain data, opinion, and non-article items.

Sections (Articles about the river scene and its evolution.)

River Conservation — news articles that present both sides of a dam or other proposed project that will damage a **popular whitewater** river run. Descriptions of a river that is **actively** being considered for Wild & Scenic status. Articles about river restoration on urban rivers, with "before" and "after" photos. Article should start off with a lead that tells the reader **why** this issue and this river are of importance to him. It must clarify which **section** of the river is involved. It should quote, or paraphrase, the dam-builders and the river runner/conservationists. It should tell paddlers what, if anything, they can do about it. The article

can be an actual trip account, but modified to discuss conservation of the river. **Photos:** Dams in progress, or sites of proposed dams. Headquarters of dam-builders. Portraits of the people involved. Action shots of kayaking, rafting, or canoeing on that river. Scenic shots. **Don't send:** Articles or photos on rivers that are too small or too flat for river running, or too obscure for a national audience. A river is "of national interest" if boaters from several other states come to run it every year.

River Access — news articles about government regulations (permit systems) on rivers, or private land problems along rivers, or cases where sheriffs close rivers in the name of safety, but boaters think they should remain open. Can be a trip account with access emphasis. **Photos:** Rangers arresting boaters. Sheriffs patrolling rivers. Landowners scowling. "Keep out" and "river closed" signs. Action or scenic shots on the river in question.

River Profiles — This is a catch-all section that has contained feature articles about paraplegic river runners, international river trips, and descriptions of several rivers in one region. We don't print straight trip accounts unless the river is of special interest for some reason. **Photos:** As needed to illustrate articles. This is a good section for special-effects photos.

River Technique — This is the section for which we most need articles. They can cover how to kayak, raft, or canoe, of course, but also many other "techniques"—how to camp in low-impact style, how to make or repair equipment, how to make a car rack, how to pack overnight gear for the river, and so on. Readers look to CURRENTS for expertise: If you're an expert on a subject, great, but if you aren't that's good too, because often we would prefer an article that interviews one or more experts on a subject, especially if it compares somewhat different viewpoints. Our readers really love such debate. **Photos:** Clear photos that show how to do something are of real value. You can often take such photos at home—don't wait for your next river trip.

River Equipment — Everything stated above under "Technique" also applies here, since these are really just how-to articles that specifically focus on how-to-equip-yourself. Again, an article that interviews equipment experts is at least as welcome as an article by the expert himself. The best experts on equipment are probably retail store staff who sell and service a lot of river gear. Note that we want to discuss the features of various

Continued

(Continued from other side.)

equipment, but not try to conclude which manufacturer's product is the "best," since this leads to endless arguments.

River Racing — We need articles about new trends in racing, or coverage of newsworthy races. We don't publish routine reports of annual races, or race results except the top finishers in national and international races. **Photos:** We already have lots of average photos of average unidentified racers. We only need close-up action photos of top racers, identified with name and home town accurately spelled.

River Media — This section strives to report and analyze how river running is being portrayed in the mass media, and what effect changing public attitudes will have on the future of river running. Analyze newspaper clippings about river drownings, or radio, television, and movies that mention river running. See whether they portray river running as dangerous, wholesome, or otherwise. **Photos:** As needed to illustrate the story.

River People — This is like *People* magazine. Subjects include long-time river runners with historical anecdotes, top racers, racers who tried to win but came up second-best, river rangers who have a tough job to do, river runners who give rangers a tough time, and so on. **Photos** are a must, either taken during the interview, or of the subject in action. For long-time boaters, historical photos showing them in their heyday.

River History — Almost the same as above, except that several people are involved and the events happened more than a decade ago.

Departments (River data, opinion, and other non-article material.)

River Reports — Bits of news that aren't worth an article. **Photos** to illustrate.

Whitewater — Flow reports and forecasts, taken from government reports. Articles about damage done by exceptionally high or low flows go in **Conservation**. Articles about new river gauges and when to run the river go in **Technique**.

Calendar — Major races, river festivals, conferences, conventions, trade shows. Actual articles on events go in **Racing, Conservation,** etc.

Reviews — Book and movie reviews. If there's a book or film you'd like to review, let us know.

Commentary — Critical or humorous opinion about the river scene.

River Trivia — Short anecdotes about the longest river, the highest river, the oldest race, the biggest raft, etc. Must be accurate and documented.

Comics, cartoons, jokes — We need more of these. We would welcome a regular comic strip. We also need humorous "filler."

Non-paying departments:
Letters to the Editor
Letters We Got Copies Of
NORS News.

Technical Points for Writers

Manuscripts must be double-spaced, and on one side of the paper only. Handwritten material may be o.k. if clear and double-spaced.

Articles should be 500 to 2,500 words (two to ten typed double-spaced pages.) Articles must be concise.

Technical Points for Photographers

Good river photos usually have one or more of these three key traits:

1. **Faces** are visible and expressive. As George Washington advised, "Don't shoot until you can see the whites of their eyes."
2. **Flesh** is visible, on both male and female subjects. Sleeveless paddlers are more interesting than those with sleeves. Muscle tension conveys action and portrays people better. We welcome photos of naked paddlers at hot springs and so on, if their private parts are not too obvious.
3. **Lighting** is dramatic. Catch the reflections on the water, the shadows in the gorge, or the glow of the clouds.

Other tips:

For river action, get right at the water's edge or **in** the water, looking upstream into the faces of the oncoming boaters. **Don't** stand up on the highway and shoot the boaters going by below.

Expose for the subject, not the water. The water is bright, so let in **much more light than your light meter says.** We need pictures of faces and people, not black silhouettes. Take steps to reduce contrast when shooting. "Burn in" the whitewater when printing, and produce a low-contrast print, since photos gain contrast in the publication process.

Photos are reproduced from black-and-white or color prints. Color photos should not have much red in them, since red reproduces as black. You can send photos for review in any form—contact sheets, little prints, big prints, or slides. Indicate whether you want us to make prints of the photos we select or you want to do it.

Technical Points for Artists

We need cartoons, comics, drawings, diagrams, maps, etc. Draw with dark black ink on white paper. Use typewriter "white out" to fix mistakes. Use a full sheet of 8 ½ x 11 paper—we will reduce it to final publication size.

Technical Points for Clipping Services

Clippings must meet two requirements: (1) They are about kayaking, rafting, or river canoeing, and (2) they contain some news. Therefore, don't send articles about motorboating, sailing, canoeing on lakes, or fishing. And don't send clippings about "my first raft trip" or "what kayaking is like," since they don't contain any news for us.

For best results, place a list of what you're sending on top, with a carbon copy of same. We will fill in payment next to the items and send back the list and a check, and keep the carbon copy in your file. Put your name clearly at the top so we can pull your file easily.

Calendar

CURRENTS is published bi-monthly, six times a year: January/February, March/April, etc. We need material by the first of the month before at the latest, so that material for the May/June issue should be sent by April 1.

<u>CutBank</u> <u>submission</u> <u>guidelines</u>

1. Mail all submissions to: CutBank, c/o English Dept, University
   of Montana, Missoula, MT 59812 (Attn: Fiction, Poetry, or Art
   Editor). Include SASE. Submit fiction, poetry, and artwork in
   separate envelopes. Please include a $3 reading fee for each
   fiction submission and a $1 fee for each poetry submission.
2. Submission and reading period: August 15 - January 1.
3. Submission length: Poetry: 3-5 poems. Fiction: up to 40
   double-spaced pages. Artwork: 2-4 photos of original.
   Photography: 2-4 black and white photos. Interviews, reviews,
   and essays by solicitation only. Queries welcome (SASE).
4. Never send original artwork. Send photos of work only. (No slides.)
5. For photography work, send black and white photos only.
6. For poetry and fiction, submit the <u>typed</u> original or a clean
   photocopy. Be sure to keep a copy for your files. Include your
   name and the page number on each page. Please do not double submit.
7. Subscription rates: One year: $9. (In Canada, add $3. In
   Europe, add $5.) Sample issue: $3. (Collector's issues are
   slightly higher.) Guidelines: SASE + $.50.
8. Rights are <u>not</u> automatically returned to author or artist on
   publication. You must write to us requesting that the rights
   be returned to you. Please enclose SASE.
9. All poetry and fiction submissions are automatically considered for the Richard Hugo Memorial Poetry Award and the A.
   B. Guthrie, Jr. Short Fiction Award, respectively. (These are
   honorary awards. Our funding guidelines prohibit us from
   awarding prize money.)

DIALOGUE, THE MAGAZINE FOR THE VISUALLY IMPAIRED

FREE-LANCE GUIDELINES

DIALOGUE welcomes the submission of free-lance material from visually handicapped authors for possible publication. Submission from new contributors are especially sought and have a good chance of being published. The best way to get an idea of the kind of material we publish is to study several issues of DIALOGUE. Every piece written by a free-lance can be identified by the inclusion of the town in which the writer lives as part of the byline.

CURRENT NEEDS: Fiction, poetry, articles and interviews.

TABOOS: Material that is religious, controversial, political or contains explicit sex.

PAYMENT: Since DIALOGUE is entirely dependent upon public contributions for its support payment is necessarily low. We think we offer an unusual opportunity for beginning writers, however, since we send an explanatory letter along with each returned manuscript. A copy of the large-print edition of the magazine will be sent to contributors whose work appears in it.

Payment is on acceptance at the following rates: $50.00 maximum for stories or articles, contributor's copies for poems, line drawings and photographs of art works.

Payment is on publication at a lower rate than the above for short filler items. No payment is currently made for short items such as "Letters to the Editor," or "What's New and Where to Get it." We appreciate information shared for "Department K-9" but cannot pay for it.

RULES: 1) No simultaneous submissions of other publications are allowed while being considered by DIALOGUE. 2) We reserve the right to do minor editing. 3) Manuscripts must be the original work of the writer, and, in most cases, must not have been previously published. If material has been previously published, state where and when.

RIGHTS POLICY: We buy all rights with a generous reprint policy.

DEADLINES: For publication in the spring issue, material must be received by December 1; for summer issue--March 1; for fall issue--June 1; and for winter issue--September 1. Check the magazine for other deadlines of features and departments such as "Classified Service" and "Vox Pop."

SPECIFIC GUIDELINES:

NONFICTION: Though the free-lance portion of any issue is generally representative of the kind of material we are buying, free-lance pieces on subjects now being staff-written are always welcome. Currently, we are especially interested in first-person travel experiences of visually handicapped persons, articles about participation in sports by the visually handicapped, information on new products useful to the blind, and features on homemaking. Queries regarding nonfiction are appreciated but not mandatory. All free-lance pieces are read, whether submitted after query or on speculation.

FICTION: We are interested in well-written stories of many types--mystery, suspense, humor, adventure, romance, fantasy, science fiction and mainstream. We prefer contemporary problem stories in which the protagonist solves his or her own problem. We are looking for strongly-plotted stories with definite beginnings, climaxes and endings. Characters may be blind, sighted or visually in between. We want to encourage any writer who shows promise, and, therefore, may return a story for revision when necessary.

POETRY: We are always eager to find really new poets, and our readers particularly enjoy poetry. Our readers are more interested in traditional forms of poetry such as blank verse and free verse than they are in avant-garde poetry. Submit one poem, complete with title, to a page. Poems should not exceed twenty lines in length. Poems may mention a supreme being, but will not be accepted if their theme or nature is religious. Submit no more than five at a time.

RECORDED INTERVIEWS: Taped interviews should be recordd on an open-reel machine at 7-1/2 inches per second or on a cassette recorder of good quality at 1 7/8 IPS. The person being interviewed should be given a seperate microphone, and ideally this mike should be of the lavalier, or clip-on, variety. This will eliminate noisy, time-consuming mike shifting between the two parties and produce a recorded signal of uniform strength and quality.

The interview should be professionally conducted and should not be over twenty minutes in length unless the subject or the guest has outstanding significance. The taping session should be preceded by careful research, and at least some of the questions should be prepared in advance.

Where possible, submit the original tape. When an edited tape is submitted, the editing should be done on an open reel machine of good quality at a tape speed of 7 1/2 inches per second.

Tapes accepted for publication will be returned only on request at the time of submission. Tapes which are not accepted will be returned as promptly as possible.

Each taped interview submitted will be evaluated on the basis of significance, content and technical quality.

ART WORK: On our front cover we are interested in displaying line drawings and photographs of paintings, sculpture, pottery and other art works by visually-handicapped artists. Dimensions of black-and-white line drawings and photographs should not exceed 4 inches long by 7 inches wide. Artists should include information about themselves and their work.

SHORT ITEMS/FILLERS: Specify what department item is for--"ABAPITA," "Recipe Round-up," "Around the House," "Vox Pop," or "Puzzle Box." Puzzle Box submissions must be complete with instructions and correct solution.

MANUSCRIPT: Material may be submitted in typed, Brailled, or recorded form.

Typed submissions should be double-spaced on standard 8 1/2 x 11-inch paper, leaving at least a one-inch margin on all sides. On the first page be sure to type your name, complete address, and date of submission in the top left-hand corner. Type title of article below these identifying data, preferably in the center of the page. On all subsequent pages be sure to include your name and the titlee of your submission in the top left corner and the page number in the top right corner.

Edit material on tape as carefully as you would a typed manuscript, making certain that each word is exactly as you intend it to appear in print. Spell any unusual words and proper nouns whose spelling is unclear or variable.

DIALOGUE cannot be responsible for manuscripts lost in the mail. Writer's are therefore advised to retain a copy of each submission.

LENGTH: Due to space limitations necessitated by quarterly publication, shorter lengths are preferred both for fiction and non-fiction. Stories and articles of more than 3,000 words are rarely used. We do occasionally run long nonfiction articles if the importance of the topic or the natuure of the material warrants it. In these cases we divide articles into two or three parts and carry them over from issue to issue.

RECEIPT/RETURN: We can only acknowledge receipt of material accompanied by a self-addressed, stamped postcard. Only submisions accompanied by a SASE bearing sufficient postage will be returned upon rejection.

TIME NEEDED FOR REPLY: At least one month.

JAMES F. VICTORIN MEMORIAL AWARD: This award was established in 1972 to recognize the best story written by a blind or visually handicapped writer published in DIALOGUE during the previous year. Annette Victorin, former Fiction and Poetry Editor, and her literary colleagues, judge which story merits receiving this $100 award.

WHERE TO SEND FREE-LANCE MATERIALS: Send all correspondence and manuscripts to Bonnie Miller, Acting Editor, DIALOGUE, 3100 S. Oak Park Avenue, Berwyn, IL 60402. For more information, telephone: (312) 749-1908.

CAT FANCY
DOG FANCY
BIRD TALK
HORSE ILLUSTRATED
magazines

Editorial Offices
P.O. Box 6050
Mission Viejo, California 92690
Telephone (714) 240-6001

Dog Fancy

WRITER'S GUIDELINES

Thank you for your interest in our publications. We would be pleased to see your material. Below we have listed some of the publication requirements of CAT FANCY, DOG FANCY, BIRD TALK and HORSE ILLUSTRATED to assist you in preparing submissions.

ARTICLES

CAT FANCY, DOG FANCY and BIRD TALK are directed at the general pet owning population and written for the adult audience. HORSE ILLUSTRATED is directed at the amateur competitor and pleasure horse owner. We suggest that you read past issues of the magazines to acquaint yourself with the types of material we use. Past issues may be obtained by sending $3.00 to the above address. We need informative articles, limited to 3,000 words, on the care of training of cats, dogs, birds, and horses (health nutrition, training, etc.); photo essays on historical and current events dealing with cats, dogs, birds and horses; how-to articles; human interest stories; and good fiction, with the animal as the primary focus of interest. We rarely use stories in which the animal speaks as if it were human. We use a breed article in each issue, but these articles are assigned. Please query if you have a breed article in mind.

Manuscripts should be typewritten, double-spaced with wide margins. We prefer that articles be accompanied with appropriate art in the form of professional quality color transparencies or black and white photographs (NOT SNAP SHOTS) or professional illustrations. Additional guidelines are available for artists and photographers.

We are always happy to review material on speculation, but with the exception of fiction, the best working procedure is to query before preparing an article. Our usual rate of payment is three to five cents per printed word, five cents if accompanied by good quality photographs. Payment is made in the latter part of the cover month in which your article appears, (i.e., if your piece was in the November issue you would be paid in the latter part of November). We buy first American rights only; all other rights revert back to the author.

We cannot assume responsibility for material submitted, but we assure you that reasonable care will be taken in handling your work. YOU MUST INCLUDE A SELF-ADDRESSED, STAMPED ENVELOPE WITH EACH SUBMISSION.

TSR, Inc.

P.O. Box 756
201 Sheridan Springs Rd.
Lake Geneva, WI 53147
(414) 248-3625
Telex 530654

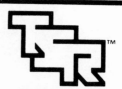

Producers of DUNGEONS & DRAGONS® Games

Dear Author:

DRAGON(R) Magazine is published on a monthly basis. Each issue of
DRAGON Magazine contains a wide variety of materials of interest to
the role-playing gamer and gaming hobbyist. The magazine includes a
complete game, game module, or playing accessories designed for use
with many of the most popular role-playing game systems. Book and
game reviews, fantasy and adventure fiction, and full-color comic
strips are some of the added features of DRAGON Magazine.

We seek fiction that is action-oriented and that has interesting
and identifiable characters. In terms of subject matter, fantasy
and adventure pieces are desired. Possible themes might be problem
solving, adventure and survival tales, quests, battles and magical
warfare, and challenging missions.

We do not seek fiction that deals primarily with philosophical,
metaphysical, or religious premises. Nor are we interested in
rehashes of other writers' works and ideas.

Submitted fiction should be written for an older adolescent and
adult audience. Extensive use of obscene language is frowned upon;
sexually explicit detail is unacceptable.

We publish stories only, no poems or plays. A query should be made
on serialized fiction and novel excerpts as these are rarely
published. Six to eight stories are published a year.

Fiction should not exceed 8,000 words in length, although we will
consider longer pieces if a query is made prior to submission.
Payment rates are 5 to 8 cents per word, and payment is made upon
acceptance for first North American serial rights. Notice of
acceptance or rejection is made within 60 days. All submissions
must include a self-addressed, stamped envelope. In no instance
can Dragon Publishing assume responsibility for manuscripts and
illustrations not specifically solicited.

Thank you for your interest in DRAGON Magazine. Please, address
all fiction submissions to my attention.

All the very best,

Patrick Lucien Price
Fiction Editor, DRAGON Magazine

Earth's Daughters

P.O. Box 41, Central Park Station
Buffalo, New York 14215

EARTH'S DAUGHTERS is a feminist literary and art periodical published in Buffalo, New York. We believe ourselves to be the oldest feminist arts periodical extant, having published our first issue in February, 1971. Since 1977, we have been organized as a collective of six women, with editorship rotating among our members. Our focus is the experience and creative expression of women.

Price and format varies from issue to issue, and includes broadsheets, topical issues and general collections. We require technical skill and artistic intensity in the work of our contributors, some of whom are Katharine Machan Aal, Olga Broumas, Gabrielle Burton, Thulani Davis, Denise Levertov, Lyn Lifshin, Marge Piercy, Janine Pommy Vega and Zana. We also publish the work of many fine "unknown" poets, writers and artists. We welcome submissions from new writers; one of our primary purposes is to publish work that otherwise might not be printed either because it is unusual, or because the writer is not well known.

Subscriptions are $10 for 3 issues, $18 for libraries and instututions. Sample copies are available for $4 which includes postage. WE URGE YOU to purchase a sample copy of our magazine. The following is a quote from Letters to the Editor in a recent CODA by Andrea Hollander Budy:
> "If you like the writing published in a particular journal or magazine, and if your own writing would seem to you to be "at home" in that publication, then you have chosen well and should send your work out to that editor. This is a journal likely to accept your writing, and even if an editor chooses not to, he or she will more likely be interested in giving you some positive encouragement." We agree.

Submissions to EARTH'S DAUGHTERS, Johnson/Box 143, Lockport NY 14094 (We have two mailing addresses, both correct; however, the Lockport address is usually much faster). Poetry can be up to 40 lines in length (rare exceptions for exceptional work), fiction, 1000 words maximum. Photocopies, dot matrix are acceptable if clearly legible. Simultaneous submissions ok, but we must be notified immediately if work is accepted elsewhere. No more than 6 poems per submission, business size envelope preferred due to space limitations of post office boxes. Self-addressed, stamped envelope (SASE) a MUST. Use sufficient postage--we will not accept mail with postage due. (We, like most other small presses, operate on a very small budget.)

Please, no "greeting card" verse or rhyme. We do many special topical issues which are announced in CODA and other small press newsletters. Yearly topics are also available after April of each year with SASE.

Once you have submitted work, please be patient. The U.S. Mail is dependable, and we have yet to lose a manuscript. Our six collective members have full time jobs, extra curricular activities and the demands of their own artistic pursuits in addition to their commitment (unpaid) to the publication of ED magazine. For this reason, we get impatient with writers who inquire too soon or too frequently as to the status of their work. We only hold work we are seriously considering for publication, and it can be up to a year between acceptance and publication. If you must contact us (change of address, notification that a simultaneous submission has been accepted elsewhere), be sure to state the issue theme, the title(s) of your work and ENCLOSE SASE.

We acquire first rights only, after which the copyright reverts to the writer. We pay in copies, and additional copies are available to contributors at cost.

We hope we haven't discouraged you! Publication of ED magazine is a labor of love, and we hope you will become one of our contributors--otherwise we could be out of business!! Good Luck.

EIDOS MAGAZINE
P.O. BOX 96
BOSTON, MASSACHUSETTS 02137-0096 USA
(617) 333-0612 • TOLL FREE (MA) 1-800-902-0548

WRITER'S GUIDELINES

EIDOS MAGAZINE: Erotic Entertainment For Women, P.O. Box 96, Boston, MA 02137-0096 (617) 333-0612. Editor: Brenda Loew Tatelbaum.

A provocative, quarterly periodical of erotic lifestyle/fantasy/entertainment for women AND men dedicated to the discussion and examination of two highly personalized dimensions of female sexuality: desire and satisfaction. Since 1983, Eidos has published personal classifieds, adult products and services, erotic art and photography, sexual advice, interviews, reviews, poetry, fiction and non-fiction directed toward an energetic and well-informed contemporary world-wide erotica readership. EIDOS MAGAZINE is published within the traditional American freedom of creative visual and written expression and is marketed within the spirit of the America Free Enterprise system. Original manuscripts and artwork returned after publication, upon request and when submitted with SASE. Reports within 8 weeks. EIDOS looks for sensuous, sensitive, sophisticated erotica depicting mutually respective sexuality and images of the human form. Alternative to commercial mainstream men's and women's magazines. More images of men are published in EIDOS than female. NOT a gay or lesbian publication. Buys one time rights only. Byline and contributor copies given. Copyrighted.

EIDOS MAGAZINE, established in 1984, is a quarterly woman's erotic arts and entertainment periodical dealing with contemporary alternative lifestyles and the sexual realities of our society, including Sexually Transmitted Diseases (STD's) and AIDS (Acquired Immune Deficiency Syndrome).

The Publisher and Editor of EIDOS, Brenda Loew Tatelbaum, is internationally recognized for her work by academicians, researchers and medical professionals, many of whom have enlisted her services in advisory or research capacities and utilize EIDOS MAGAZINE as a conduit between the lifestyle community and the professional world. Many well-known and eloquent authors have been published in EIDOS, enabling the free flow of timely information and ideas to EIDOS readers.

Brenda Loew Tatelbaum and EIDOS MAGAZINE were the first in their industry to address the AIDS problem, not only by supplying `safer sex' information and free condoms to EIDOS readers but also by actually participating in the first `Safer Sex and AIDS March' in history, in April, 1987, in Boston, Massachusetts. In addition, Ms. Tatelbaum donates advertising space in EIDOS as a public service to those fighting AIDS and STD's and is actively working to generate information and funds to help in the battle to find a cure for AIDS.

Ms. Tatelbaum has demonstrated commitment and has been outspoken when others have not. She has often been wrongly criticised for her efforts.

It is the position and policy of EIDOS MAGAZINE and its Publisher/Editor, Brenda Loew Tatelbaum, to exercise the traditional American right of free speech and to promote that same right for all, guaranteeing the freedom to choose in all areas of life and lifestyles; further, guaranteeing protection to those who make their choices; specifically, guaranteeing the free flow of alternative lifestyle ideas between and amongst all those individuals opting to receive those ideas; to promote the rights of the producers of those ideas and to encourage and promote the growth of the erotic arts and sciences; to protect the rights of all those in American society who freely choose and value their sexual preference and lifestyle.

Results of a "Readership Survey" conducted by *EIDOS MAGAZINE* March 1987

WHO READS EIDOS?

1. Are you a regular reader of EIDOS? — Yes 50%   No 50%

2. How often during the month do you glance through EIDOS? — 1-3X 51%   4-6X 24%   7X or More 25%

3. How many persons in your household read EIDOS? — 1-3 81%   4 or More 6%   Did Not Respond 13%

4. Where do you pick up EIDOS? — Mail Order 59%   Friend 18%   Bookstore 9%   Subscription 5%   Newsstand 5%   Conferences 4%

5. What other magazines do you read? — 1-3 Others 50%   4-9 Others 45%   10 or More Others 5%

6. What newspapers do you read? — Only 1 25%   2-4 Papers 70%   5 or More 5%

7. In which cities do you shop the most? — Only 1 82%   2 or More 18%

8. What is your occupation? — Professional 48%   Business 44%   Student 8%

9. What is your income? — Under $20,000 36% $20-50,000 53%   Over $50,000 11%

10. How long have you lived at your present address? — 3 Months-5 Years 42%   6-10 Years 20%   11-26 Years or More 38%

11. What is your age? — 18-35 41%   36-45 36%   46-62 14%   over 62 9%

12. Name your favorite retailer. — Small Boutique 48%   Major Retail Chain 31%   Restaurant 21%

13. Do you own your own home? — Yes 68%   No 32%

14. Next major purchase? — Car 31%   Home Electronic Equipment (Computer, VCR, Color TV) 31%   Home/Condo 18%   Medically-Related Health/Fitness 10%   Clothes 9%

Writers Guidelines for Eldritch Tales

Eldritch Tales is a magazine devoted to supernatural horror fiction in the tradition of Poe, Lovecraft, Bloch and King. I would suggest that would-be contributors read the works of these authors and see what I need. What we **don't** need are mad slasher stories in the mold of the *Halloween* and *Friday the Thirteenth* movies, also we are not interested in Sword and Sorcery or Hard Science Fiction stories. I would suggest that you should read the magazine. A sample copy is $6.00, it'll give you a very good idea of what we want.

All manuscripts **must** be **typed double-spaced** with your name, address and word count at the top of the first page and each page should have the story title, author's name and page number at the top.

Individual requirements are as follows:

FICTION: All stories should be no longer than 10,000 words and should be within the contents of the contents of the publication (see above). All stories should be well-written and be original. We mean that we don't want stories that are rip-offs of other stories, and no stories involving characters created by other authors, unless you have permission from either the author or his estate. The one exception is, of course, Lovecraft's Cthulhu Mythos, and even then, be yourself, **don't** try to copy Lovecraft's style, write them the way you would any other story, otherwise leave well enough alone. If you are attempting any mythos material, I would recommend Dirk Mosig's excellent essay, "H. P. Lovecraft: Myth-Maker" which differentiates Lovecraft's own mythos stories to those of his successors, especially those of August Derleth's, it's in the excellent collection, *H. P. Lovecraft: Four Decades of Criticism.*

NON-FICTION: Same word limits as fiction and it also should be in the framework of the publication, supernatural horror in literature, film, television, radio and even comic-books. We have a regular film column, called "The Eldritch Eye," but if you think that you can add some further insight into the genre, you're welcome to try. Book reviews are a regular feature of our publication, all such should be no longer than 2,000 to 3,000 words, unless you are doing a survey of several similar works, in which case, we will let you go a little longer.

POETRY: Shouldn't be any longer than **two** manuscript pages, and should also be within the contents of this publication.

ARTWORK: Send samples of your artwork and if we like it, we will assign a story for you to illustrate. We will take independent illos for cover (front and back), frontispiece, book review section and assorted spots. **Please** no more than four illos per story. Also please be original, no copies of established illustrators. Also, **please, no work needing halftones.**

TABOOS: Sex is permissible, if handled discreetly, we are not a pornographic publication. Nudity is also permissible in the artwork as long as it is in good taste. Blood and gore in both fiction and art is also permissible as long as there is more to the story than that (for example, I consider *Dawn of the Dead* to be a much better film than any of the *Friday the Thirteenth* films, as *Dawn* had a lot more going for it than the gore, while with the *FtT* films that's all there is to them).

PAYMENT: Fiction and Non-Fiction both are paid 1/4 cent per word. $1.00 minimum payment. Poetry is paid 10 cents per line. Minimum payment is also $1.00. Artwork payment is on several layers; covers are $15.00 each. All full page interior illos are $10.00 each and spots are either $5.00 or $1.00 depending on size. **All** payment is upon publication.

Send work to: Crispin Burnham
Editor/Publisher, *Eldritch Tales*
Yith Press
1051 Wellington Road
Lawrence, KS 66044

THE WORLD'S LEADING MYSTERY MAGAZINE

380 LEXINGTON AVENUE • NEW YORK, N.Y. 10017 • 212-557-9100

<u>Ellery Queen's Mystery Magazine</u> is always in the market for the best detective, crime, and mystery stories being written today -- by new writers as well as by "name" writers. We have no editorial taboos except those of bad taste. We publish every kind of mystery: the suspense story, the psychological study, the deductive puzzle -- the gamut of crime and detection from the realistic (including the policeman's lot and stories of police procedure) to the more imaginative (including "locked rooms" and "impossible crimes"). We need private-eye stories, but do not want sex, sadism, or sensationalism-for-the-sake-of-sensationalism. We especially are interested in "first" stories -- by authors who have never published fiction professionally before -- and have published more than 600 first stories since <u>EQMM</u>'s inception.

<u>Ellery Queen's Mystery Magazine</u> has been published continuously since 1941, and critics agree it is the world's leading mystery magazine. From the beginning there have been three criteria -- quality of writing, originality of plot, and professional craftsmanship. These criteria still hold and always will. The most practical way to find out what <u>EQMM</u> wants is to read <u>EQMM</u>: every issue will tell you all you need to know of our standards and of our diversified approach.

We use stories of almost every length. 4,000-6,000 is the preferred range, but we occasionally use stories of 10,000 words. Short-shorts of 1,500-2,000 words are also welcome. Our rates for original stories are from 3¢ to 8¢ a word.

We are also looking for fine reprints -- any type of crime, detective, or mystery story, no matter where it has been published before (providing the author owns and controls the reprint rights), and no matter how long ago the story first appeared.

We urge you to support the high standards of <u>EQMM</u> by writing the best mystery stories of our time, and by giving <u>EQMM</u> first chance to publish them. Note to beginners: It is not necessary to query us as to subject matter or to ask permission to submit a story. We do not want fact-detective cases or true stories; this is a fiction magazine. All manuscripts should be typed on one side of the paper and double-spaced, preferably with a fresh ribbon in the typewriter. Please enclose a self-addressed stamped envelope of suitable size in case the manuscript must be returned; if outside the U.S., use International Postal Reply coupons for return postage. Please do not ask for criticism of stories; we receive too many submissions to make this possible.

ENFANTAISIE
2603 SE 32nd Avenue
Portland, OR 97202   **WRITER'S GUIDELINES**

ENFANTAISIE welcomes items appealing to children between the ages of 12 and 17. With the exception of pedagogical essays, all material we publish is written in French and edited for ease of reading, since we are widely used as a teaching instrument in French classrooms. We buy first rights, and we accept reprint submissions.

Manuscripts are preferably submitted in French, but they may be in English or Italian for translation into French. Those submitted in French, requiring little or no editing, are awarded a higher fee. Our fees are shamefully modest: $20 per feature needing translation plus 3 complimentary copies of the issue in which the item appears. Authors generally find that the prestige of being published in a high-quality educational magazine compensates for the meager stipend.

Stories in ENFANTAISIE run to about 1000 words. We reserve the right to edit for length and expression, and to stray from the original when translating in order to meet linguistic and pedagogical requirements. Poetry must be submitted in French.

We prefer fiction pieces relating in a realistic way to everyday situations in a youngster's life, such as conflicts with parents, siblings and friends concerning social obligations, household chores, gift giving, decison making, school problems, misunderstandings, etc. Humor, unexpected plot twists and surprise endings are welcome.

The following stylistic considerations apply: 1) No "syrupy" or overly cute point of view in the narrative voice; 2) No lengthy introspection or stream of consciousness; 3) No complex imagery or rich vocabulary as this is a handicap with regard to translation into simplified French; 4) A strong moral tone should be avoided; no religious references or inspirational messages. 5) Dialogue should be a strong component.

Manuscripts are to be submitted with SASE for reply and ms return. A sample copy for writers can be purchased for $3.00 (for rush add 9" x 12" SAE plus 4 first-class stamps). In the case of manuscript acceptance, the sample copy charge will be refunded upon request.

THE EOTU GROUP
1810 W. STATE #115
BOISE, IDAHO 83702

WRITER'S GUIDELINES

FICTION: Experimental. I'm looking mostly for stories that show an artistic integrity, a determination inside the writer to create something new at the edges of fiction; a new style, new ways to develop characters, or new paths of plot lines. Or if not something new, the story must do the traditional very, very, well.
     If you aren't sure your work is right for Eotu, send it anyway. Let me decide.

MECHANICS: Manuscripts should be typed, double-spaced, on white 8 1/2 X 11 paper. Your name, address, and word count should appear on the title page. Your name and the story's name should also appear on each page of your manuscript.
     Maximum word count, about 6,000 words.
     Don't send me simultaneous submissions. I'll report back to you in 4-6 weeks.
     Submit the manuscript with a Self-Addressed Stamped Envelope.

ILLUSTRATIONS: Black ink on white. Reproductions are okay if the lines are clear. Prefer size between 3 x 4 inches to 8 1/2 x 11 inches. Submit as many as you wish, just include your name, address, and title of work on each piece of your work. Submit with Self-Addressed Stamp Envelope.

RENUMERATION: I buy 12-15 stories per issue, 7-8 illustrations. Payment is $5-$25 for fiction, for First North American Serial Rights. $5 for one-time rights for illustrations. Payment is on acceptance. You will also receive a complimentary copy of the issue in which your work appears.

NOTE: EOTU is a bi-monthly publication and is available for a single issue price of $4.00. A year's subscription (six issues) is $18.00
     Thank you for your interest. I look forward to reading your story.

Larry D.Dennis
Editor

EFQ Publications

Post Office Box 4958
San Francisco, CA 94101

Erotic Fiction Quarterly

Thank you for your inquiry.

EFQ is buying creative short fiction manuscripts with sexual themes for a small, quality literary journal which
is published only occasionally at this time. No particular
slant is required and there are essentially no restrictions
on content, style, explicitness, etc. However, we do not
use standard pornography or men's magazine-type stories.
Also, no contrived or formula plots or gimmicks, no broad
satire or parody, no obscure "literary" writing, and no
poetry. (We DO use graphic erotica, but it must be original
and delightful, unlike anything else on the market.)

Writers who have something positive to express, in fiction,
regarding human sexual expression or interaction, including
atitudes, emotions, roles, etc., are encouraged to submit
exciting short stories (average length 1500 words) they
feel are special. Any heartfelt and intelligent fiction
with real characters will be carefully considered.

Always include a STAMPED, SELF-ADDRESSED ENVELOPE for return
of manuscript or reply. Non-returnable copy OK. EFQ cannot
be responsible for material lost in the mail. Payment is
minimum $35 on acceptance.

--EDITOR, Erotic Fiction Quarterly

ESPIONAGE

ESPIONAGE MAGAZINE, A LEO 11 PUBLICATION

WRITERS' GUIDELINES

ESPIONAGE MAGAZINE. LEO 11 PUBLICATIONS, LTD.
P.O. Box 1184, Teaneck, NJ 07666

Editor/Publisher: Jackie Lewis (201)836-9177
Associate Publisher: Jeri Winston (201)569-4072

Spy stories only. 9 - 12 stories per issue (bi-monthly).
Byline given. Pays $.03 - .08 per word, payment upon
publication. 1000 - 9000 words in length, fiction and
non-fiction. Historical articles and authentic biographies also accepted. We publish every type of spy story;
no gratuitous gore, horror or explicit sex. Anecdotes,
cartoons and games also accepted (payment for these
on request). We buy first and second serial (reprint)
rights. Photocopied submissions acceptable; multiple,
simultaneous submissions not acceptable. We do not
like queries and ask that you not send them to us.

All materials must be accompanied by a stamped self-
addressed envelope (SASE). We report in one month's
time.

We thank you for your interest.

Jackie Lewis
Editor/Publisher

January 24, 1985

writer's guide

Evangel

for ACTION and EVANGEL
Department of Christian Education
901 College Avenue
Winona Lake IN 46590

action!

is an 8-page take-home paper for children in grades 4-5-6, and needs stories about children in that age bracket. Because the paper's purpose is to supplement and strengthen the concepts learned in Sunday school, each story must have a Christian frame of reference, and should deal with a moral or ethical choice confronting the hero. Situations at home, in school, or on the playground should provide lots of possibilities for action and dialogue.

THE STORY PROBLEM must have significance (be worth worrying about), and the hero who copes with it must be a believable person, with a few weaknesses to balance his strengths. Fiction is limited to 1,000 words, for which we pay $25.

SHORT FEATURES (300-500 words) are also needed. Craft instructions (with photo or sketch), nature oddities, and interviews with children are highly prized, and rewarded with $15. A photo-interview can be about the child's pet, unusual experience, or some special project.

BRIEF NATURE POEMS are accepted for $5. Cartoons $10.

evangel

is an 8-page take-home paper for young adults, and needs stories about young people involved in family and/or occupational crises. Fiction is expected to show how Christ can help a person make satisfactory decisions in practical, everyday affairs, but these improved judgments cannot come easily. The tension between opposite possibilities must be strong to be believable. Stories need not end "happily." However, the implications of a better solution should be clear. Fiction between 1200-1500 words; payment is $35-$40.

PERSONAL EXPERIENCE articles are the favorite type of non-fiction (1000 words-$25).

Preferred stories are those about God's help in crisis situations, giving hope to readers who may face a similar crisis. Relationships, family budgeting, work problems are likely topics. Remember, anecdotes and dialogue add color.

SHORT, filler-type (300-500 words) devotional items are also welcome. These should be centered around a single idea or incident which leads into a brief, cogent observation about life and/or God. $10-$12.

POEMS may be about nature, the human experience, or about God. They should be tightly focused, and present a single, sharp picture. Concrete words are preferred over abstractions, to appeal to the reader's emotion or thought. Five dollars for a poem.

HOW TO IMPRESS AN EDITOR

THE FIRST CLUE to hit the editor's desk is the stamped, self-addressed return envelope that pops out of your just-opened script. This means the editor is dealing with a professional! (We cannot return scripts without a return envelope.) Next thing noticed is the name and address typed in the upper left corner of page one, and the word count in the upper right. A pro, for sure. Starting the story halfway down page one gives the editor room to mark instructions for the printer.

NO EDITOR can help being impressed by black, clean type on fresh, untattered paper. (Editors know you have to circulate scripts to many magazines in order to stay in business, but when a script becomes yellow with age and crumbles as it comes out of the envelope, it's time for retyping.) Scripts of one to five pages should be folded twice and mailed in a number-10 envelope; 6 to 10 pages should be folded once and mailed in a 6 x 9 envelope. Only larger scripts should be shipped flat. (Proper shipping preserves freshness.)

PAYMENT is made "on publication." Actually, your check should arrive at the time your story goes to press: from three months ahead for EVANGEL to nine months ahead for ACTION.

We hope to find a script from you soon!

EXPRESSO TILT WRITER'S GUIDELINES

The emphasis of Expresso Tilt is both literary and comic. Our focus is on America's trash culture, especially as it is enhanced by the media. A few subjects that interest us are The Gipper, junk food, superheroes, game shows, Buford Pussor, photoboothography, dating habits, talk radio, X-rated westerns, and true love. We will, however, consider all work submitted. We are looking for quality first.

We print mostly non-fiction feature stories, short fiction (to 4000 words), poetry, and comics. We enjoy poetry that is short and humorous and avoid sentimentality, morbidity, violence, obscenity, the muse, and self-pity.

All contributors are paid in copies. We will consider photocopied submissions and simultaneous submissions. Include an SASE. We are now reading material for the 6th and 7th issues.

Samples copies of #5 are $1.75. We recommend that you review a sample copy before submitting material. Back issues: $3. Three-issue subscriptions: $5.

737 Wharton Street, Phila., PA 19147

CONTEST LISTINGS

We have compiled detailed information on over 500 writing contests sorted into categories - poetry and fiction. The contests are listed chronologically, according to entry date. The listings do not include fellowships or awards based on previously published work. These are contests anyone, beginner or professional, can enter simply by submitting work. Most of the awards include cash and publication. Our reseach is thorough, and we update the listings regularly.

Prices and specs per listing:

Poetry:	51 pages	300 entries	$7.50
Fiction:	31 pages	200 entries	$6.00

$12.50 for both. Postage included! And it's tax deductible!!! Such a deal!!! This collection of information cannot be found elsewhere. Write to: **Expresso Tilt, 737 Wharton St., Philadelphia, PA 19147**

SUBSCRIBE TO EXPRESSO TILT

Here's you big chance, folks. Get the next three issues for a dirt-cheap $5. Remember, Expresso Tilt is non-profit, which means that each fun- filled issue costs us a serious chunk of coinage. But you can help make our lives just a little bit more wonderful by subscribing. WAH—HOO!!!!

Back issues are also available. Fill out the order form below, and receive our limited no Joyce Carol Oates warranty. Join in the fracas! Who knows what we'll pull next?

BACK ISSUES

( ) #1 - The Gipper issue. Rare and wonderful. Leonard Nimoy - $3
( ) #2 - Only 1500 printed. Lawn Ornaments! Amundson! Love Connection.
      The Shaggs. Two Zym's. $3
( ) #3 - Great fiction. Miss Ardor debuts. Man of the Year! Trash Picking.
      Talk Radio. Ed MacMahon. $3
( ) #4 - Photoboothography! James Hampton! Vanna White! Frederick's!
      Kenny Be's debut! 32 pages or pure Tilt-o-matic!! $2
( ) #5 - Adult Westerns! Creek Charlie! Ivan E. Roth! Party Tips!!!
      Exclamation points and more...36 pages!! $2
( )   Subscription-Next 3 issues for $5. Postage included! Such a deal!
_____ Total (Send money to Expresso Tilt, 737 Wharton, Phila., PA 19147.)

Name _____

Address _____

Family
MAGAZINE

P.O. Box 4993   Walnut Creek, CA 94596   (415) 284-9093

FAMILY magazine is an 80 page glossy magazine that caters to the U.S. military wife. Published ten times per year (plus two special issues), it has a circulation of 525,000. FAMILY is distributed free of charge at U.S. commissaries around the world at the mid-month pay day.

The FAMILY reader is young (53% are between 26-35 and 24% are between 18-25), married, and has at least one child under the age of six. Ninety-nine percent have graduated from high school; only 13 per cent are college grads. Over half work, at least part time, and most of the others would like to have a job. Because their husbands are in the military, they move often--many even once a year. They spend a lot of time away from their husbands who may be gone for a year at a time.

FAMILY is interested in articles of particular interest to these young women. Most of the stories we reject are not badly written, just inappropriate. We are interested in any article that speaks to the situation military wives find themselves in. We do not want stories about finding a man (they already have one) retiring or aging (they're too young) or anything too technical. The backbone of FAMILY is recipes, travel stories and human interest stories usually written by military wives to military wives.

Our departments are all set; we are only interested in features and short fiction. Payment for both fiction and nonfiction varies, depending on length and the experience of the writer. The range is between $100 and $300 and the word length is usually between 1000 and 3000 words. Virtually all of FAMILY is freelanced.

We are also in the market for both black and white and color photos of food and families--children, adults, men and women. Payment for black and white photos is $25 per photo, color is negotiated with the photographer.

It is best to submit a complete manuscript or in the case of photographs, sample photos. Payment is upon publication and we usually hold manuscripts for at least six months before printing. Always enclose a stamped, self-addressed envelope. Sample copies are $1.25.

THE MAGAZINE OF Fantasy and Science Fiction

EDWARD L. FERMAN, PUBLISHER, BOX 56, CORNWALL, CONNECTICUT 06753 / 203-672-6376

NOTES FOR CONTRIBUTORS

— We have no "formula," but you should be familiar with the magazine before submitting. Send $3.00 for one sample copy, $5.00 for two.

- Do not send us queries or portions of stories; we prefer to see completed manuscripts.

- We cannot use: non-fiction, poetry, stories over 25,000 words. Best length is under 10,000 words.

- All manuscripts should be typed, double-spaced. Submissions of clear photocopies and clear, dark dot matrix mss. is OK.

- Include return postage and allow at least 8 weeks for a decision. Please indicate if ms. is disposable.

- Payment is ~~4-6¢~~ 5-7¢ a word on acceptance. We buy first NA and foreign serial rights and an option on anthology rights. All other rights are retained by the author.

Farmer's Market

Farmer's Market, PO Box 1272, Galesburg, IL 61402. John E. Hughes, Jean C. Lee, and Gail Nichols, Editors. Poetry, fiction, articles, art, photos, interviews, satire, plays, non-fiction. Interested in high-quality work, especially as it reflects the voice and vision of the Midwest. Prefer no more than 40 manuscript pages submitted at one time. Include SASE.

Festivals

160 E. Virginia St., Suite 290   San Jose, CA 95112

WRITER'S GUIDELINES

Thank you. We appreciate your interest in writing for FESTIVALS. We welcome unsolicited articles. We encourage you to familiarize yourself with our editorial goals.

Our main goal is to promote the discovery of the sacred in ordinary living. We see this being done in a variety of ways: storytelling, home ritual, community festivals, ethnic customs, religious practice, prayer and meditation, awareness exercises, study, the discovery of new symbols, and the rediscovery of ancient ones. We like articles written from your own experience and tradition — whatever it is — and articles that share how you have discovered a sense of sacrament in your own life.

Get to know FESTIVALS. We are more likely to publish your article if you are a reader of the magazine and are familiar with the issues we discuss. Think about the subjects you know well and those for which little information is available. We cover major feasts (Christmas, Hannukah, Easter, Passover, Thanksgiving, Memorial Day), but we're also interested in little known or all-but forgotten celebrations that might be adapted for the modern world. Celebrations, in fact, are legion. They take place on special occasions: anniversaries (of birth, death, first meetings, marriages, business startups), times of transition (graduation, marriage, arrivals and departures, moving into a new home, entering adolescence, retirement), and key times of the year (agricultural festivals, solstice celebrations, May Day, Thanksgiving, etc.).

FESTIVALS grew out of the Catholic/Christian tradition but, in keeping with the practice of the church from the earliest times, it is open to "all that is good and holy" from any tradition. Since current FESTIVALS readers come from a variety of religious traditions — and may or may not attend a regular place of worship — it is best to either avoid terms that may be peculiar to your tradition or to explain them in a way that anyone can understand.

Generally, first-time writers should concentrate on writing how-to articles or sharings of festivities that have worked for them. However, we also use interviews, profiles, in-depth essays, reports, and stories. Here it is best to query first.

Style: If you are in touch with the way we approach subjects — sometimes with reverence, sometimes with humor, always with the conviction that everything in the universe is connected to the Great Mystery — you can write *about* almost anything. Take your style cue from the name, FESTIVALS, and the particular "festival" you are writing about. Some articles might be solemn; others might be celebratory, fun-loving, playful, entertaining, even boisterous — but somehow in touch with that deep thing that made you want to celebrate in the first place. Don't write with a lot of extra adjectives and exclamation points, but don't be afraid to have fun either.

Some departments are open to your contributions:

— *Pilgrimage* takes readers beyond travel to journey as a religious or spiritual experience. Contributions can focus on travel-as-ritual, meaningful places to visit, the right ways to pilgrimage, or even psychological journeys.

— *Breaking Bread* is about eating-as-ritual and includes recipes, tips on hospitality, and seasonal suggestions for celebrations that involve food or drink.

— *Male&Female* is about rituals and celebrations that enhance relationships, particularly between the sexes.

— *Good Medicine* focuses on rituals, herbs, and techniques anyone can use to heal both body and soul.

— *Off the Beaten Tract* presents serious scholarship on Scripture (or other sacred writings) in an entertaining manner.

— *Around the Hearth* is our letters section and includes short sharings of real-life celebrations as well as reader-commentary on previously published articles.

Length is not a significant consideration for us. We generally recommend 4-8 typewritten double-spaced pages or 1000-2000 words. Say what you have to say, and let us edit as necessary.

Typewrite your articles, double-spaced, with one-inch margins all around. Ordinarily, submitting manuscripts on magnetic media or via modem is not useful for beginning writers, but we sometimes do this with regular writers.

Photos and illustrations are welcome accompaniments to articles. Photos should be high contrast, 5"X7" or 8"X10". Pen and ink illustrations work best.

Please do not send us an article that you have already submitted elsewhere unless you have had that article returned or have heard that it is not going to be used. However, if your article has *already* been published elsewhere and you think it might be useful as is or adapted for FESTIVALS, send it in. We sometimes reprint articles.

Send us a stamped self-addressed envelope (S.A.S.E.) with your article if you want it returned. We may not return it otherwise. Always keep a copy of the original for your files.

Please put your name, address, and phone numbers on the first page of your manuscript.

Bio-Notes. Please include brief biographical information for use at the end of your article and perhaps a photo of yourself. A cear snapshot will do.

Our procedure is to read and consider your article soon after we receive it, but there are some built-in delays that might slow down our response. Ordinarily, we try to read your manuscript right away as soon as we open the mail, but if we are overloaded, we may put it aside for a few days. If we read it and think it has possibilities, we may pass it on to another editor who may or may not work in this office. Please be patient with us, but if you do not hear from us in six weeks, send us a reminder notice.

If we decide to publish your article, it may take months — sometimes longer than a year — before it reaches the printed page. This is partly due to the seasonal nature of FESTIVALS and partly due to the normal lag-time in magazine publishing. Normally, we will tell you what our plans are, but as publication time nears, plans can change and your article can be bumped to a later issue (which could mean next year if you've written a seasonal article). Rather than letting this happen twice, we may try to use a smaller portion of your article right away or return it so that your article can have another chance in the market.

Rejection! Our hardest task is sending back articles we cannot use. We do this with a short note, usually saying we cannot use it without going into the whys and wherefores. We believe you deserve a personal note from a real human being, but we do not have the time to do literary criticism. We evaluate articles in light of our editorial focus, what articles we have on hand, the substance, and the style. Manuscripts are rejected for all kinds of reasons, quality being only one of them. Most are rejected for other reasons. So don't take it personally. We can only accept about one manuscript in every 20.

Compensation is a challenging question for a small magazine. FESTIVALS carries very little advertising and does not yet make a profit, which means that subscribers and the publisher (a small family-owned company) must pay the bills. Thus, we cannot pretend to be a money-making market for you. Still, we think you should receive something for your work. Each author receives a one-year complimentary subscription for themselves or a friend and five copies of the issue they were published in. Additional copies are available on request. We negotiate other terms with writers who have written for us before, sometimes a small cash stipend and sometimes products and services offered by the publisher.

Fine Madness

18 July 1987

I'm very happy that you are interested in our journal. Fine Madness's sample copies are available for your perusal (for you to see the kinds of poems, short stories and reviews which our editors choose to print) for $3.00, postage paid. Our yearly subscription rate is $7.00, plus postage ($1.80).

We want writers with their own, distinctive voices, and writing which shows that a mind is working, not just a tongue. We are open to almost any style of poetry or prose, provided that the form works for the piece and not against it.

However, we do want you to send original, typed manuscripts (no blurred photocopies or smudged carbons, please). Also, no simultaneous submissions (they often waste our time), no previously published work, and a self-addressed, stamped return envelope (an SASE) must be included with your manuscript if you want us to return it to you (or respond in any way). We would also appreciate it if you would type your name and address in the upper left-hand corner of every page you submit.

We would like to see 1 to 5 poems (no more than 10 pages total) per manuscript. We publish both long and short poems, but no single poem over ten pages can be considered. We also publish short prose and short fiction pieces, but at this time we cannot consider anything longer than 2500-3000 words. We try to respond within 3 months to all manuscripts submitted with an SASE. We buy first North American serial rights and anthology rights (in case we are able to bring out The Best of Fine Madness sometime in the future). Payment is a year's subscription to Fine Madness plus two contributor's copies of the issue in which your work appears and a discount on additional copies of that issue. (This is, we know, small payment, but we hope that the chance to place your work before an interested public will be 'compensation,' too.)

Since 1985, we have been offering two yearly cash prizes, The Kay Deeter Memorial Awards ($50 apiece). Recipients will be selected by the editors from that year's contributors to the magazine. The first awards were made to Glyn Jones (for "Shader's Vision," which appeared in Vol. 1, No. 1) and to Melinda Mueller (for "The Botanist," which appeared in Vol. 2, No. 2). The awards for 1986 are being made to Kaija Berleman (for "The Voyeur Meditates Upon the Human Spine," which appeared in Vol. 3, No. 1) and to David Hopes (for "In the Valley of Dry Bones," which appeared in Vol. 3, No. 2).

I hope that this note has answered your questions, and that you will consider submitting your work to Fine Madness in the future. Sincerely,

James Snydal
Fine Madness
P.O. Box 15176
Seattle, WA   98115-0176

FIRST HAND LTD.

P.O. Box 1314, Teaneck, New Jersey 07666 (201) 836-9177

Publishers of FirstHand and MANSCAPE Magazines

WRITER'S GUIDELINES FOR: FirstHand Magazine
                          Manscape Magazine
                          Manscape 2 Magazine

All three of the above magazines use unsolicited erotic fiction manuscripts, ranging in length from 10 to 20 double-spaced typed pages. Our average story length is fifteen pages. Manuscripts longer than 20 pages will be considered only if they are exceptional in some way. Material should be written in the first person and deal explicitly with homosexual experiences. All stories must contain some graphic sex scenes and should convey a positive attitude toward gay people and gay sex.

FirstHand also uses short non-fiction articles (2-3 double-spaced typed pages) highlighting practical information on safe sex practices, health, travel, books, video, fashion and other advice/lifestyle/ consumer-related topics of interest to gay or single men. These appear in our "Survival Kit" section, and should be written in the second or third person. We prefer for writers to query us first about ideas for "Survival Kit," but we will consider unsolicited submissions.

Poetry: Both FirstHand and Manscape 2 use poetry, generally not more than a page in length. Poems need not be graphically sexual but must deal directly with gay themes.

All three magazines are very reader-oriented in that a large part of every issue is comprised of letters from our readers describing their personal experiences, fantasies and feelings. Our readers are from all walks of life, all races and ethnic backgrounds, all classes, all religious and political affiliations, etc. They are a diverse group and many live in far-flung rural areas or small towns. For some of them, our magazines are the primary source of contact with gay life, in some cases the only support for their gay identities. Our readers are very loyal and most save every issue. We return that loyalty by trying to reflect their interests. For instance, we strive to avoid the exclusively big-city bias so common to national gay publications.

FirstHand deals with the "vanilla" side of gay sexuality: first homosexual experiences, romantic same-sex relationships, and the more common sexual practices such as oral and anal sex. Manscape has a similar format but focuses on gay sexual fetishes such as enemas, watersports, fisting, etc. Manscape 2 carries the kink a bit further, has a large-size format (8 x 11) and includes photo spreads.

All characters in stories must be at least eighteen years of age. We do not use material dealing with scat or double-fisting, or the injection of foreign objects (other than dildoes) into the body. Also, all participants in sexual acts must be willing: rape is a taboo subject as far as we're concerned, except in prison stories, where it is an unavoidable reality. Don't include heavy drug use in your stories--an occasional joint is okay but that's it. We don't even mention poppers, which have been pretty conclusively linked to AIDS. If you can write a <u>hot</u> safe sex story (condoms, sex toys, JO, phone sex, voyeuristic sex, etc.) by all means do so, and we'll be happy to read it.

<u>Manscape 2</u> also prints non-fiction full-length articles, which consist of varying topics of interest such as interviews with people of interest to gay men, information about AIDS, leather-Levi oriented articles and how-to articles concerning kinkier sex. If you would like to write a non-fiction piece, you would be well-advised to consult with us first about topic, length, etc. But we will also read unsolicited non-fiction.

<u>Pseudonyms</u>: Please be sure, if you intend to use a pseudonym, to put it in the by-line, under the title. There has been some confusion in the past with writers about this, and we would like to avoid more.

<u>Simultaneous Submissions</u>: We feel this practice to be not entirely ethical (submitting the same manuscript to several magazines at the same time, to see who responds the quickest). The writer thereby wastes the valuable time of the editor(s) who did <u>not</u> get back to him first--time that could have been better spent in other ways. For this reason, we do not like to deal with writers who practice this tactic. Owing to the enormous amount of submissions we receive, it usually takes from two to four weeks to respond to manuscripts or queries.

<u>Pay Scale</u>: We normally purchase all rights to stories and articles, for which we pay $150.00. Occasionally, we will buy First North American Serial Rights, for which we pay $100.00. For Survival Kit items, the pay scale is $35.00 (2 pages); $50.00 (3 pages); and $70.00 (4 pages). We favor articles of two to three pages for <u>Survival Kit</u>, preferring to present more and varied topics to fewer longer ones. A four-page item should be concerned only with a subject of major importance. For <u>poetry</u> we pay $25.00 per poem. We occasionally <u>reprint</u> articles which have appeared elsewhere and payment for these is on a case-by-case basis.

All manuscripts must be typed and double-spaced with right and left margins of at least one inch. The writer's name and address should appear in the upper right hand corner of the title page. Material which is seasonal or in any way timely should be submitted at least seven months in advance.

We sincerely appreciate your interest in our magazines and look forward to seeing your work in our pages.

Cordially yours,

Lou Thomas
Editor

the florida review

Department of English • University of Central Florida • Orlando, Florida 32816

Dear Contributor:

Thank you for your interest in The Florida Review. We are looking for fiction (up to 7,500 words) and poetry (any length). We are especially interested in new writers.

Payment, made on acceptance, is $5 per published page for fiction, and $15 per poem. All contributors receive three complimentary copies of the issue their work appears in. One-year subscriptions are $7, two-year subscriptions are $11, and single copies are available for $4 each.

We publish fiction of high "literary" quality -- stories that delight, instruct, and aren't afraid to take risks. We aren't especially interested in genre fiction (science fiction, romance, adventure, etc.), though a good story can transcend any genre. We welcome experimental fiction, so long as it doesn't make us feel lost or stupid.

We are looking for clear, strong poems, poems filled with real things, real people, real emotions, poems that might conceivably advance our knowledge of the human heart.

Address manuscripts to Pat Rushin, Fiction Editor, or Judith Hemschemeyer, Poetry Editor, at The Florida Review, Department of English, University of Central Florida, Orlando, FL 32816. Please include SASE.

We will be looking forward to seeing your work. Good luck!

The Editors

Footwork

Footwork is interested in fiction which shows a serious concern with

literary values; we do not want slick or formula stories. Because of

space limitations, stories of 3,000 words or less have the best

chance of publication. Rights revert to author on publication.

Frank
An International Journal of
Contemporary Writing & Art

Frank -- Fiction Writers' Guidelines

Frank welcomes unsolicited manuscripts of previously unpublished fiction, poetry, drama, short essays, translations, portions from longer works, interviews, black and white photography, drawings, reproductions of paintings and sculpture, and other forms of reproducible and original work.

All submissions must be accompanied by SASE or International Reply Coupons. Payment is in copies. It is highly appreciated when contributors are familiar with **Frank** and also agree to support the journal by subscribing.

Subscriptions (four issues): 125 FF/ $20.00 US/ $25.00 CAN./ £12.00. Back issues available at: 40 FF/ $5.00 US/ $6.00 CAN/ £3.00. Checks should be made payable to **Association Frank**. Tax deductible in that **Frank** is a Non-Profit Organization under California State Law.

Frank is a highly eclectic forum for creative work of varying styles, genres, voices, and sensibilities that favors work that conveys a sense of necessity, engagement, and serious, substantative innovation. The journal attempts to combat cultural ethnocentricity and welcomes work from diverse regions and translations from languages often ignored or little known to English-language readers. Additionally, **Frank** is particularly open to work that falls between existing genres.

Some recent contributors include: Robert Coover, John Berger, E.M. Cioran, Hélène Cixous, Edmond Jabès, Stephen Dixon, Raymond Carver, Hubert Selby, John Sanford, Claude Simon, Rikki Ducornet, Yilmaz Güney, Tom Waits, Henri Michaux, James Tate, Winfried Weiss, Alan Ginsberg, Yashar Kemal, Paul Bowles, Italo Calvino, William Burroughs, Lawrence Ferlinghetti, James Laughlin, Edouard Roditi, Derek Walcott, Breyten Breytenbach, Carl Andre, Stefan Brecht, Michel Butor, Edouard Glissant, Rodrigo Rey Rosa, Tomas Transtromer, and Foreign Dossiers on Nordic and Turkish, with Portugeuse, Pakistani, Filipino, and Central African dossiers in preparation.

Send all submissions, subscriptions, and enquiries to:

David Applefield, Editor
6 rue Monge
75005 Paris   or
France

Garrett White, US Editor
414 South Genesee
Los Angeles, CA 90036

GUIDELINES FOR SUBMISSIONS TO THE <u>FRIEND</u>

ADDRESS: The <u>Friend,</u> 23rd Floor, 50 E. North Temple, Salt Lake City, Utah 84150

The <u>Friend</u> is published by The Church of Jesus Christ of Latter-day Saints for boys and girls up to twelve years of age. All submissions are carefully read by the <u>Friend</u> staff, and those not accepted are returned within two months when a self-addressed stamped envelope is enclosed. Manuscripts without self-addressed stamped envelopes will not be returned nor will there be any response to them. Submit seasonal material at least eight months in advance. Query letters are not encouraged. The <u>Friend</u> purchases all rights to manuscripts accepted. Authors may request rights to have their work reprinted after their manuscript is published.

Special needs are:

1. SHORT STORIES AND ARTICLES: Stories should focus on character-building qualities and should be wholesome without moralizing or preaching. Boys and girls resolving conflicts is a theme of particular merit. Since the magazine is circulated worldwide, the <u>Friend</u> is interested in stories and articles with universal settings, conflicts, and characters. Biographies of living people are not accepted.

    Other suggestions include rebus, picture, holiday, sports, and photo stories, or manuscripts that portray various cultures. Short stories and articles of not more than 1,000 words are preferred. Very short pieces (up to 250 words) and nonfictional articles are desired for younger readers and preschool children; the <u>Friend</u> is particularly interested in stories with substance for tiny tots. Appropriate humor is a constant need. Our current supply of science articles is overstocked, although we are always on the lookout for those of exceptional merit. Serials are rarely accepted.

2. POETRY: Poems should be uplifting and of substance, evoking positive emotions and worthy aspirations without overattention to rhyme. Nature poems and those with a clever play on words are also desirable. Stories written in rhyme are seldom used in the <u>Friend.</u> Picturable poems with catchy cadences, suitable for preschoolers, are of special interest.

3. ACTIVITIES: The <u>Friend</u> features many handicraft, science, and homemaking projects. Cartoons, games, and puzzles about pets, nature, history, religion, and other subjects are also featured.

4. ILLUSTRATION: Artwork is not accepted through free-lance submission; art assignments are made to artists by our designers.

PAYMENT: Stories and articles are purchased for 8¢ a word and up; poems for $15 minimum per poem; recipes for $10; and activities and games for $10 and up. Additional payment may be made for outstanding manuscripts. The <u>Friend</u> does not pay for children's contributions.

MANUSCRIPT PREPARATION: Manuscripts should be accurately typed and double-spaced on one side of 8 1/2" x 11" white paper. Name, address, and social security number should be included with each manuscript.

ACCEPTED MANUSCRIPTS: Two copies of the issue containing an accepted contribution will be sent to the author upon publication. Accepted manuscripts may not appear for a year or longer.

FICTION GUIDELINES: THE GAMUT

THE GAMUT is a general interest magazine that publishes sharply focused, well-researched articles on nearly any subject in the sciences, arts, social sciences, business, or industry. We also like to publish good fiction and poetry when we can. THE GAMUT is a regional magazine, and we are of course interested in supporting area writers, but we are open to submissions from elsewhere.

Our only requirement is work of high quality. We are, however, usually not interested in genre fiction or fiction for specific age groups. Although we do not publish a great deal of fiction, we believe in its importance. Above all, writers who wish to be published in our magazine should care about the quality of their writing.

o **Editing** The editors may suggest some revision or ask for clarification. Any editorial revisions are submitted to the author for approval. Pre-publication galleys are sent to the author for final proofreading.

o **Length** Preferred length is 1000-6000 words, though longer stories will be considered.

o **Honorarium** Payment of $25 to $150 upon publication, except CSU authors, who receive five copies of the issue in which their work appears. Remunerated authors receive two copies. All authors may buy up to ten extra copies for half the cover price.

o **Manuscripts** Typing or word-processing double-spaced, on 8 1/2" x 11" paper with dark ribbon and margins of one inch all around is acceptable. Diskettes bearing WordStar files are also welcome, but must be accompanied by hard copy.

o **Title Page** Articles should have a title page containing the working title, the author's name, address, phone number and social security number, the number of pages, and the approximate number of words in the manuscript.

o **Multiple Submission** Acceptable if mentioned in original contact. As a rule, material must not have been previously published.

o **Cover Letter** Although it is not necessary, a letter briefly describing publishing history or other relevant information is appreciated.

o **Rights** THE GAMUT receives first serial rights plus right to reprint. Material is copyrighted by Cleveland State University, but all rights (except those aforementioned) revert to the author after publication.

o **Return of Ms.** Unsolicited mss. will be returned only if accompanied by a stamped, self-addressed envelope.

o **Sample Copy** A sample copy costs $2.50--check or money order.

      For further information, write: THE GAMUT
                                      Mary Grimm, Managing Editor
                                      RT 1216
                                      Cleveland State University
                                      Cleveland OH 44115

            or call: 1-216-687-4679

DUGENT PUBLISHING CORP.
2355 Salzedo St., Coral Gables, Florida 33134/(305) 443-2378

Gent   GUIDELINES FOR WRITERS

DUGENT PUBLISHING CORP. publishes three magazines, Cavalier, Gent and Nugget. We buy all fiction and articles from freelance writers. Each magazine has its own editorial slant and a description of each magazine's special needs follows:

CAVALIER is a sophisticated men's magazine aimed at the 18 to 35 year old male. We feature beautiful girls and entertaining fiction and articles. Stories must be professionally written and presented (first-timers welcome) and articles must be carefully researched and documented, if necessary. Subject matter for both stories and articles can vary from serious to sex to humor, keeping our readership in mind.

FICTION: We buy all types of fiction -- all kinds of plots, but they must be well-plotted and exceptionally well written. We are looking for good, solid stories...no intellectual or obtuse exercises and no poetry. We prefer at least one very graphic and erotic sexual encounter in each story and we are also interested in scenes of girl/girl fighting, or boy/girl fighting within the context of a story whether it is murder, science fiction, sex, horror or whatever. Length: 1,500 to 3,500 words. Pay from $200 to $300.

ARTICLES: Also cover a wide range but within the restriction that it must be a subject of interest to our readers, not dated material (since we have a four month lead time) and, preferably, that it be on a subject that is somewhat off-beat and not something that will be extensively covered by the media nationally. Please query first with a brief but comprehensive outline. First time writers may be asked to submit the finished article on speculation, but we give firm assignments to regular contributors. Where necessary, material must be carefully researched and documented. We are not interested in expose type articles, politics, historical figures or current events unless different and off-beat. Pay is similar to fiction but we pay additional for photos if submitted with article (and if professional and appropriate) and length is the same as for fiction. Our most urgent need is for non-fiction and we welcome beginners.

GENT: Specializes pictorially in large D-cup cheesecake and prefers both fiction and non-fiction articles gauged to the subject of breasts, bras, fat women, lactation, etc. Fictional female characters should be described as extremely large busted with detailed descriptions of breasts. Fiction length can vary from 2,500 to 3,500 words. Articles from 1,500 to 3,000 words. Payment is from $125 to $150 (with more for specialized material and articles with photos) upon publication. Query first on non-fiction articles, with brief comprehensive outline.

NUGGET: This magazine is primarily concerned with offbeat, fetish oriented material (sado-masochism, TV, TS, B&D,WS, amputees, fetishism, etc) and we prefer both fiction and articles slanted to this variety of subjects. Payment, length, etc., same as GENT magazine. Query first on articles.

WE DO NOT PUBLISH material on minors, religious subjects or on characters or subjects that might be considered libelous. Interviews (query first) must be accompanied by permission of the interviewee and supporting documentation. ALWAYS enclose self addressed stamped envelope for returns.

Georgia Journal

Agee Publishers, Incorporated
P.O. Box 526, Athens, GA 30603.
(404) 548-5269

GUIDELINES FOR SHORT FICTION

Georgia Journal publishes short fiction up to 2,500 words. Stories should be strong in narrative line and characterization and may be serious or humorous. Quality writing and good taste are essential requirements for us. We do not use previously published work. We have considered an excerpt from an unpublished novel, and would do so again if we could find one that stands on its own and possesses the same merit we would expect of any short fiction.

Stories may have a Georgia slant, but this is not essential. We cannot use experimental fiction and formula stories. Some writers have sent us science fiction and fantasy, but we have yet to see a story we felt our readers would enjoy. We have bought light fiction, and we would like to see more.

Georgia Journal buys first serial rights and presently pays $25 per story upon acceptance. Ours is a quarterly regional magazine that appeals to a sophisticated audience. Too often we receive sentimental reminiscences thinly disguised as fiction. We have published new writers, and we hope to do so again. Sometimes we will give an author feedback with a rejection if we see possibilities in a story, but with increased submissions we cannot do this as frequently.

Writers should send complete manuscripts which are typed, double-spaced on 8½ x 11 inch white paper. Photocopied submissions are acceptable, as are computer printouts (no dot-matrix). Submissions without a self-addressed, stamped envelope will not be returned. While we assume that all writers keep a file copy of each manuscript and that many writers send stories by first-class for added assurance, Georgia Journal cannot be responsible for lost manuscripts.

Writers unfamiliar with Georgia Journal may send $3 for a sample copy. Our publication is copyrighted.

Address fiction to Hugh Agee, Fiction Editor, Georgia Journal, P.O. Box 526, Athens, GA 30603. Reports on submissions within 6 weeks.

GOOD HOUSEKEEPING

959 EIGHTH AVENUE, NEW YORK, NEW YORK 10019 – (212) 262-3630 – FICTION DEPARTMENT

FICTION GUIDELINES

We are always pleased to read and consider short fiction which authors feel might be right for GOOD HOUSEKEEPING. We look for stories of emotional interest to women--courtship, romance, marriage, family, friendships, personal growth, coming of age. The best way to know if your story is appropriate for us is to read several of our recent issues. (We are sorry, but we cannot furnish free sample copies of the magazine.) Owing to the thousands of manuscripts we receive, the odds are long that your story will be published, so please be sure before you take the time and expense to submit it that it is our type of fiction. The number of manuscripts we receive also means that we cannot give individual criticism, but you may be assured that all material is given careful consideration.

We prefer manuscripts to be typewritten, double-spaced, between 1,000-3,000 words and accompanied by a short cover letter list- ing your previous publishing credits. Make sure your name and address appears on the manuscript itself and that you have retain- ed a copy for yourself. A self-addressed envelope large enough to hold the manuscript and sufficient postage should be included for its return. Please stick the stamps to the envelope so they won't get lost, use your own address as the return address, and you will receive an answer within one month. As is the case with most magazines, we cannot take responsibility for unsolicited manuscripts, and these guidelines should not be construed as a solicitation.

GOOD HOUSEKEEPING pays current market rates on acceptance, with prices varying according to length and merit of the material.

We hope that the above information is helpful to you and thank you for your interest.

THE FICTION EDITORS

grain

BOX 1154 REGINA, SASKATCHEWAN   S4P 3B4

HOW TO SUBMIT YOUR WORK TO *grain*

The manuscript:

Do not send already published work.
Do not send your only copy of a manuscript.
Multiple submissions are not acceptable.
We discourage computer-printed manuscripts.
Type your work double-spaced on one side of the paper.
Do not allow more than three small corrected errors on a page.
Type your name and full address on the first page of the manuscript.
On subsequent pages type your name and the title of the piece.

The covering letter:

Make your covering letter brief.
Include a biographical statement of two or three sentences.
Let us know if you are just beginning to send your work to magazines.
Type your full address, postal code and phone number on the letter.
Resist the temptation to explain your work; it should be able to do that for itself. Resist the temptation to be funny or to vent your feelings on being rejected. The professional way to deal with rejection is to improve the work and send it elsewhere.

Mailing:

Enclose a stamped self-addressed envelope large enough to contain the manuscript and attached to it with a paper clip.
Submissions from outside Canada require sufficient international reply coupons to cover return postage. Foreign stamps are not valid in Canada.
If you want immediate acknowledgement of your submission, enclose a stamped self-addressed postcard.

General advice:

Read back issues of the magazine before submitting. *grain* publishes literary, not popular, writing.
If you are a beginning writer, study your craft. Learn from good writers and consult them before you submit.

Useful texts:

The Canadian Writer's Market
The Canadian Author's Guide

(Grain continued)

MARKETING POETRY

by JOSEPH BRUCHAC

A. Ten Tips on Submitting:

More than 90% of the outlets for serious poetry pay only in copies. This does not mean, however, that one should be less than professional when submitting work to ANY publication. Here are some simple rules to be followed when submitting your work:

1. Always type your manuscripts. Single-spaced is acceptable.
2. Put your name and address on each page -- usually the upper right hand corner.
3. Always enclose a stamped self-addressed legal-sized envelope (with sufficient postage).
4. Do not submit the same poems to more than one place at the same time.
5. Keep accurate records of what you have sent out, when and where.
6. A cover letter is not necessary with your submission. If you MUST SEND ONE, KEEP IT SHORT AND SIMPLE. Your poems SHOULD speak for themselves. A list of prior publications may be a good indication that you are a serious and practicing poet, but it is the actual poem itself which will be accepted or rejected, not the cover letter.
7. When sending out poems, a group of from 4 to 6 poems is about right for a single submission. Too many can make it hard for an editor, too few may not give a good enough sample of your work.
8. When rejected, use it as an opportunity to read your own poems with fresh insight -- as if they were written by someone else. Submission to magazines can be part of the creative process.
9. When rejected, try again. But if the pages on which your poems are typed become stained, torn, or terminally creased, make fresh copies.
10. Though photocopies are now much less frowned upon than in the past, many editors prefer to receive only typed originals. (Use of a word processing program with a microcomputer makes this much easier than in the past.)

B. Finding the Markets:

The following are the publications which I would most highly recommend to the serious poet in search of markets. In no case, however, should such publications or lists of markets take the place of reading actual copies of the magazines which are publishing poetry. Further, I think it is the responsibility of the poet to be part of the AUDIENCE and the support network for contemporary poetry by SUBSCRIBING TO AND BUYING at least a few literary magazines each year. If we don't support them, how can we expect others to do so?

1. AWP NEWSLETTER, Old Dominion University, Norfolk, Va. 23508. $7/yr. This is a newspaper format publication which provides news relating to the various creative writing programs in the United States. It always contains market listings. Further, AWP sponsors numerous competitions open to the public which offer prize money and publication to the winners.

2. CODA, Poets and Writers, Inc., 201 West 54th Street, NYC 10019. $12/yr. Published on newsprint in an 8½ by 11 format, CODA is one of the most useful publications for literary writers. In addition to information about prize competition and markets, each issue contains news and informational articles covering many subjects. Recently these have included contracts, royalties, chapbooks, what to do when your editor leaves your publishing house, and using word processors in writing.
Poets and Writers, Inc. also publishes a number of directories and guides including *A Writer's Guide to Copyright* ($3.95), *Literary Agents: A Writer's Guide* ($4.95), and *A Directory of American Poets and Fiction Writers* ($14.95).

(Note: CODA is changing its name to POETS & WRITERS and will publish 6 times yearly.)

3. THE INTERNATIONAL DIRECTORY OF LITTLE MAGAZINES AND SMALL PRESSES, edited by Len Fulton and Ellen Ferber, Dustbooks Press, PO Box 100, Paradise, Ca. 95969. $17.95 (yearly publication). Regarded as the only comprehensive guide to the constantly changing world of small press publishing, this book is a must for the poet. If you do not have one, find a library which does. The current edition is 581 pages long and contains information about thousands of magazines and presses.
Dustbooks Press also publishes *Small Press Review* ($27 a year - monthly) which contains reviews of small press publications, as well as additional and updated listings of magazines and presses, contests, and markets.

4. LITERARY MARKETS, 4340 Coldfall Road, Richmond, British Columbia V7C 1P8, Canada. $9/yr. for 6 issues. This is one of the newest editions to market listings. Published as a 5-6 page photocopied, stapled newsletter, it often contains listings not found elsewhere and is a good way to keep up to date on opportunities for publishing in both the United States and Canada.

5. WRITER'S MARKET, 9933 Alliance Road, Cincinnati, Ohio 45242. $17.95 (yearly publication). Though less focussed on small press and poetry then the other publications listed thus far, this is a useful book for the writer in general. Published by *Writer's Digest*, which is also recommended, especially for Judson Jerome's monthly columns on poetry. ($15/yr. 12 issues)

6. Poet's Market, edited by Judson Jerome. 9933 Alliance Rd., Cincinnati, Oh. 45242 This is the newest (and, to my mind, the best) of the "markets" books focussing on poetry. With 1,500 listings and good evaluations of poetry publishers, as well as articles on marketing your work, this may well be the book to have for placing your poems. (Yearly publication. 1987 version sells for $16.95.)

HADASSAH

MAGAZINE

50 WEST 58th STREET NEW YORK, N.Y. 10019   (212) 355-7900   Telex: HADASS 425191

Writer's Guidelines

Thank you for your inquiry about writing an article for Hadassah Magazine. As a matter of policy, the magazine does not assign articles to authors who have not previously written for us. We do, however. give a careful and considered reading to all manuscripts submitted to us. Many articles which appear in Hadassah Magazine were unsolicited. We would suggest, however, that you first submit to us your story idea, so we can let you know whether it is one in which we are interested.

We want stories on Jewish life here, in communities around the world and in Israel, both fiction and nonfiction. They should focus on shared Jewish experiences, but be told in fresh new ways, whether dealing with past traditions or grappling with new problems. While holiday stories, immigrant sagas and Holocaust tales are all important themes, we receive many of them. Therefore, to be of interest to us, the quality of writing and angle of the story must stand out.

We are interested in unusual current events for our "Currents" column, and in articles for our "Travel" and "Parenting" columns-- although these must conform to our guidelines and should be discussed with the editors first.

We appreciate objective, lively writing, with lots of quotes and without the author's voice intruding. Speeches and research reports do not usually translate into a publishable feature.

The optimum length of our articles is 1,500 words (and up to 2,500 words for fiction). We pay a minimum of $300 for a feature article (less for book reviews), payable upon publication. Travel stories are $400 for all-time rights. If you have pictures related to your story, include them. We pay for each photo used. To help expedite correspondence, please enclose a self-addressed, stamped envelope.

We welcome hearing from you.

--The Editors

ROSE GOLDMAN, Chairman   •   ALAN M. TIGAY, Executive Editor   •   NANCY MARGOLIS Associate Publisher/Advertising Director

HELICON NINE

GUIDELINES FOR CONTRIBUTORS

Helicon Nine provides a forum for the creative accomplishments of women in the fields of literature, music, the visual and the performing arts. It juxtaposes works from one generation with another, thereby covering the broad range of past and present talent. In addition to publishing the works of eminent and aspiring artists, the editors hope to reawaken interest in women artists of the past whose works have continued to inspire subsequent generations of fellow artists, yet who have been themselves overlooked by history.

Helicon Nine is a bit larger than most "little magazines" (7″ x 10″), it is richly illustrated with color reproductions and photographs. Each issue includes a recording of a live musical performance, a reading, or an interview. It has a long shelf life, as it is designed to be read many times for pleasure and for information. Separately, the issues will stand on their own merit; together, they will provide a rich documentation of the ongoing history of women in the arts.

Subscription price is $18.00 for 3 issues; single copy, $8.00; double copy, $12.00. It is offset in black ink; has perfect binding. Circulation is 3,500.

Contributors and featured artists include: Virgil Thomson, Alice Neel, Anne Roiphe, Francine de Plessix Gray, Ned Rorem, Audrey Flack, Merce Cunningham, Marian McPartland, Marya Mannes, Miriam Shapiro, John Perreault, Dame Ethel Smyth, Carmen Orrego, Helen Hardin, June Jordan, Ntozake Shange, Georgia O'Keeffe, Willa Cather, Joyce Carol Oates, Richard Kostelanetz, John Tibbetts, Mary Lou Williams, James Dickey, Grace Paley and others.

Subscriptions are held by public libraries, art museums, universities and colleges nationwide, among them Harvard, Yale and Stanford Universities, The Smithsonian, Lincoln Center for the preforming Arts, the San Francisco Museum of Modern Art, the National Gallery, Washington, D.C.

Helicon Nine will obtain first rights and reassign them to the author immediately upon publication. Payment will be in contributor's copies. Artists are encouraged to send slides or transparencies and color separations when available. All submissions should be addressed to the Editor, with a return stamped and self-addressed envelope enclosed. There are no limitations on the number or length of submissions.

P.O. Box 22412 • Kansas City, Missouri 64113
913/345-0802

HIGH ADVENTURE

High Adventure is a quarterly Royal Rangers magazine for boys. Designed to provide boys with worthwhile,
enjoyable, leisure reading; to challenge them in narrative
form to higher ideals and greater spiritual dedication;
and to perpetuate the spirit of the Royal Rangers program
through stories, ideas, and illustrations.

16 pages, size 8 1/2 X 11; four color

TIPS TO WRITERS

1. *Read the magazine.* Become familiar with the type of
material used and editorial style. A sample copy will
be mailed to you on request.

2. *Know the readership.* Recognize the age level, interests, and needs of the readers. Slant the material
accordingly.

3. *Give attention to writing style.* Watch grammar and
spelling. Don't overwork adjectives; use action verbs.
Avoid long, involved sentences (shoot for average of
15 words). Beware of cliches and hackneyed express-
ions.

4. *Be accurate.* Check your own work. Watch spelling
of proper names. Be sure quotations are accurate
and give scource. If Scripture passages are quoted
from a version other than King James, identify the
version. If you quote extensively (more than 50
words) from published material, especially copyrighted
material, enclose a letter from the publisher giving
reprint permission.

PREPARING AND SUBMITTING MANUSCRIPTS

1. *The manuscript.* Should be typed, double-spaced, with ample margins, on one side of sheet. Name, address and social security number of writer in upper left-hand corner; approximate number of words in upper right. Number each page; do not staple pages together.

2. *Carbon copy.* Keep a carbon copy as the editor cannot be responsible for loss of manuscript in mail or otherwise. Do not send carbon copy; it is hard to read, and the editor hesitates to use it in case the original has been sent to another publisher.

3. *Return postage.* Accompany free-lance manuscripts with a self-addressed envelope and sufficient postage for return of manuscript if necessary.

4. *New writers.* If writer is unknown to editor a letter of introduction is appreciated giving personal background, church affiliation, whether layman or minister, etc.

5. *Seasonal material.* Should be sent 6 months in advance.

6. *Payment.* Usual rates are 2¢ a word for first or all rights.

7. *Cartoons.* $7.50.

8. *Puzzles.* $10.00

9. *Jokes.* $1.00 - $2.00

10. *Rejections.* Do not be discouraged by rejections. Space in periodicals is at a premium, and the amount of free-lance materials some accept is quite limited. A rejection may not mean that the material lacks merit but rather that it does not fit current needs of the periodical.

11. *Address:* Address all inquiries and manuscripts to:

    The Editor
    High Adventure
    1445 Boonville Ave.
    Springfield, MO 65802

FREE-LANCE OPPORTUNITIES

Articles: Christian Living
          Devotional
          Holy Spirit
          Salvation
          Self Help

Biography

Cartoons

Feature Stories

Fiction

Fillers

How-to-Do-It Features

Missionary Stories

News Items

Photographs: Color

Puzzles

Testimonies

CRAFTS

We want fresh, novel, tested ideas, with clear directions. We require a well-made sample to be submitted with each craft idea. Project must require only salvage materials or inexpensive, easy-to-obtain materials. The wider the age range, the better; especially desirable if easy enough for primary grades or preschoolers. We are particularly interested in ideas for projects that result in the creation of interesting toys and games and attractive, useful gift items.

VERSE

We seldom buy verse.

FINGER PLAYS/ACTION PLAYS

Should have lots of action. Must be easy for very young child to grasp and for parents to dramatize, step-by-step, with hands, fingers, and body movements. Should not be too wordy. $25.

GENERAL INFORMATION

We don't pay persons under 15 for contributions.

No inquiries needed. We buy all rights, including copyright, and do not consider material previously published.

All material is paid for on acceptance.

Be sure to enclose with manuscript a self-addressed, stamped envelope for its possible return.

HIGHLIGHTS FOR CHILDREN is published monthly (except bimonthly July-August) for children from 2 to 12. Circulation is over 1,500,000. Sold by subscription only.

FICTION

We carry stories up to 900 words appealing to both girls and boys. Stories should begin with action rather than description. Create a story which children 8 to 12 will want to read, capturing interest in the first few sentences. If children 3 to 7 will also enjoy hearing this same story, it is especially valuable to us. We print no stories just to be read aloud and we seldom choose rhyming stories.

Our greatest current need is for stories for beginning readers, (600 words or under) having strong plot and great suspense, short sentences, and much action.

We like stories in which listeners or readers can imagine themselves the leading character and wish to emulate the traits of this person—stories which don't emphasize money values, but imperishables. Any moral teaching must be indirect and subtle. We particularly need stories with female leads, humorous stories, stories with urban settings, and stories of adventure. We welcome stories that accurately portray other cultures and religious observances, and stories that leave a good emotional and moral residue.

Suggestions of war, crime, and violence are taboo. HIGHLIGHTS aims to exalt the preciousness of every person regardless of sex, family background, social

Highlights® for Children

EDITORIAL REQUIREMENTS AND PAYMENT SCHEDULES

Editorial Offices, 803 Church Street, Honesdale, Pa. 18431

status, religion, race, or nationality. We aim to foster wholesome human relations.

We accept a story on its merit whether written by a novice or by an experienced writer.

FACTUAL FEATURES

We are always looking for gifted writers, especially engineers, scientists, historians, artists, musicians, etc., who, having a rich background in their respective fields, can interpret to children useful, interesting, verifiable facts. References or sources of information must be included with submission. Photos or art reference material are helpful when we evaluate such submissions.

Also, we want authors who write from firsthand experience and can interpret well the ways of life, especially of children, in other countries; who show appreciation of cultural differences; and who don't leave the impression that our ways always are the best. In short, writers who can help foster world brotherhood.

Biographies stressing the early lives of individuals who have made significant contributions through their own efforts are particularly welcome.

Science and other factual articles within 900 words, $60 and up.

PARTIES

We want original party plans for children, giving clever ideas and themes clearly described in 300 to 800 words, including drawings or samples of items to be illustrated. $30-$50.

THE HORROR SHOW

AN ADVENTURE IN TERROR

PUBLISHED BY: PHANTASM PRESS, 14848 Misty Springs Lane, Oak Run, CA 96069
EDITOR: David B. Silva

Published quarterly, **THE HORROR SHOW** is dedicated to contemporary tales of the macabre, fine illustrations, and inside tips on the horror field. There is no other magazine in America quite like it. Each new issue is a grand collection of never-before-seen tales.

FICTION: we're looking for solid horror fiction, not overly graphic nor overly violent, always set in a contemporary setting, and original in its premise. We are not interested in science fiction, sword & sorcery, or other genres which can easily be found in numerous other publications. A logical twist or surprise at the end is generally appreciated, but not necessary. More important is originality, strong characterization, a sense of mood. Try to avoid insect, dog, cat, mad slasher, and simplistic ghost stories. Maximum length is a firm 4,000 words.

NON-FICTION: generally runs 1600-1800 words and is on assignment. If you have an idea, please make a proposal. We're looking for informative articles that have insight into the horror field, horror writers, etc. Must be well done, and keep in mind we already have a regular book reviewer, movie reviewer and interviewer.

ILLUSTRATIONS: new artists are asked to send photocopies of their work. We use black and white illustrations only, on assignment, generally tied directly to a story. Currently, we're carrying a backlog of artists, so the market is not easy to break into. Full-page illustrations pay $7.50, partial page $5.00, front cover $15.00.

PAYMENT: 1/2 - 1 1/2 cent per word, plus a contributor's copy. This is for first time rights only, all rights revert back to you upon publication. **THE HORROR SHOW** is copyrighted, all included material is protected. No simultaneous submissions or previously published material. Always include a SASE. Response time is generally three weeks to four weeks.

THE HORROR SHOW
For those wishing to partake in the terror ...

[ ] FALL '84 - $4.95   [ ] FALL '86 - $4.95
[ ] WINTER '85 - $4.95   [ ] JAN. '87 - $4.95
[ ] SPRING '86 - $4.95   [ ] FULL SUBSCRIPTION (4 ISSUES) - $14.00
[ ] SUMMER '86 - $4.95   [ ] CAN'T GET ENOUGH (8 ISSUES) - $26.00

NAME: _____
ADDRESS: _____
CITY: _____ STATE: _____ ZIP: _____

Foreign orders: please add $1.00 for singles, $2.00 for subscriptions. Foreign checks and money orders should be made out to: David Silva. All others to: Phantasm Press, 14848 Misty Springs Lane, Oak Run, CA 96069.

CAT FANCY
DOG FANCY
BIRD TALK
HORSE ILLUSTRATED
magazines

Editorial Offices
P.O. Box 6050
Mission Viejo, California 92690
Telephone (714) 240-6001

Horse Illustrated

WRITER'S GUIDELINES

Thank you for your interest in our publications. We would be pleased to see your material. Below we have listed some of the publication requirements of CAT FANCY, DOG FANCY, BIRD TALK and HORSE ILLUSTRATED to assist you in preparing submissions.

ARTICLES

CAT FANCY, DOG FANCY and BIRD TALK are directed at the general pet owning population and written for the adult audience. HORSE ILLUSTRATED is directed at the amateur competitor and pleasure horse owner. We suggest that you read past issues of the magazines to acquaint yourself with the types of material we use. Past issues may be obtained by sending $3.00 to the above address. We need informative articles, limited to 3,000 words, on the care of training of cats, dogs, birds, and horses (health nutrition, training, etc.); photo essays on historical and current events dealing with cats, dogs, birds and horses; how-to articles; human interest stories; and good fiction, with the animal as the primary focus of interest. We rarely use stories in which the animal speaks as if it were human. We use a breed article in each issue, but these articles are assigned. Please query if you have a breed article in mind.

Manuscripts should be typewritten, double-spaced with wide margins. We prefer that articles be accompanied with appropriate art in the form of professional quality color transparencies or black and white photographs (NOT SNAP SHOTS) or professional illustrations. Additional guidelines are available for artists and photographers.

We are always happy to review material on speculation, but with the exception of fiction, the best working procedure is to query before preparing an article. Our usual rate of payment is three to five cents per printed word, five cents if accompanied by good quality photographs. Payment is made in the latter part of the cover month in which your article appears, (i.e., if your piece was in the November issue you would be paid in the latter part of November). We buy first American rights only; all other rights revert back to the author.

We cannot assume responsibility for material submitted, but we assure you that reasonable care will be taken in handling your work. YOU MUST INCLUDE A SELF-ADDRESSED, STAMPED ENVELOPE WITH EACH SUBMISSION.

<u>GUIDELINES</u> <u>FOR</u> <u>HOR-TASY</u>   6/82

<u>HOR-TASY</u> is an anthology of psychological horror & pure fantasy.

Our definition of psychological horror is horror dealing with the
human mind, horror coming from within a person to be used against
either himself or another person. We want to be able to feel the
horror that is present in the story. We want to understand why the
horror is occuring & where it is headed. We want the horror to be
so realistic & vivid that it could very well be possible. We also
want it to be well-written, but we've found that experience has
very little to do with an acceptance here. <u>Everyone</u> is considered
equally here. We don't care how much or how little you've been
published elsewhere--our only concern is the story you offer for
potential use in <u>H-T</u>.

We are <u>not</u> interested in stories making constant references to one's
sanity or insanity, nor do we want stories involving psychiatrists.
We do not want stories dealing with monsters, zombies, ghosts,
spooks, vampires, hexes, voodoo dolls, "things", "creepies-in-
the-dreams", or the all-too-common haunted houses.

Our definition of pure fantasy is fantasy involving myths, legends,
faërie tales (on an adult level), magic (but not sword & sorcery),
& other fantasies along that line. Again, we want the story to
be vivid & realistic, along with being well-written. Everyone is
also considered equally in the fantasy department. Names mean
nothing to us--only the story. Famous names in one circle are
totally unknown in another circle, anyway.

<u>HOR-TASY</u> so far has run 72 pages for both #1 & #2. This will be
roughly a guideline for future issues. Story length is of no
concern to us as long as the story <u>needs</u> that length. It's
possible that we may even publish a story-within-a-story <u>if</u> it's
what we want. Extremely short stories, however (1-3 pages) usually
lack the character development that we look for.

Please keep in mind that these are only <u>guidelines</u> & that they
are flexible.

If you have any questions, we'll be happy to answer them (please
send along an SASE, though) & we'll try to guide you closer to
what we're looking for if we return your story.

<u>HOR-TASY</u>; Ansuda Publications; PO Box 158; Harris, IA 51345 USA

EDITORIAL GUIDELINES

INDIVIDUAL MAGAZINE NEEDS

MUCH OF THE MATERIAL USED IN ALL OF OUR MAGAZINES IS HEALTH-RELATED. THIS INCLUDES STORIES, POETRY, ARTICLES, AND ACTIVITIES.

TURTLE MAGAZINE FOR PRESCHOOL KIDS (ages 2 to 5)
HUMPTY DUMPTY'S MAGAZINE (ages 4 to 6)
CHILDREN'S PLAYMATE MAGAZINE (ages 5 to 7)

TURTLE uses bedtime or naptime stories (approximately 200 to 600 words) that can be read to the child. HUMPTY DUMPTY'S MAGAZINE and CHILDREN'S PLAYMATE use easy-to-read stories for the beginning reader. Fiction can be 500 to 800 words. All of these magazines use short, simple poems or stories in rhyme. Games and crafts should involve a minimum of adult guidance and have clear, brief instructions. Humorous stories and poems are especially needed. In HUMPTY DUMPTY and CHILDREN'S PLAYMATE, healthful recipes requiring little or no need for the stove are used.

JACK AND JILL (ages 6 to 8)
CHILD LIFE (ages 7 to 9)
CHILDREN'S DIGEST (ages 8 to 10)

Stories may run from 500 to 1800 words. Articles may run from 500 to 1200 words. When appropriate, articles should be accompanied by photographs or transparencies. Nonfiction material should list sources of information. We may use factual features dealing with nature, science, and sports—also some historical and biographical articles. Preferred fiction includes realistic stories, adventure, mysteries, and science fiction. Humorous stories are highly desirable. Also needed are healthful recipes (see page 2).

SAMPLE COPIES

We regret that we are unable to provide free sample copies of the magazines. Individual copies may be obtained for seventy-five cents each by writing to Children's Better Health Institute, P.O. Box 567, Indianapolis, IN 46206.

Children's Better Health Institute
Benjamin Franklin Literary & Medical Society, Inc.
1100 Waterway Boulevard
P.O. Box 567
Indianapolis, Indiana 46206

TURTLE MAGAZINE FOR PRESCHOOL KIDS

HUMPTY DUMPTY'S MAGAZINE

CHILDREN'S PLAYMATE MAGAZINE

JACK AND JILL • CHILD LIFE • CHILDREN'S DIGEST

Our goal at the Children's Better Health Institute is to provide children with good reading that not only entertains but also educates, primarily about good health. We have a constant need for high-quality stories, articles, and activities with an exercise, nutrition, safety, hygiene, or other health-related theme. Our emphasis is preventive medicine, and we are seeking material that will encourage young readers to practice better health habits.

Health information may be presented in a variety of formats. We are looking for fresh, creative ways to encourage children to develop and maintain good health. Fiction stories that deal with a health theme need not have health as the primary subject but should include it in some way in the course of events. Main characters in fiction stories should adhere to good health practices, unless failure to do so is necessary to a story's plot. Word and math puzzles, games, and other activities can also successfully convey health messages if they are enjoyable to youngsters and age-appropriate. We also use factual articles that teach scientific facts about the body or nutrition. Writers should avoid an encyclopedic or "preachy" approach. We try to present our health material in a positive manner, incorporating humor and a light approach wherever possible without minimizing the seriousness of what we are saying.

In all material, please avoid references to eating sugary foods, such as candy, cakes, cookies, and soft drinks. In recipes submitted for publication, ingredients should be healthful. Avoid sugar, salt, chocolate, red meat, and fats.

We are also interested in material with more general themes. We are especially in need of holiday material—stories, articles, and activities. Send seasonal material at least eight months in advance. Also remember that characters in realistic stories should be up-to-date. Many of our readers have working mothers and/or come from single-parent homes. We need more stories that reflect these changing times but at the same time communicate good, wholesome values.

GENERAL INFORMATION

MANUSCRIPT FORMAT

Manuscripts must be typewritten and double- or triple-spaced. The author's name, address, telephone number, Social Security number, and an approximate word count must appear on the first page of the manuscript. KEEP A COPY OF YOUR WORK. We'll handle your manuscript with care, but we cannot assume responsibility for its return. Please send the entire manuscript; queries are not necessary. The editors cannot criticize, offer suggestions, or enter into correspondence concerning unsolicited manuscripts that are not accepted, nor can they suggest other markets for material that is not published. MATERIAL CANNOT BE RETURNED unless it is accompanied by a self-addressed envelope and SUFFICIENT return postage.

PHOTOS

WE DO NOT PURCHASE SINGLE PHOTOGRAPHS. We do purchase short photo features (up to 6 or 8 pictures) or photos that accompany and help illustrate editorial matter. (Please include captions.)

REVIEW TIME REQUIRED

Time required to review manuscripts properly is about eight to ten weeks. Each manuscript is carefully considered for possible use in *all* the magazines, not only that one to which it was originally addressed; therefore, if a manuscript is returned, it should not be resubmitted to a different youth publication at this address.

RATES AND PAYMENT POLICIES

Fiction and articles: approximately six cents a word. Poetry: $7.00 and up. Photos: $7.00 minimum. Puzzles and games: no fixed rate. Payment is made upon publication. Each author will be sent two complimentary copies of the issue in which his or her material is published. Additional copies may be purchased for seventy-five cents each.

RIGHTS

We prefer to purchase all rights. Simultaneous submissions are not accepted.

CHILDREN'S CONTRIBUTIONS

Except for items that may be used in the children's columns that appear each month, the editors do not encourage submissions from children. Even highly talented young people are not usually experienced enough to compete on a professional level with adult authors.

LARRY FLYNT PUBLICATIONS

HUSTLER ARTICLE SPECIFICATIONS

Dear Contributor:

HUSTLER wants articles that contain information that is daring, new, different and controversial, dealing primarily with sexual topics. Since HUSTLER's standards are special, the magazine seldom buys articles on speculation, but gives all submissions fair consideration. The best approach is to submit a written proposal outlining not only the topic, but how it will be presented for the HUSTLER audience. Tell who you'll talk to, what areas you'll cover, and how it's new or something that hasn't been dealt with in other media. When a proposal is accepted, the assignment is made by contract.

HUSTLER presents information to its audience in clear, straight-forward language. The magazine provides sexual information and entertainment to a diverse but regular readership. Articles must be third-person reportage.

ARTICLES

Maximum length: 4500 words   Fee: $1500 (+); some expenses

Article topics must be presented with impact through concise, fact-filled coverage. All facts and quotes are double-checked by our Research Department, and documentation must acompany the article. We are primarily interested in sexual topics that are current, of interest to a wide audience, and particularly those that are not being covered openly, if at all, by nonsex media. Social, legal, religous and political topics will also be considered.
Query first.

PERSONALITIES

Maximum length: 4500 words   Fee: $1500 (+)

HUSTLER publishes profiles and interviews that reveal new and different information about celebrities, uncover the upcoming stars and leaders, and present the personalities the other media can't get. The magazine wants ideas, opinions and personal

experiences that haven't been expressed before, or haven't
seen print. All sides of the personality must be shown.
Interviews are acceptable most often when the person's viewpoint is the central issue, and that person is outspoken and
informative, or when they reveal, in the personality's own
words, a candid or intimate side.
Query first.

FICTION

Maximum length: 3000 words   Fee: $1000 (+)

HUSTLER wants erotic fiction that conveys an interesting
story line, with at least two imaginatively written sex scenes
that grow logically from the action and chatacters. The plot
should not serve merely as a vehicle to describe sex acts,
and the sex should not souund contrived or forced. Plots
should have tension and conflict--adventure, mystery, action,
horror, fast living--that have images and experiences the
average reader can relate to. The story should be told in a
fast-paced, straightforward way. Brisk dialogue that both
moves the story forward and tells about the characters is best.

HUSTLER does not buy poetry. Please do not submit stories
with sex with minors, incest, homosexual themes or blasphemy.

LARRY FLYNT PUBLICATIONS

Hustler Letters

HUSTLER LETTERS Magazine specifications

and guidelines

All submissions should be   typed in straight-forward
style. They must be readable, but not overly academic or literary.

All manuscripts or letters must have a stamped and addressed
envelope if the contributor expects their materials to be returned
(if deemed unacceptable), or if a response is requested by the
contributor. If a manuscript does not contain a SASE and is rejected,
it will then be destroyed. Please allow six weeks for response.

HUSTLER LETTERS

Maximum length: 1,000 words, or five typed, double-spaced pages
Rate of payment: $25.00 (upon publication)

These erotic letters relate all types of sexual experiences:
Kinky, straight, oral, anal, bondage and discipline, S&M, etc.
They should be written in first-person, conversational or
confessional style with little or no dialogue.
Please refrain from letters about sex with minors, beastiality,
incest, and homosexuality.

FICTION

Maximum length: 4,000 words
Rate of payment: $500.00

HUSTLER LETTERS wants erotic fiction that conveys an interesting
story line, with at least two imaginatively written sex scenes
that grow logically from the action and the characters.
The plot should not serve merely as a vehicle to describe sex acts,
and the sex should not sound contrived or forced. Plots should have
real-life tension and conflict(adventure, mystery, horror
fast-living) that have images and experiences the average reader
can relate to. Brisk dialogue that both moves the story forward
and reveals the most about the characters involved is best.

Please do not submit stories with homosexual themes, beastiality,
incest, or sex with minors.
We do not publish assumed names or pseudonyms on the fiction manuscripts.

2029 CENTURY PARK EAST, SUITE 3800, LOS ANGELES, CALIFORNIA 90067 (213) 556-9200

Healthy tooth

Enamel
Dentine
Pulp
Cement

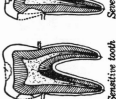

*Sensitive tooth
Decay down
to dentine*

*Severe decay
Decay deep
into dentine*

*Final stage
Decay has
extended to pulp*

*Overseas orders, please
add $2.00 postage.*

WHAT YOU CAN BE

A SUBSCRIBER

Send $6.00 (U.S.) for
three issues per year.

Name _____

Address _____

City, State _____

ZIP _____

WHAT WE WANT

SUBMISSION GUIDELINES

image accepts submissions of any
kind.
Poetry, fiction, prose, reviews,
essays, plays, scripts: send 5-10
pages. For longer works contact
the editors.
Photographs, pen and ink, collages
and other artwork –send samples
if possible. Black and white preferred. Sizes should be no larger
than 8.5" by 5.5".

You send it we'll look at it. You
must be original. No sloppy attempts. We have no limitations
other than these. Be sure to enclose a SASE with your submission.
If you fail to do this we will send
you dirty socks and/or underwear.

Payment is one copy and cash if
we have extra. In the past we have
paid $1-$100 for works we have
accepted.

If you're not sure, send for a
sample copy. Only $3.00, postage
included.

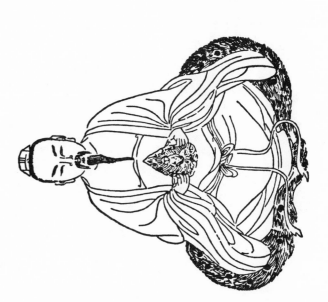

IMAGE MAGAZINE
P.O. BOX 28048
ST. LOUIS, MO. 63119

WHO WE ARE

image magazine is a first-class
effort. image magazine has been
published since 1972.

image magazine is generally published three times each year. The
issues are 40-180 pages long,
usually perfect bound.

image has readers in all parts of
the known world, from Brooklyn
to Kuala Lumpar.

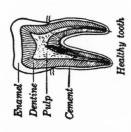

Indiana Review

316 North
Jordan
Avenue
Bloomington
Indiana
47405

812·335·3439

Indiana Review is a triquarterly magazine of new poetry and fiction. Although we do publish a number of established writers--Raymond Carver, Charles Baxter, Susan Engberg, William Kloefkorn, Lisel Mueller, Madeline DeFrees, and Albert Goldbarth-- we are more interested in the work itself than the name attached to it. As a result we publish innovative work by many newcomers.

Indiana Review is committed to publishing significant amounts of fiction--usually six or seven short stories per issue. We look for work that has a distinctive style and that uses language adeptly, and for stories whose content has depth and significance. Payment for works of short fiction is $25 per story.

Although we emphasize our fiction, Indiana Review still maintains a high profile in poetry, accepting about twenty poems per issue. Again, the emphasis is on style, on careful use of language, and we lean toward poems that have some scope and ambition. Poetry pays $5 per published page.

Indiana Review is also accepting essays for publication. Our new series addresses the lack of attention paid to individual contemporary poems and stories. Payment for each essay published is $200. Length of essays should be 1,000-2,000 words. Manuscripts are accepted and read year round.

Subscriptions to Indiana Review are $10/year ($4 per single issue); $18/2 years. In addition, there are Supporting, Donor, and Patron subscriptions available for $25/year, $50/year, and $100/year respectively (tax deductible). Supporters, Donors, and Patrons are acknowledged at the beginning of each issue.

All manuscripts must be accompanied by a self-addressed, stamped envelope. Address submissions and correspondence to Indiana Review, 316 N. Jordan Avenue, Room 302, Bloomington, IN., 47405.

We do not accept simultaneous submissions.

* * * * * * *

Policies:

Innisfree is sent to subscribers. A free copy will be sent to anyone interested in subscribing. Additional copies and any extra back copies are available at a cost of $1.50 per copy plus $1.00 for postage and handling, if applicable. Subscription rates are available for $2.50 an issue or $20.00 a year.

Eight issues will be published a year. Submission deadlines are:

January 15	June 1	October 15
March 1	July 15	December 1
April 15	September 1	

A submission is any number of pages you care to send. Please mail submissions typed and **double-spaced** (except for short poems).

The magazine will be mailed within two weeks from the cut-off date.

Rates may change with costs of publication. Fees pay for postage, envelopes, and copying charges, not for the right to have published anything submitted. The editors make all decisions on inclusion or exclusion of copy. Monies contributed for postage, etc., do not guarantee acceptance of submitted materials.

We hope this publication will provide a place to express thoughts, relate experiences, and set up a dialogue with members about philosophical ideas.

Any suggestions or comments are welcomed.

The Editors
Mary Kennaugh
Rex Winn
P. O. Box 93
Manhattan Beach, CA 90266

LEXINGTON LIBRARY, INC.

355 LEXINGTON AVE., NEW YORK, NEW YORK 10017   (212) 391-1400

Intimacy

Dear Writers and Photographers:

Here are the payment rates for JIVE and INTIMACY. Where variance (range) in payment rate appears, it gives the editor leeway to evaluate (Length, quality, etc.) the material in question. Any exceptions to the indicated rate structure must be pre-approved by the publisher, John J. Plunkett.

EDITORIAL	PAYMENT RATE
Standard Confession Stories	$ 75-60
Special Features	100-75
Service Articles	100-75
Horoscope	100
Advice	75
Reprint Fee (Story/Service Article)	50

PHOTOGRAPHY	
Cover Photo (Color)	$ 250
B/W Confession Story Photos	80 ea.
B/W Service Article Photos	40 ea.
B/W Reprint	25

Most assignments are given on speculation. However, we do request that photographers present samples of their work, as well as 35 mm slides of models whom they feel are cover material. Photographers should supply their models with model releases.

LEXINGTON LIBRARY, INC.

355 LEXINGTON AVE., NEW YORK, NEW YORK 10017   (212) 391-1400

STORY GUIDELINES FOR ROMANTIC MAGAZINES JIVE & INTIMACY

Dear Writer:

For JIVE and INTIMACY magazines, we strive for the stories to lean toward romantic lines. This does not mean that the stories should not have true-to-life experience plots. We simply want to project romance, love and togetherness, rather than to overwhelm our readers with violence or anything too depressing.

Make the stories believable. We do not want to deviate from reality. All endings cannot be happy ones, but we want to try, whenever possible, to cast an optimistic outlook as much as possible.

Hopefully, you can follow these guidelines and will soon be sending in your manuscripts. There is no limit as to how many you can submit at one time. It is good to submit material as frequently as you can, so that outlines for upcoming months can be made. Here are the guidelines:

1. Stories must be written from a young, black female perspective with romance in mind (this is not to discourage male writers, you may use a pen name).

2. Stories must be true-to-life confessions with interesting plots.

3. Stories need to exude an aura of romance.

4. Stories should have at least two descriptive love scenes.

5. Stories must be written in the first person.

6. Stories must be typed and double-spaced, with each page numbered and identified either with your name or the title of your work.

7. Stories should be 3,000 - 4,000 words (between 12 to 15 typed pages).

Allow at least 90 days for confirmation of acceptance or rejection. If we do accept the story, you will receive a release form in the mail. If we do not accept it, your story will be returned if you enclose a self-addressed stamped envelope with it.

Thank you for your interest in our publications.

Sincerely,

Nathasha Brooks

The Editor

LEXINGTON LIBRARY, INC.
355 LEXINGTON AVE., NEW YORK, NEW YORK 10017   (212) 391-1400

<u>POETRY GUIDELINES</u>

Dear Poet:

We welcome poetry that deals with romance, love, and normal sex between
a heterosexual couple. Poems should not be derogatory or stereotypical
towards Black people in any way, form or fashion. Our people should be
seen in as positive a light as possible in any poems submitted.
Poems should be written in free verse, blank verse or Haiku. If you are
writing poems in Haiku, please say so somewhere on your work. Cute, rhyming
poems are NOT acceptable. Poems dealing with cultural issues are also
acceptable.

All poems should be typewritten, preferably double spaced on white
bond paper. Please edit your work before sending it in, use a dictionary,
thesaurus, style book or any helpful writer's aids to familiarize yourself with
any problem areas.

Poems should be at least five lines long, but never over twenty-five
lines.

Payment for poems upon publication is ten dollars per poem. All unused
poems will be returned to the poet.

Yours truly,

Nathasha Brooks

Nathasha Brooks
Editor

LEXINGTON LIBRARY, INC.

355 LEXINGTON AVE., NEW YORK, NEW YORK 10017   (212) 391-1400

Dear Writer:

For our magazines, we strive for the stories to lean towards romantic lines. As well as following the original guidelines, we would like you to know that we welcome black male writers to send us stories from their perspectives also. All writers are entitled to write special feature articles too.

Black women like to know what black men are thinking, in terms of romance and relationships in the '80's. Therefore, your stories, ideas, and articles would be graciously appreciated and accepted.

Dear men, please don't hesitate to let JIVE & INTIMACY know what you are thinking, feeling, doing, or wanting concerning romance.

We welcome your response, and wish you success in your endeavors.

Sincerely,

The Editors

CONFIDENTIAL MEMO TO: Potential *In Touch* writers
FROM: An unidentified source close to the editor
RE: HOW TO BREAK INTO *IN TOUCH*

1. Take the editor to lunch.

2. Send an unsolicited manuscript that shows the editor that you're *in touch* with our **13-19 YEAR OLD READERS.** *In Touch* is published in conjuction with the Aldersgate Graded Curriculum to reinforce each week's session. Because of this, most writing is on an assignment basis. However, **WE ARE CONSTANTLY LOOKING FOR NEW WRITERS.**

3. Write **NONFICTION:** Testimonies, observations on contemporary issues, how-to articles, humor, interviews with famous or newsworthy Christians. Remember, most teens hate to read. You must grab them by their Nike's in the first paragraph. **500-1,000 WORDS.**

4. If you write fiction, you can still break in. Write a **TRUE EXPERIENCE** told in fiction style, a **HUMOROUS PIECE OF FICTION**, or a C.S. Lewis-type **ALLEGORY. 500-1,000 WORDS.**

5. We are not using poetry, cartoons or puzzles.

6. Send a **SEASONAL ARTICLE** at least nine months in advance.

7. Type double-spaced on 8 1/2 by 11-inch paper. Your name, address, social security number, and word count should be in the upper left-hand corner. Also include what rights are being offered. Indicate Reprint Rights if the article has already been published. No manuscript will be returned unless it is accompanied by a **SELF-ADDRESSED STAMPED ENVELOPE. NO QUERIES**, please.

8. INCLUDE PHOTOS if available. We need *Seventeen* and *Campus Life*-type cover shots and candid close-ups of faces. We do NOT need teens sitting in meadows reading Bibles in soft focus. Some of our readers are offended by excessive jewelry, shorts, low necklines, and short hem lengths.

9. Understand the **OFFICIAL *IN TOUCH* PASSWORD:** *Wesleyan-Arminian-evangelical-holiness manuscript.* Roughly translated, that means articles should reflect a joy and excitement in a personal relationship with God resulting in a transformed life, holiness of heart, and effective Christian service. We attempt to encourage (without being "preachy"), a biblical life-style, witnessing, sexual purity, and abstinence from all things harmful to the body and soul.

10. Tell us you read *In Touch* every week and think the editor is doing a great job.

DECISION TO BUY OR RETURN A MANUSCRIPT/PHOTO IS BASED ON THESE TEN PRINCIPLES (or at least several of them!): You should receive a response in two to four weeks (depending on when the editor can take some time off). **Payment is made on acceptance.** Our rate is from 2 to 4 cents per word, depending on the amount of editing required. Photos are purchased separately from $15.00-25.00. **We buy one-time rights only.** You may sell your work to other markets.

In Touch
Box 2000
Marion, IN 46952

James Watkins, Editor
David Keith, General Officer

The <u>Iowa Review</u> publishes stories, poems, essays, interviews, and reviews. Possibly there are other literary forms that could persuade us. We have no set guidelines as to content or length. We look for what we take, at the time, to be the best writing available to us.

We request that all manuscripts be accompanied by self-addressed, stamped envelopes. Please allow us two to three months to read your manuscript and make a decision. Often, though, we do respond much more quickly.

Payment is one dollar per line or a minimum of twenty-five dollars for poems and ten dollars per page of prose. You also get two copies of the issue in which your work appears and a year's subscription. We make additional contributor's copies available at a discount of thirty percent.

We can mail you a sample copy of a recent issue for $5.00. Subscriptions are $15.00 per year.

Thank you for your inquiry.

The
Iowa Review
308 EPB The University of Iowa Iowa City, Iowa 52242

ISAAC ASIMOV's SCIENCE FICTION MAGAZINE
380 LEXINGTON AVE · NEW YORK, NY 10017

Isaac Asimov's Science Fiction Magazine is an established market for science fiction stories. We pay on acceptance. Beginners get 6.0 cents a word to 7,500 words, 5.0 cents a word for stories longer than 12,500, and $450 for stories between those lengths. We pay $1 a line for poetry. Poems should not exceed 40 lines. We buy first North American serial rights plus certain non-exclusive rights, which are explained in our contract. The contract also sets forth the additional money we pay you if a story is picked up in one of our anthologies. We very seldom buy stories longer than 15,000 words, and we don't serialize novels. We do not publish reprints, and we don't want to see "simultaneous submissions" (stories sent at the same time to a publication other than IAsfm). IAsfm will consider material submitted by any writer, previously published or not. We've bought some of our best stories from people who have never sold a story before.

In general, we're looking for "character-oriented" stories, those in which the characters, rather than the science, provide the main focus for the reader's interest. Serious, thoughtful, yet accessible fiction will constitute the majority of our purchases, but of course there's always room for the humorous as well. (No puns, please!) Fantasy is fine, but no Sword & Sorcery or cute little elves, trolls, or dragons. Neither are we interested in explicit sex or violence. A good overview would be to consider that all fiction is written to examine or illuminate some aspect of human existence, but that in science fiction the backdrop you work against is the size of of the universe.

Manuscripts submitted to IAsfm must be neatly typed, double-spaced on one side of the sheet only, with one-inch margins, on bond paper (no erasable paper, please). Any ms. longer than 5 pages should be mailed to us flat. Dot-matrix printouts are acceptable only if they are easily readable. When using a word processor, please do not justify the right-hand margin. If sending a printout, separate the sheets first. The title page should include the title of your story, your name and address, and the number of words in your story. Enclose a cover letter if you like. All manuscripts must be accompanied by a self-addressed stamped envelope large enough and carrying enough postage to return the ms. If you wish to save on postage, you may submit a clear copy of your story along with a standard long (no. 10) envelope, also self-addressed and stamped. If you mark your copy "DISPOSABLE," you will receive our reply (but not your ms.) in the small envelope. We do not suggest that you have us dispose of your original typescript. If you live overseas or in Canada, use International Reply Coupons for return postage.

Finally, we regret that it has become necessary for us to use form letters for rejecting manuscripts, but time limitations are such that we have no choice. Unfortunately, we are unable to provide specific criticism of each story. Our response time runs from two to five weeks. If you have not heard from us within two months, send a letter of inquiry along with a self-addressed stamped envelope. It is unfortunately still possible for manuscripts to get lost in the mail.

Thank you for your interest in IAsfm and good luck!

Gardner Dozois
Editor

EDITORIAL GUIDELINES

INDIVIDUAL MAGAZINE NEEDS

MUCH OF THE MATERIAL USED IN ALL OF OUR MAGAZINES IS HEALTH-RELATED. THIS INCLUDES STORIES, POETRY, ARTICLES, AND ACTIVITIES.

TURTLE MAGAZINE FOR PRESCHOOL KIDS (ages 2 to 5)
HUMPTY DUMPTY'S MAGAZINE (ages 4 to 6)
CHILDREN'S PLAYMATE MAGAZINE (ages 5 to 7)

TURTLE uses bedtime or naptime stories (approximately 200 to 600 words) that can be read to the child. HUMPTY DUMPTY'S MAGAZINE and CHILDREN'S PLAYMATE use easy-to-read stories for the beginning reader. Fiction can be 500 to 800 words. All of these magazines use short, simple poems or stories in rhyme. Games and crafts should involve a minimum of adult guidance and have clear, brief instructions. Humorous stories and poems are especially needed. In HUMPTY DUMPTY and CHILDREN'S PLAYMATE, healthful recipes requiring little or no need for the stove are used.

JACK AND JILL (ages 6 to 8)
CHILD LIFE (ages 7 to 9)
CHILDREN'S DIGEST (ages 8 to 10)

Stories may run from 500 to 1800 words. Articles may run from 500 to 1200 words. When appropriate, articles should be accompanied by photographs or transparencies. Nonfiction material should list sources of information. We may use factual features dealing with nature, science, and sports—also some historical and biographical articles. Preferred fiction includes realistic stories, adventure, mysteries, and science fiction. Humorous stories are highly desirable. Also needed are healthful recipes (see page 2).

SAMPLE COPIES

We regret that we are unable to provide free sample copies of the magazines. Individual copies may be obtained for seventy-five cents each by writing to Children's Better Health Institute, P.O. Box 567, Indianapolis, IN 46206.

Children's Better Health Institute
Benjamin Franklin Literary & Medical Society, Inc.
1100 Waterway Boulevard
P.O. Box 567
Indianapolis, Indiana 46206

TURTLE MAGAZINE FOR PRESCHOOL KIDS

HUMPTY DUMPTY'S MAGAZINE

CHILDREN'S PLAYMATE MAGAZINE

JACK AND JILL • CHILD LIFE • CHILDREN'S DIGEST

Our goal at the Children's Better Health Institute is to provide children with good reading that not only entertains but also educates, primarily about good health. We have a constant need for high-quality stories, articles, and activities with an exercise, nutrition, safety, hygiene, or other health-related theme. Our emphasis is preventive medicine, and we are seeking material that will encourage young readers to practice better health habits.

Health information may be presented in a variety of formats. We are looking for fresh, creative ways to encourage children to develop and maintain good health. Fiction stories that deal with a health theme need not have health as the primary subject but should include it in some way in the course of events. Main characters in fiction stories should adhere to good health practices, unless failure to do so is necessary to a story's plot. Word and math puzzles, games, and other activities can also successfully convey health messages if they are enjoyable to youngsters and age-appropriate. We also use factual articles that teach scientific facts about the body or nutrition. Writers should avoid an encyclopedic or "preachy" approach. We try to present our health material in a positive manner, incorporating humor and a light approach wherever possible without minimizing the seriousness of what we are saying.

In all material, please avoid references to eating sugary foods, such as candy, cakes, cookies, and soft drinks. In recipes submitted for publication, ingredients should be healthful. Avoid sugar, salt, chocolate, red meat, and fats.

We are also interested in material with more general themes. We are especially in need of holiday material—stories, articles, and activities. Send seasonal material at least eight months in advance.

Also remember that characters in realistic stories should be up-to-date. Many of our readers have working mothers and/or come from single-parent homes. We need more stories that reflect these changing times but at the same time communicate good, wholesome values.

GENERAL INFORMATION

MANUSCRIPT FORMAT

Manuscripts must be typewritten and double- or triple-spaced. The author's name, address, telephone number, Social Security number, and an approximate word count must appear on the first page of the manuscript. KEEP A COPY OF YOUR WORK. We'll handle your manuscript with care, but we cannot assume responsibility for its return. Please send the entire manuscript; queries are not necessary. The editors cannot criticize, offer suggestions, or enter into correspondence concerning unsolicited manuscripts that are not accepted, nor can they suggest other markets for material that is not published. MATERIAL CANNOT BE RETURNED unless it is accompanied by a self-addressed envelope and SUFFICIENT return postage.

PHOTOS

WE DO NOT PURCHASE SINGLE PHOTOGRAPHS. We do purchase short photo features (up to 6 or 8 pictures) or photos that accompany and help illustrate editorial matter. (Please include captions.)

REVIEW TIME REQUIRED

Time required to review manuscripts properly is about eight to ten weeks. Each manuscript is carefully considered for possible use in *all* the magazines, not only that one to which it was originally addressed; therefore, if a manuscript is returned, it should not be resubmitted to a different youth publication at this address.

RATES AND PAYMENT POLICIES

Fiction and articles: approximately six cents a word. Poetry: $7.00 and up. Photos: $7.00 minimum. Puzzles and games: no fixed rate. Payment is made upon publication. Each author will be sent two complimentary copies of the issue in which his or her material is published. Additional copies may be purchased for seventy-five cents each.

RIGHTS

We prefer to purchase all rights. Simultaneous submissions are not accepted.

CHILDREN'S CONTRIBUTIONS

Except for items that may be used in the children's columns that appear each month, the editors do not encourage submissions from children. Even highly talented young people are not usually experienced enough to compete on a professional level with adult authors.

The James White Review

A GAY MEN'S LITERARY QUARTERLY

SUBMISSION GUIDELINES FOR
The James White Review

We would appreciate poets sending us no more than eight poems per issue, or no more than 250 lines of poetry, whichever is smaller. This does not preclude the submission of a single poem of more than 250 lines. Writers of prose should limit themselves to three submissions per issue, no one of which may exceed 22 pages typewritten, double-spaced. Also regarding prose, we strongly advise clean, double-spaced, type-written copy; hand-written copy that is in any sense unclear or ambiguous will be automatically dropped from consideration. It is wise to have your name on every page of prose or poetry submitted to us. *We also strongly encourage the submission of artwork: sketches, photos, compositions. Please send copies and not the originals, we are not responsible for lost or damaged artwork.* Deadline for graphics will be the same date as deadline for poetry and prose submissions. Send SASE for return.

Submission Deadlines

November 1	February 1
May 1	August 1

SUBSCRIBE

Name _____

Address _____

_____

City/State/ZIP _____

Back Issues: $ 2.00/indicate:

When ordering eight or more, $1 each (except Fall '83, Winter '84)

Minnesota residents, add 6% sales tax

☐ Summer 1986
   Spring 1986
☐ Winter 1986
☐ Fall 1985
☐ Spring/Summer 1985
☐ Winter 1985
☐ Fall 1984
☐ Summer 1984
☐ Spring 1984
☐ Winter 1984 ($ 3.00)
☐ Fall 1983 ($ 3.00)

☐ One year subscription: $ 8
☐ Canada: $ 10
☐ Two years: $ 14
☐ Foreign: $13
☐ Institution: $ 10
☐ *The Salt Ecstasies* by James L. White: $ 6
☐ JWR Sustainers Club: $ 30.00/year

Gifts to *The James White Review* are tax deductible.

The James White Review
P.O. Box 3356, Traffic Station
Minneapolis, MN 55403

The review is mailed in an envelope displaying our name and return address.

A red circle on your address label indicates a subscription about to expire. Subscriptions begin with the issue following receipt of your order; to begin a subscription with the current issue, add $1. Please send change of address notification; the post office usually does not forward bulk mail.

For information about The James White Review, contact Phil Willkie at (612) 291-2913 or Greg Baysans at (612) 874-0553

LEXINGTON ⌊⌊⌊ LIBRARY, INC.

355 LEXINGTON AVE., NEW YORK, NEW YORK 10017   (212) 391-1400

Jive

Dear Writers and Photographers:

Here are the payment rates for JIVE and INTIMACY. Where variance (range) in payment rate appears, it gives the editor leeway to evaluate (Length, quality, etc.) the material in question. Any exceptions to the indicated rate structure must be pre-approved by the publisher, John J. Plunkett.

EDITORIAL	PAYMENT RATE
Standard Confession Stories	$ 75-60
Special Features	100-75
Service Articles	100-75
Horoscope	100
Advice	75
Reprint Fee (Story/Service Article)	50

PHOTOGRAPHY	
Cover Photo (Color)	$ 250
B/W Confession Story Photos	80 ea.
B/W Service Article Photos	40 ea.
B/W Reprint	25

Most assignments are given on speculation. However, we do request that photographers present samples of their work, as well as 35 mm slides of models whom they feel are cover material. Photographers should supply their models with model releases.

LEXINGTON LIBRARY, INC.
355 LEXINGTON AVE., NEW YORK, NEW YORK 10017 (212) 391-1400

POETRY GUIDELINES

Dear Poet:

We welcome poetry that deals with romance, love, and normal sex between a heterosexual couple. Poems should not be derogatory or stereotypical towards Black people in any way, form or fashion. Our people should be seen in as positive a light as possible in any poems submitted.
Poems should be written in free verse, blank verse or Haiku. If you are writing poems in Haiku, please say so somewhere on your work. Cute, rhyming poems are NOT acceptable. Poems dealing with cultural issues are also acceptable.

All poems should be typewritten, preferably double spaced on white bond paper. Please edit your work before sending it in, use a dictionary, thesaurus, style book or any helpful writer's aids to familiarize yourself with any problem areas.

Poems should be at least five lines long, but never over twenty-five lines.

Payment for poems upon publication is ten dollars per poem. All unused poems will be returned to the poet.

Yours truly,

Nathasha Brooks

Nathasha Brooks
Editor

LEXINGTON LIBRARY, INC.

355 LEXINGTON AVE., NEW YORK, NEW YORK 10017   (212) 391-1400

Dear Writer:

    For our magazines, we strive for the stories to lean
towards romantic lines. As well as following the original
guidelines, we would like you to know that we welcome black
male writers to send us stories from their perspectives also.
All writers are entitled to write special feature articles too.

    Black women like to know what black men are thinking,
in terms of romance and relationships in the '80's. Therefore,
your stories, ideas, and articles would be graciously appreciated and accepted.

    Dear men, please don't hesitate to let JIVE & INTIMACY
know what you are thinking, feeling, doing, or wanting concerning romance.

    We welcome your response, and wish you success in your
endeavors.

            Sincerely,

            The Editors

LEXINGTON LIBRARY, INC.

355 LEXINGTON AVE., NEW YORK, NEW YORK 10017   (212) 391-1400

STORY GUIDELINES FOR ROMANTIC MAGAZINES JIVE & INTIMACY

Dear Writer:

For JIVE and INTIMACY magazines, we strive for the stories to lean toward romantic lines. This does not mean that the stories should not have true-to-life experience plots. We simply want to project romance, love and togetherness, rather than to overwhelm our readers with violence or anything too depressing.

Make the stories believable. We do not want to deviate from reality. All endings cannot be happy ones, but we want to try, whenever possible, to cast an optimistic outlook as much as possible.

Hopefully, you can follow these guidelines and will soon be sending in your manuscripts. There is no limit as to how many you can submit at one time. It is good to submit material as frequently as you can, so that outlines for upcoming months can be made. Here are the guidelines:

1. Stories must be written from a young, black female perspective with romance in mind (this is not to discourage male writers, you may use a pen name).

2. Stories must be true-to-life confessions with interesting plots.

3. Stories need to exude an aura of romance.

4. Stories should have at least two descriptive love scenes.

5. Stories must be written in the first person.

6. Stories must be typed and double-spaced, with each page numbered and identified either with your name or the title of your work.

7. Stories should be 3,000 - 4,000 words (between 12 to 15 typed pages).

Allow at least 90 days for confirmation of acceptance or rejection. If we do accept the story, you will receive a release form in the mail. If we do not accept it, your story will be returned if you enclose a self-addressed stamped envelope with it.

Thank you for your interest in our publications.

Sincerely,

Nathasha Brooks

The Editor

The Journal

The Literary Magazine of The Ohio State University

GENERAL GUIDELINES

Published: twice a year. Subscriptions: five dollars per year.
Established: 1972. Circulation: 1000.

Payment: in contributor's copies, and, when funds are available,
a small stipend will also be paid. Each contribution is automatically
entered into competition for the annual President's Awards: $100
for poetry and $100 for fiction.

The Journal aquires all rights, but will reassign rights following
publication.

We are interested in fiction, poetry, nonfiction and book reviews.
Unsolicited manuscripts will not be read during the summer months.

Fiction and Poetry: no restrictions as to category or type. Fiction:
maximum length, 6000 words, typed. Poems: typed, one per page.
Address correspondence to the Editors.

Nonfiction and Reviews: material of interest to an audience
knowledgeable of literature and the arts, not neccesarily of an
academic nature.

Self-addressed, stamped envelope required.
Reports in four to six weeks.

Sample copy available for three dollars.

The Ohio State University ■ Department of English ■ 164 West 17th Avenue ■ Columbus, Ohio 43210 ■ (614) 292-4076

Journal of Polymorphous Perversity ®

A publication of Wry-Bred Press, Inc.

10 Waterside Plaza, Suite 20B, New York City 10010 (212) 689-5473

PUBLICATION GUIDELINES

The Wall Street Journal called JPP "...a social scientist's answer to Mad Magazine." JPP publishes humorous and satirical articles that spoof psychology, psychiatry, medicine, mental health, and scientific journals themselves.

What Kinds of Articles Are You Looking For? First, our editorial aim is to publish funny, humorous fiction which closely parallels real scientific journals both in content and format. This means that the topic must in some way relate to psychology, behavior, or mental health, that the successful article is one usually written in scientific structure and jargon, and that it is not written in the first person (unless a first person narrative is meant to support some kind of clinical vignette). We do not publish short stories, poetry, or cartoons, rather creative writing. (For examples, see below.) A good way to prepare for submitting an article to us is by going to the library and reading through some real mental health journals. Remember: A large number of our readers are those who read these journals and want to be entertained by spoofs of them.

How Do I Submit an Article? We welcome submission of manuscripts in triplicate. We do not accept simultaneous submissions or materials which have already appeared in print elsewhere. If you wish your manuscript returned, please include a SASE. Keep a copy of your manuscript--we cannot take responsibility for lost manuscripts.

How Long Can the Article Be? We prefer articles no longer than 8 typed double-spaced (4 typeset) pages, although we will consider longer articles.

Examples of Articles Published in the JPP
 Psychotherapy of the Dead (Presents the problem--"It is time to 'bury the myth' that certain people are untreatable by modern psychotherapy*"; Review of the Literature; Transference and Counter-Transference Problems, Problems with Patients Paying Bills; Conclusion; 3 typeset pages)
 The Etiology and Treatment of Childhood (Reviews the [fictitious] literature on childhood as a "disorder," addresses 5 core features of the syndrome [congenital onset, dwarfism, emotional lability and immaturity, knowledge deficits, and legume anorexia*], reviews sociological, biological, and psychological models of childhood, and presents a case study ["Billy, age 8,...stood only 4' 3" high...His sexual experience was nonexistent. Indeed, Billy considered women 'icky.'*]"; 5 typeset pages, including 26 full reference citations)
 New Improved Delusions (Brief introductory paragraph of the problem leads into a list of 50 new delusions, e.g. "Hells Angels are holding Tupperware parties under my bed*"; 2 typeset pages.)
 A Modern Day Psychoanalytic Fable (The tale of Cinderella retold from a humorous psychoanalytic slant; 4 typeset pages)
 Journel [sick] of Schizophrenic Processssssssssssssssssss (A seemingly psychotic ad, psychotically typeset, announces a new journal)
 Cancer and Tobacco: A Bum Rat (Complete experimental study, with Abstract, Subjects, Procedure, Results, Discussion, Conclusion, and Reference sections, 1 Figure, 1 Table; 3 typeset pages)
 A Brief Report of a Psychodiagnostic System for Mental Health Clinic Patients: Parking by Diagnosis (Brief introductory paragraph introduces 12 drawings; 1 typeset page, including all drawings)
*Material copyright 1984, 1985, 1986, 1987 by Wry-Bred Press, Inc.

KALEIDOSCOPE: International Magazine of Literature,

Fine Arts, and Disability.

Published 2/yr. (January, July)

326 Locust Street, Akron, Ohio 44302.

Telephone: (216) 762-9755

Editor/Publication Director: Dr. Darshan Perusek

Senior Editor: Gail Willmott

Guidelines: Kaleidoscope is a forum for disability-related
literature. It is open to both disabled and non-disabled
writers. Disabled writers may write on any topic, although
we prefer that they offer fresh and original perspectives
on disability; non-disabled writers, on the other hand,
must limit themselves to the experience of disability.
The criteria for good fiction apply in every case: thought-
provoking subject matter, effective handling of technique,
fresh language and imagery, and, in general, a mature grasp
of the art of story-telling. Avoid the stereotypical and
the sentimental.

Length: Maximum, 5000 words.

Reporting Time: 6 - 8 weeks. Minor editing to be expected.
                 Substantive editing with author's approval.

Payment: $25. Copyright reverts to author.

NOTES TO PROSPECTIVE CONTRIBUTORS

Kalliope publishes poetry, fiction, interviews, reviews
and visual art by and about women and women's concerns. We
are open to drama, experimental form and informal essays
as well. Please submit poems in groups of 3-10, one long
or two short fiction pieces or essays. Art work in groups
of 5-10. Send glossy B&W prints os visual art (no color
reproductions, please). We welcome an artist's statement
of 50-75 words. Please include SASE, a short contributor's
note and phone number with all submissions. Foreign contributor's should send U.S. postage or international postage
coupons. Payment is in copies. Copyright reverts to
author/artist upon request. Because each submission is
reviewed by several members of the Editorial Collective
response time may be 3-6 months. Thank you, in advance,
for your patience. Sample copies of Kalliope are available
for $3.50 plus $1.50 postage and handling, please specify
preferred issue, or current series.

Editorial Offices: Department of English / Denison Hall / Kansas State University / Manhattan, Kansas 66506 / Phone: 913-532-6716

June 17, 1987

Dear Prospective Contributor:

You inquire about guidelines on submissions. We have no special or unusual requirements, but we look for the best poems and stories among those submitted each year. We prefer to see submissions typed and certainly sent with a SASE if you wish them considered and returned. We do occasional special numbers on area history, literary criticism and art history, which are announced in numbers of KQ.

We pay only in two contributor's copies, and in two series of awards yearly. The KQ/Kansas Arts Commission awards for fiction and poetry number about 10 to 12 yearly, and are between $25 and $250 (or $300). All writers published in KQ during a year are eligible. And present or former Kansans are eligible for a similar series of Seaton awards yearly--some occasionally receive an award under both series. Our judges are nationally known writers like Marilyn Hacker, R.V. Cassill, Dave Smith, and Anne Tyler.

If you wish to know more about the magazine, sample copies are available at $5.00.

Sincerely,

Harold W. Schneider
Editor, KQ

HWS:hb

Kansas Quarterly

THE KINDRED SPIRIT
Writer's Guidelines

THE KINDRED SPIRIT   Sample Copy: $1/$3 overseas
Michael Hathaway, editor   1 year sub.: $4 (4 issues)
Rt. 2 Box 111 $8 overseas, U.S. Funds
St. John, Ks. 67576

All submissions should be legible, typed or printed neatly. Clean Xeroxes are ok.
Previously published and simultaneous submissions are ok, too. The Kindred Spirit
is copyrighted, writer's retain all rights to their work. If material has been
previously published, we like to know where and when so we may print acknowledgement
to the mag or press. All submissions must include a self-addressed stamped
envelope (SASE) with sufficient postage. Any submission without SASE goes in the
trash.

POETRY GUIDELINES
We prefer short experimental unrhymed poetry under 30 lines. But since we like to
present a large varied selection of poetry styles and subjects, we will read and
consider any style (traditional, concrete, rhymed, surreal, avant garde, haiku,
etc.), any length and almost any subject. This excludes gross violence, chauvenism/
sexism, racism, and anything that glorifies the killing of animals or people. We
also won't consider self-indulgent therapeutic poetry or goopy Helen Steiner Rice/
greeting card verse. We like unique writing that has any of the following: powerful
feelings, vivid imagery, guts, substance, originality, creative style, punch, twist
or humor. The best way to get an idea as to what we use is to get a sample copy,
which is only $1.00.

FICTION GUIDELINES
We prefer experimental stories, but will read traditional styles if they have
very clever, witty and/or vivid dialogues and characters. Word limit is no more
than 4,000 words. We use very few short stories and are usually backlogged with them,
but if you think your story fits our guidelines, please send it.

Thank you for your interest in The Kindred Spirit. We wish you lots of luck
and success with your writing endeavors, and look forward to hearing from you
in the future.

Sincerely,

Michael Hathaway

The Kindred Spirit
A Poetry Journal

KS is a quarterly 16-pg. tabloid magazine of modern poetry/art/fiction and, since 1982, has been publishing some of the most talented/inspiring/bizarre/innovative poets and poetry of our time. Each issue features several poets. Each feature includes several poems by the poet and usually a photo and short biography. Also included in each issue: fiction, art, reviews of new poetry books/mags and market news and other items of interest to today's poets and poetry readers.

A year's subscription is $4, this includes 4 issues. A sample copy (current issue) is $1. We also welcome all poetry, art, review submissions or review materials accompanied by a SASE. We prefer short unrhymed poetry, mostly avant garde, experimental, surreal, haiku but will consider any style if it is good. We are also interested in seasonal material. Deadlines: Winter-Oct. 1; Spring-Jan. 1; Summer-Apr. 1; Autumn-July 1). SASE for yearly contest info. We welcome all correspondence.

> Also available from The Kindred Spirit: **Stream Of Consciousness** by Rochelle Lynn Holt. ($7.95 ppd.) Gwendolyn Brooks said about this book: ''I enjoyed these poems.'' Anais Nin called Rochelle Holt ''the Queen of Creativity.''

Shadows of Myself by Michael Hathaway ($4 ppd.) Poetry written and published during high school years, 1976-1980.

Send to:

Michael Hathaway

Rt. 2 Box 111

St. John, Ks. 67576

_____ 1-year subscriptions to KS ($4 per year)

_____ Sample copy (current issue) ($1)

_____ Back Issues—complete set $6, or $1 ea. specify issue #'s:_____

_____ copies of **Shadows of Myself** by Michael Hathaway ($4 ppd.)

_____ copies of **Stream of Consciousness** by Rochelle Lynn Holt ($7.95 ppd.)

Name:_____

Address:_____

City:_____ State:_____ Zip:_____

Allow 3-6 weeks for delivery of books

Editorial Guidelines
Short Story Submissions
Lake Effect

All submissions must be double spaced on 8½ x 11 one-sided sheets of white paper or printed out on standard computer paper. Author's name, address and phone number must appear in upper right hand corner of each page.

Author should retain a copy of any and all pieces submitted. *Lake Effect* is not responsible for any loss or damage to manuscripts submitted for consideration.

All material must be original and previously unpublished.

The editorial staff of *Lake Effect* reserves the right to accept or reject any material submitted for publication for whatever reason it deems in the best interest of *Lake Effect*. Further *Lake Effect* is not obliged to reveal the reasons for acceptance or rejection to the authors, their agents or the general public.

The editorial staff of *Lake Effect* will make efforts to insure that material printed in *Lake Effect* is free of typographical errors. However it does not guarantee to the authors that their submission to *Lake Effect* will be printed exactly as submitted. In other words, the author, when submitting material for possible publication in *Lake Effect* accepts the risk that some unintentional error may occur in the final printed form.

The editorial staff of *Lake Effect* may provide some limited editing to assist the authors of works accepted for publication.

If a piece is rejected by the editorial staff for publication in a particular issue of *Lake Effect,* it may be submitted to and will be considered again for a later edition of *Lake Effect* if resubmitted by the author.

Lake Effect acquires on publication first North American serial rights. Ownership of the work resides with the author.

Manuscripts should be sent to *Lake Effect*, P.O. Box 315, Oswego, N.Y. 13126 and will be returned if an envelope and sufficient return postage is included.

Submissions should be limited to two per issue: maximum 5,000 words each.

the LAKE STREET REVIEW

Woneta Eddy

SEEKS SUBMISSIONS

The LAKE STREET REVIEW, an annual literary magazine, needs material for its 22nd issue. Deadline is October 1, 1987. We need poetry, **prose (500 to 4,500 words)**, songs (with musical notation) and drawings (black and white). Payment is in copies. Copyright reverts to the author upon publication. **Reporting time is no longer than two months following the deadline.** Please use proper postage and enclose a stamped, self-addressed envelope for return of your work.

The LAKE STREET REVIEW is available in many area bookstores, including Orr Books, Savran's, and B. Dalton–Dinkytown in Minneapolis, and Hungry Mind, Odegard Books, Micawber's and Bryan's Bookshop in St. Paul.

Our address for copies, $2 each; $4 for a two issue/two year subscription, submissions, or enquiries is: LAKE STREET REVIEW, Box 7188, Minneapolis, MN 55407.

Deadline in 1988 is 1-15-88

L
a
k
e

S
t
r
e
e
t

R
e
v
i
e
w

Box 7188, Powderhorn Station
Minneapolis, Minnesota 55407

1-1-87

PRESS RELEASE

The LAKE STREET REVIEW announces the publication of its 21st issue, 1987. This issue of the annual literary magazine features a ten year index of authors and artists and the particular works they have published in the LSR from 1976 to 1986, issues one through twenty. This fourteen page index is in addition to the usual lively and engaging assortment of poetry, prose and artwork.

Fiction in the 21st issue features Roger Sheffer's short story, "The Anatomy of Singing," in which a young tenor's admiration for his chorale director deepens and broadens as he learns of her life-threatening illness and contemplates her musical legacy. In "Rocks, Roots, and Weeds" by Kent Meyers, a boy struggles with the primordial as he constructs a tunnel system beneath his family's farm, while a drifter in Laurel Ostrow's "Measures" suddenly becomes a carnival's "All Knowing Guesser" and contends with the realities of ages and weights that change drastically before his very eyes. Mary S. Griggs and Kathleen Patrick also contribute fiction to this issue.

Poetry in this issue is evocative and very wide-ranging: the reader will listen to a children's band concert in Chernobyl, puff down jogging paths after elusive balls, then sense the anxiety of career machinists at a bankrupt railroad. The eve of All Saints Day, Biker Bob's living room, and a crowded rush-hour bus are also part of the poetic tour, as well as the body and rage of a wounded bear.

Poets and artists in this issue include Emilio De Grazia, Sue Doro, Paul Ruffin, Kathy Force, Robert Schuler, Cary Waterman, Michael Finley, Waneta Eddy, Steve Eide, John Ekholm, James P. Lenfestey, Anne Marshall Runyon, Dale Jacobson, and Jay Moon.

Copies may be ordered from the LAKE STREET REVIEW at Box 7188, Minneapolis, MN 55407—$2 each; $4 for a two issue/two year subscription.

Bookstores may wish to order from Bookslinger Distribution, 213 East 4th Street, St. Paul, MN 55101, (612) 221-0429.

Deadline for submissions to LSR #22 is October 1, 1987.

Thank you.

Sincerely yours,

Kevin FitzPatrick

Kevin FitzPatrick
Editor

SEE REVERSE SIDE FOR SUBMISSION DETAILS

LAKE SUPERIOR MAGAZINE

Editorial Guidelines

Editorial Deadlines - Jan. / Feb. . . . . September 15   Mar. / Apr. . . . November 15   May / June . January 15
Jul. / Aug. . . . . March 15   Sept. / Oct. . . . . May 15   Nov. / Dec. . . . . . July 15

Categories -

Nonfiction - Persons, places and events in the Lake Superior region (contemporary; historical with current tie).

Fiction - Pertinent to the region or specific issue's theme.

Shore Lines - Short pieces and / or photos on events and highlights from our region.

Life Lines - Short articles about individual people who work and play in our region, their life styles and impact.

Poetry - Used sparingly, if appropriate and well-done.

Cartoons - Pertinent to the region; funny, not too political.

Photographs - As a complete picture essay or to illustrate an article.

Illustrations - Normally assigned, although freelance submissions will be considered.

Copy Material -

Lake Superior Port Cities, Inc., receives many queries on duplicate subject matter. We reserve the right to accept or reject a specific query based on quality, appropriateness and editorial subjectivity. We *prefer* short queries, naming possible sources, although manuscripts will be considered. If this is your first submission, send a sample of your work. A simple query would not apply, of course, if yours is a humor piece or otherwise heavily dependent on style. Enclose a self-addressed, stamped envelope if you wish your material to be returned. Persons whose manuscripts are accepted for publication must be able to assume responsibility for permission to publish photos and names of individuals and places. Secure written permission to protect yourself when appropriate. Short biographical information on the writer should also be submitted.

Payment - We pay up to $400, according to writer's experience, length and importance of story. You will be asked to sign a standard agreement on rights to your work. Lake Superior Magazine is copyrighted. We normally ask for First North American serial rights, and sometimes Second serial rights. This is to allow us to reprint your material or include it in any special publications. Before reprinting your article, we would first notify you. We reserve First serial rights for 90 days following the month of publication. Payment is made within 30 - 60 days of publication. You will receive one copy of the publication in which your work appears, with additonal copies available at wholesale cost.

Appearance - Please double-space and leave reasonable 1" margins! Dot matrix computer printouts are acceptable if used with dark ribbon. Put your name, address and telephone number in the upper left-hand corner of the first page of your manuscript. Put the total number of words in the upper right-hand corner.

Word Processing - Submissions on computer discs or by telecommunication possible; information available upon request.

Photographs -

When you query, send duplicates (if available and of good quality). But originals *only* are used for final publication. Enclose a self-addressed, stamped envelope for return.

Black and White - 5 x 7 or 8 x 10 glossies. B & W pictures are rare these days. We encourage these for the magazine.

Color - 35 mm, 2¼, 4 x 5 or 8 x 10 transparencies.

Cutlines or complete identification should accompany all photographs; photos numbered to coincide.

Photographer is responsible for proper attribution and release for use. Written permission may be necessary from the subject of a photograph, and at the very least should be held by the photographer for personal protection.

Payment - We pay $15 for each B & W print used and $25 for each color transparency used. Cover photo pays more. Combination writer/photographer stories are handled as a package. Payment is made within 30 - 60 days of publication.

Copyright - As with editorial material, we ask for First North American serial rights with 90-day protection for all photography and illustrations used.

Please take care! Watch depth of field, focus, shutter speed, lighting. Only the best is used.

325 Lake Avenue South   Duluth, Minnesota 55802   (218) 722-5002

8-15-86

L'Apache
P. O. Drawer G
Wofford Heights, CA 93285

WRITER'S GUIDELINES

The editors at **L'Apache** will consider any manuscript or poem, as long as it is written in good taste. We prefer short fiction, articles and poetry on the Indians, or any ethnic group.

One way for a writer to get an immediate rejection is to include sex, drugs, or violence in their writing. Stories, or poetry can be written, alluding to love, without descriptive scenes or four-letter words.

Although we prefer typewritten, double spaced submissions on 8 1/2 x 11 white paper, **L'Apache** will not reject a manuscript or poem simply because a writer does not have access to a typewriter. All we ask is that you print, or write legibly.

In the beginning **L'Apache** tried to answer within three weeks. We have been flooded with hundreds of manuscripts and have found it impossible to answer within that time. **L'Apache** reads every submission, making notes and trying to help each writer with suggestions. We do not *"Speed read"* them.

We suggest that you maintain a professional attitude, realizing that most large publishers do not even promise to return a manuscript; they are often farmed out to *"readers"*, and they certainly do not take a personal interest in each writer, and offer suggestions, as we do at **L'Apache.**

One *"poet"* in Vancouver, B.C. sent a scathing letter, poorly typed on cheap paper threatening **L'Apache** and writing, *"One could give you the benefit of the doubt: death, accident, fire, evacuation of the community due to a natural disaster. In the absence of anything confirming any of the above, I can only assume that either apathy or rudeness can account for your failure to return my material . . . I don't even think you'll have what-ever it takes to send my poems back . . . etc., etc."* Threats to "expose" **L'Apache** were a part of the poet's letter.

In checking, the poems *had* been sent back, prior to receiving the diatribe, with notes on the poems.

Whether you have been published or not, at least, have a professional attitude. Put yourself in the publisher's place. If you have an attitude like the Vancouver *"poet"* please send your submissions elsewhere, or better yet, keep them, and spare the poor publisher.

Please send a short bio with your submission and a 4x5 black and white glossy photo (optional).

University students and professors all over the world have a good chance of being published. Foreign translations are especially welcome. Good Luck.

Lighthouse

timeless stories and poems for family reading

Lighthouse Publications • P.O. Box 1377 • Auburn, WA 98071-1377

Writer's Guidelines

If you would like to submit material for our consideration, it should meet the following criteria:

1. Must be **your** original work.
2. Has never been published.
*3. Should be from one of the following categories: fiction story, poetry, **your** true personal experience, children's story or poetry. (Any length accepted. Each poem on a separate sheet for evaluating purposes.)
4. Should be typed, preferably double-spaced.
5. Must have your name, address, and S.S.# on it.
6. Must have self-addressed stamped envelope if you want it returned. (We are not responsible for lost, stolen, destroyed or unreturnable material.)

If your story or poem is accepted, a fee will be paid **upon publication.** Rates include up to $15 for a poem, and up to $100 for a story.
Material can be published again **after our use.**

* 1. Please do not send fiction stories that are based on, or include, characters and/or events in The Bible, or other real people.
2. If there is a message in your story, we prefer it to be subtly hidden in the action of the story.

GUIDELINES FOR LIGUORIAN AUTHORS

LIGUORIAN is a leading Catholic magazine written and edited for Catholics of all ages. Our purpose is to lead our readers to a fuller Christian life by helping them to better understand the teachings of the gospel and the Church and by illustrating how these teachings apply to life and the problems confronting them as members of families, the Church, and society.

1. Articles and stories should not exceed 2000 words. Style and vocabulary should be popular and readable. Use an interest-grabbing opening, state why the subject is important to readers, use examples, quotes, anecdotes, make practical applications, and end strongly.

2. LIGUORIAN does not consider simultaneous submissions or articles previously accepted or published elsewhere.

3. Manuscripts should be typewritten -- double spaced -- and should include your name, address and Social Security number. Address manuscript to Editor, LIGUORIAN Magazine, Liguori, MO 63057. Your manuscript will not be returned unless it is accompanied by a self-addressed stamped envelope.

4. Please allow six to eight weeks for our response regarding your manuscript.

5. LIGUORIAN assumes no responsibility for material damaged or lost. Please keep a copy of any manuscript submitted.

6. We pay 7 to 10 cents a published word on acceptance. NOTE: No check may be issued without a Social Security number.

7. Before you write for LIGUORIAN, it is advisable to read and study several issues of the magazine.

8. LIGUORIAN receives over two hundred manuscripts every month. Of that number we can only accept eight or ten. Your manuscript stands a better chance of acceptance if it is neatly presented, carefully written and then polished, and on a topic of special interest to our readers.

Good luck and we hope to be hearing from you soon.

The editors of LIGUORIAN

Reprinted with permission, LIGOURIAN 1987

EDITORS: Walter Cummins
Martin Green
Harry Keyishian

The
LITERARY
An International Quarterly
REVIEW

Fairleigh Dickinson University · 285 Madison Avenue, Madison, New Jersey 07940 ·

GUIDELINES FOR CONTRIBUTORS

MAJOR INTERESTS: TLR has an international focus and welcomes work in translation.

CONTENT: TLR uses original poetry, fiction, translations into English, essays, and review-essays on contemporary writers and literary issues.

LENGTH: We have no length restrictions for fiction and poetry. However, unusually long works must meet a very high standard of excellence. In general, essays should be under 5,000 words and review-essays from 1,500 to 2,500 words. Review-essays should include several books of common interest.

STYLE: We have no preconceptions about style or format, accepting work that ranges from the traditional to the experimental. However, we expect our contributors to have a strong understanding of technique and a wide familiarity with contemporary writing. All editorial decisions are made on the basis of quality alone.

NUMBER OF SUBMISSIONS: We prefer to read one story, essay, or review-essay by an author at any one time, and no more than six poems. S.A.S.E. must be included for return of manuscript.

MANUSCRIPT FORMAT: All submissions whould be typed on 8½ by 11 paper with fiction and essays doublespaced and poems either single- or doublespaced. Photocopies and dot-matrix printouts are permissible if they are clear.

EVALUATION TIME: We try to read manuscripts within two or three months after receiving them.

PUBLICATION TIME: Accepted manuscripts usually appear within one year to eighteen months, often sooner, depending on our commitment to special issues.

COMPENSATION: Writers receive two copies of the issue in which their work appears and are eligible to compete for three to five annual Charles Angoff cash awards.

COPYRIGHT: We copyright all material in TLR. Authors are granted reprint rights upon request and receive any royalties paid to the magazine.

SPECIAL ISSUES: We welcome proposals for special issues, for example, work from a single nation in translation, such as Brazilian short stories or current Italian fiction and poetry. Guest editors, unfortunately, cannot be compensated; but several have received grants with our cooperation.

SAMPLE COPIES: Sample copies are available at $4.50, prepaid.

LONE STAR
publications of humor

P.O. Box 29000
Suite #103
San Antonio, Texas 78229

GUIDELINES FOR WRITERS & ARTISTS

Thank you for your interest in **LONE STAR PUBLICATIONS OF HUMOR**. **LONE STAR** specializes in humorous and humor-related publications and services for the professional humorist and comedy connoisseur. All unsolicited submissions are automatically considered for inclusion in one or more of our current publications and projects.

We are seeking the following types of humorous and humor-related material from freelancers:

Short Stories & Essays on anything topical or timeless. Length: 500-1200 words. (Anything longer than 1500 words will be returned--unread--to the sender.) Do not send us short stories that go on for several pages before reaching the first--and usually the last--"punchline." There must be humor <u>throughout</u> the piece.

Interviews & Profiles of anyone professionally involved in humor. Length: 500-800 words.

News Items & Opinion Pieces on anything concerned with comedy. We welcome reviews of stand-up comedians, humorous plays, humorous books, etc. Length: 500-800 words.

Poetry of any type (traditional, light verse, clerihews, limericks, free verse, cheap verse, designer verse, etc.) as long as it's funny. Maximum length: 60 lines.

Jokes, Gags, Anecdotes, etc. All material must be original. We prefer to receive joke and gag submissions on index cards--one joke/gag per card.

Letters to the Editor on any aspect of humor. There is no payment for letters accepted for publication, but each letter writer receives a contributor's copy.

(Continued on next page)

****

ABOUT LONE STAR ANNUAL EVENTS

Every year, **LONE STAR** sponsors four events: Humorists Are Artists Month/HAAM (March), International TWIT Award Month (April), Be Nice to New Jersey Week (second week of July) and Be Kind to Editors and Writers Month (September). All are listed in the current edition of **CHASE'S ANNUAL EVENTS** (published by Contemporary Books, Chicago). Those interested in contributing--either as a writer or artist--to these celebrations should first send a 9" x 12" envelope and three first class postage stamps for more information. Please include a note saying, "I want to contribute" along with your request for materials.

GUIDELINES FOR WRITERS & ARTISTS-continued

Cartoons. We're seeking single panel and multi-panel cartoons on topical/timeless subjects. All artwork should be clean, black & white and camera-ready. Please don't send us wash drawings. (Use of "Zip-A-Tone" or another shading film is okay.)

Performable (oral) One-Liners & Jokes on timeless and timely subjects. We prefer to receive at least 10 one-liners or jokes on one topic and no more than 40 jokes per submission. Bylines will be given only to writers contributing 5 or more joke/one-liners to a publication.

A self-addressed envelope and adequate return postage must be included with every unsolicited submission or query. (Warning: Submissions without SASE will not be returned and may be used to stuff ballot boxes during the next Texas election.) Those who have the bad taste to mail their submissions "postage due" can expect to have them promptly returned--unpaid for and unread. Writers from the school of "Disposable Photocopies are Cheaper than SASEs" should indicate this preference by including a brief note with their photocopied materials.

Originality is a must. If any material is found to be copied from another source, **LONE STAR** will no longer consider work from the author/artist.

A few words about style: If the words "wacky", "zany" or "crazy" are part of your humor vocabulary, it's not likely that your endeavors will be suitable for **LONE STAR**. REMEMBER: The best humor closely resembles reality.

Allow 8 to 16 weeks for a response on your submission or inquiry. Because of an ever-increasing workload, we have little time to make personal comments on freelance material. We hope you will not feel slighted by form letter replies.

It is highly recommended that you purchase samples of our publications before sending in your creative works. Back issues of **LONE STAR: A MAGAZINE OF HUMOR** are available for $6 each. Please write for current prices on other **LONE STAR** publications.

PAYMENT: $7-$30 for short stories, essays, interviews and profiles;$4-$12 for opinion pieces/reviews;$2-$5 for short verse;$1-$5 per joke/one-liner;$5-$30 for cartoons. Inquire for current rates on photographs and newsclippings. We purchase variable rights. If your work has been previously published, please let us know where and when. Our policy is "payment-on-publication", but we often manage to pay before.

****

ABOUT THE EDITOR

Comedy writer **Lauren Barnett** has been the editor and publisher of **LONE STAR** publications for five years and a selling humorist for seven years. She has written humor for stand-up comedians, broadcasters, public speakers and cartoonists. Barnett's cartoons and writing have been published in numerous periodicals including **INNERVIEW, THE JOURNAL OF IRREPRODUCIBLE RESULTS** and **COMPUTER WORLD.** She is also the creator and sponsor of four humor "events" which have received extensive national and international media attention: Humorists Are Artists Month, International TWIT Award Month, Be Nice to New Jersey Week and Be Kind to Editors and Writers Month. All are listed in the 1987 edition of **CHASE'S ANNUAL EVENTS** (Contemporary Books, Chicago). Barnett is among those catalogued in **WHO'S WHO IN U.S. WRITERS, EDITORS & POETS** and **THE INTERNATIONAL AUTHORS & WRITERS WHO'S WHO.**

The MacGuffin

Schoolcraft College

18600 HAGGERTY ROAD • LIVONIA, MICHIGAN 48152-2696

TELEPHONE 313-591-6400

Arthur J. Lindenberg
Editor

GUIDELINES FOR SUBMITTING FICTION

THE MACGUFFIN staff will consider manuscripts of short fiction and parts of novels of up to 4,000 words. We consider all kinds of fiction except for hard or soft core pornography.

1. Please include a self-addressed, stamped envelope (SASE) or sufficient International Reply Coupons.

2. Please do not send simultaneous submissions.

3. Allow eight weeks for consideration. The editorial offices are closed for six weeks, from July through mid-August.

4. Upon acceptance, a note will be sent to the contributor along with a request for brief biographical information.

5. THE MACGUFFIN is copyrighted. Upon publication, all rights revert to contributors.

6. At this time, payment is limited to two contributor's copies.

7. Sample copies are available for $2.50.

485 MADison Avenue, N.Y., N.Y. 10022-5852   (212) 752-7685

Dear

OK. You say you want to write for MAD. You read it as a kid, loved it, and always thought it would be a lot of fun to come up with stuff like that. Well, here's your chance!

MAD is now actively seeking to expand its freelance writing staff. We're looking for writers who are clever, offbeat and, most importantly, <u>funny</u>. We want to infuse new life, energy and a fresh look into the magazine.

Still interested? Good. Here's what we want from you:

1) ARTICLES: On anything or everything that catches your fancy and is funny. Especially prized are articles on current hot trends. (i.e. This weeks; topics might be rock videos, computers, etc.) Send us a paragraph or two explaining the premise of your article with 3 or 4 examples of how you intend to carry it through, describing the action and visual content of each example. Rough sketches are welcomed but not necessary. Remember! No straight text pieces! MAD is a visual magazine!!

2) COVER IDEAS: Preferably with Alfred E. Neuman in the gag, though we will eagerly consider anything that is funny.

3) DON MARTIN GAGS: Two to eight panel cartoon continuities in the style and tradition of MAD's maddest artist. (Sketches not necessary.)

4) EVERYTHING ELSE: Anything you think is funny, even if you've never seen anything like it before in MAD.

Here's what we <u>don't</u> want from you:

1) MOVIE & TV SATIRES: Unless they're entirely different in format or approach than the one we're currently using.

2) REWRITTEN MAD-LIKE STUFF: Nothing turns us off faster than an article that begins "You Know You're A_____When…" We've done it to death!

3) ACUTELY TOPICAL MATERIAL: Always remember it takes six months from typewriter to newsstand! Very topical material could be dead and forgotten!

A few final thoughts: Always include a self-addressed stamped envelope with each submission. You can include more than one idea in a submission. Each is judged on its own merit. have fun! Don't be afraid to be stupid and don't self-edit yourself because <u>you</u> don't think it's what <u>you</u> think <u>we're</u> looking for. Sometimes <u>we</u> don't know what we're looking for until we see it! Make us earn our money as editors!

Don't be discouraged if you're rejected your first or second time out. Writing for MAD isn't a piece of cake. That's why we pay top rates—on acceptance!

We're waiting to hear from <u>you</u>! This is your big chance! Don't blow it! Hit those keys!!!

MAD-ly,
The Editors

P.S. Have a nice day.

350 Madison Avenue
New York, New York 10017
212 880-8800

WRITERS' GUIDELINES (FICTION)

<u>Mademoiselle</u> has a long tradition of publishing fiction of literary
quality. We are looking, in particular, for stories of interest
to young, single working women. But since these young women
are vital and socially aware, and concerned with understanding
both themselves and the world they live in, we are open to any
good story that offers fresh insights into universal human experiences.

We look for good writing, strong voices, generally classic form.
We very much welcome male point-of-view stories about personal
relationships. (We are less interested in male stories of
sports triumphs or war exploits.) We are not interested
in science fiction, mysteries, genre fiction (historical
romances etc.), surprise endings or highly experimental
prose that comes to no conclusion. We do not publish poetry.

If you have publishing credentials, you should say so.
Otherwise, no cover letter is necessary. Submissions
should be typed, double spaced, 25 lines to a page.

Short shorts: 7-9½ pages (1500-2500 words), $1,000
Short stories: 10-25 pages (15 pages is ideal) (2500-6250 words),
$1,500-2000. Pay on acceptance. SASE required for return of
manuscript.

MAGICAL BLEND

P.O. Box 11303
San Francisco, CA 94101

WRITER'S GUIDELINES

Thank you for your interest in *Magical Blend* magazine. *Magical Blend* welcomes submissions of articles and fiction in keeping with our editorial policy of positivity, growth, and alternative paths to enlightenment. Payment is in contributor's copies only.

Although *Magical Blend* prefers to avoid hard-and-fast rules, the sections below should answer any questions you have concerning editorial requirements for written submissions.

LENGTH

Magical Blend has published articles ranging from 540 words to 13,000 words. Our primary consideration is not so much with quaantity as with quality. An article should be long enough to adequately cover the subject matter but should not be padded just to fill up space. Problems with length generally fall into two categories: (1 the article is not long enough to do more than introduce the subject matter leaving the reader with a dissatisfied "hunger" for specific information or else (2 the article rambles on, repeats itself, and gets lost in superfluous digressions. We cannot overstress the importance of discipline and self-editing in submissions. The rule of thumb is—long enough to adequately cover the subject matter and no longer.

Concerning the length of fiction, we are more inclined toward shorter pieces of 1,000 to 3,000 words. Length of fiction depends largely on the genre of the piece. "Message" stories tend to be short and to the point whereas fiction "Atmosphere" stories which concentrate more on mood, feeling, and description than on a particular message, are generally longer. As with articles, we are more concerned with the quality of fiction than with the length, but a 6,000 word story, for example, would encounter more obstacles in reaching publication than a 3,000 word story.

SUBJECT MATTER

The slant of an article is often more important to *Magical Blend* than subject matter. Our editorial slant of positivity and creativity allows for a wide range of possible subjects if they are approached from an attitude emphasizing these two criteria. For example, any individual, company, product or organization that is far-sighted and actively involved in improving the quality of life here on earth is a good candidate for a short (500-to 1,500-word) profile.

Readers of *Magical Blend* are interested primarily in personal and planetary growth and are anxious to read articles that reflect their own high aspirations on spiritual, physical, psychological, philosophical and social levels. The key word here is "aspiration." Any article that encourages the reader to aspire to his or her highest self is a good candidate for publication. However, please be wary of a common trap many writers fall into when approaching such a piece—avoid cliches and generalizations that result in frothy enthusiasm but lack clarity, direction, and insightfulness. **Be specific and give the reader tangible information!**

We are particularly interested in well-researched articles that deal with the history, philosophy, and personalities of religious and mystical schools of thought. (Examples might be: the life and philosophy of Meister Eckhart; the precepts of Buddhism, Sufism, etc.; th.e personalities and objectives of the Golden Dawn; or the teachings of the 19th-century American transcendentalists.) In short—any article that deals with the past, present or future of mysticism and metaphysics if approached from a positive, noncombative slant.

Submissions of fiction should stress the magic and mysterious events of life that lift us from the mundane and transport us to the mythic and spiritual realms. Endings should be upbeat and positive. *Magical Blend* is not looking for "doomsday" scenarios. Fantasy and humor are welcome.

FICTION VS. ARTICLES

Because of space limitations and the sheer amount of fiction we receive, we advise potential contributors to consider submitting articles as they are much more likely than fiction to reach publication.

RESPONSE TIME

Submissions may require up to two months to answer.

A FINAL NOTE

In preparing these guidelines, we have tried to be precise and informative—exactly the qualities we urge potential contributors to strive for in their writing. *Magical Blend* applauds your creativity and appreciates your interest. We look forward to your query and/or submission. Good luck!

FIRST HAND LTD.

P.O. Box 1314, Teaneck, New Jersey 07666 (201) 836-9177

Publishers of FirstHand and MANSCAPE Magazines

WRITER'S GUIDELINES FOR: FirstHand Magazine
                          Manscape Magazine
                          Manscape 2 Magazine

All three of the above magazines use unsolicited erotic fiction
manuscripts, ranging in length from 10 to 20 double-spaced typed
pages. Our average story length is fifteen pages. Manuscripts
longer than 20 pages will be considered only if they are
exceptional in some way. Material should be written in the first
person and deal explicitly with homosexual experiences. All stories
must contain some graphic sex scenes and should convey a positive
attitude toward gay people and gay sex.

FirstHand also uses short non-fiction articles (2-3 double-spaced
typed pages) highlighting practical information on safe sex practices,
health, travel, books, video, fashion and other advice/lifestyle/
consumer-related topics of interest to gay or single men. These
appear in our "Survival Kit" section, and should be written in the
second or third person. We prefer for writers to query us first
about ideas for "Survival Kit," but we will consider unsolicited
submissions.

Poetry: Both FirstHand and Manscape 2 use poetry, generally not
more than a page in length. Poems need not be graphically sexual
but must deal directly with gay themes.

All three magazines are very reader-oriented in that a large part
of every issue is comprised of letters from our readers describing
their personal experiences, fantasies and feelings. Our readers
are from all walks of life, all races and ethnic backgrounds, all
classes, all religious and political affiliations, etc. They are
a diverse group and many live in far-flung rural areas or small
towns. For some of them, our magazines are the primary source of
contact with gay life, in some cases the only support for their gay
identities. Our readers are very loyal and most save every issue.
We return that loyalty by trying to reflect their interests. For
instance, we strive to avoid the exclusively big-city bias so common
to national gay publications.

FirstHand deals with the "vanilla" side of gay sexuality: first
homosexual experiences, romantic same-sex relationships, and the
more common sexual practices such as oral and anal sex. Manscape
has a similar format but focuses on gay sexual fetishes such as
enemas, watersports, fisting, etc. Manscape 2 carries the kink
a bit further, has a large-size format (8 x 11) and includes photo
spreads.

All characters in stories must be at least eighteen years of age.
We do not use material dealing with scat or double-fisting, or the
injection of foreign objects (other than dildoes) into the body.
Also, all participants in sexual acts must be willing: rape is a

WRITER'S GUIDELINES   Page 2

taboo subject as far as we're concerned, except in prison stories, where it is an unavoidable reality. Don't include heavy drug use in your stories--an occasional joint is okay but that's it. We don't even mention poppers, which have been pretty conclusively linked to AIDS. If you can write a hot safe sex story (condoms, sex toys, JO, phone sex, voyeuristic sex, etc.) by all means do so, and we'll be happy to read it.

Manscape 2 also prints non-fiction full-length articles, which consist of varying topics of interest such as interviews with people of interest to gay men, information about AIDS, leather-Levi oriented articles and how-to articles concerning kinkier sex. If you would like to write a non-fiction piece, you would be well-advised to consult with us first about topic, length, etc. But we will also read unsolicited non-fiction.

Pseudonyms: Please be sure, if you intend to use a pseudonym, to put it in the by-line, under the title. There has been some confusion in the past with writers about this, and we would like to avoid more.

Simultaneous Submissions: We feel this practice to be not entirely ethical (submitting the same manuscript to several magazines at the same time, to see who responds the quickest). The writer thereby wastes the valuable time of the editor(s) who did not get back to him first--time that could have been better spent in other ways. For this reason, we do not like to deal with writers who practice this tactic. Owing to the enormous amount of submissions we receive, it usually takes from two to four weeks to respond to manuscripts or queries.

Pay Scale: We normally purchase all rights to stories and articles, for which we pay $150.00. Occasionally, we will buy First North American Serial Rights, for which we pay $100.00. For Survival Kit items, the pay scale is $35.00 (2 pages); $50.00 (3 pages); and $70.00 (4 pages). We favor articles of two to three pages for Survival Kit, preferring to present more and varied topics to fewer longer ones. A four-page item should be concerned only with a subject of major importance. For poetry we pay $25.00 per poem. We occasionally reprint articles which have appeared elsewhere and payment for these is on a case-by-case basis.

All manuscripts must be typed and double-spaced with right and left margins of at least one inch. The writer's name and address should appear in the upper right hand corner of the title page. Material which is seasonal or in any way timely should be submitted at least seven months in advance.

We sincerely appreciate your interest in our magazines and look forward to seeing your work in our pages.

Cordially yours,

Lou Thomas
Editor

© 1987 by FirstHand Ltd.

LT/hs

The Massachusetts Review

VOL. XXVII, NO. 3-4

Editors: Mary Heath, John Hicks, Fred Robinson; *Associate Editors:* Paul Jenkins, Dale Peterson; *Art Editor:* Lisa U. Baskin; *Secretary:* Carol Fetler; *Business:* Mary Heath, Rita Gabis; *Editorial Assistants:* James Haug, Ruth Stemmer; *Poetry:* Anne Halley, Paul Jenkins; *Fiction:* Corinne Bliss, Joan Bramwell, Julia Demmin, Charles Moran; *Criticism and Cultural Theory:* Neal Bruss, Jules Chametzky, Arlyn Diamond, Sara Lennox, Shaun O'Connell, Esther Terry; *Public Affairs:* Milton Cantor, Jan Dizard, Philip Green, William McFeely, Robert Paul Wolff; *Film and Popular Culture:* Jack Shadoian; *Art and Photography:* Oriole Farb Feshbach, Jerome Liebling; *Theater:* Doris Abramson, James Ellis.

Contributing Editors: *Leonard Baskin, David R. Clark, Sidney Kaplan, William Kennick, Richard C. Lyon, Leo Marx, B. L. Reid, Seymour Rudin, Leone Stein, Jean Sudrann, Mike Thelwell, F. S. Troy, Frederick Turner.*

Editorial and business office: Memorial Hall, University of Massachusetts, Amherst, Mass. 01003. *Subscriptions:* $12.00 a year, $4.00 a copy, in the U.S.A.; $14.00 foreign, including Canada. *The Massachusetts Review* is published four times a year by The Massachusetts Review, Inc. Second class postage paid in Amherst, Mass. 01003 and at additional mailing offices; return postage guaranteed. Postmaster: send address changes to The Massachusetts Review, Memorial Hall, University of Massachusetts, Amherst, MA 01003. Manuscripts must be accompanied by return postage. No poetry or fiction accepted from June to October. Copyright 1986 by The Massachusetts Review, Inc. *National distributor:* B. DeBoer, 113 E. Centre Street—Rear, Nutley, N.J. 07110. Printed by Commonwealth Press, 44 Portland St., Worcester, Mass. 01608. The staff is grateful to the Associate Alumni of the University of Massachusetts and to other patrons for their assistance, to the Coordinating Council of Literary Magazines, and to the Massachusetts Council on the Arts & Humanities.

MR is indexed in the following publications: *Abstracts of English Studies; America: History & Life; Annual Bibliography of English Language & Literature; Historical Abstracts; Index to Little Magazines; MLA—International Bibliography; Sociological Abstracts; Social Sciences & Humanities Index.*

Charter member Association of Literary Magazines of America
ISSN 0025—4878

MR
THE MASSACHUSETTS REVIEW
PUBLISHED INDEPENDENTLY WITH THE SUPPORT AND CO-OPERATION OF AMHERST, HAMPSHIRE, MOUNT HOLYOKE, AND SMITH COLLEGES, AND THE UNIVERSITY OF MASSACHUSETTS

Dear

Thank you for your interest in The Massachusetts Review, a quarterly of literature, the arts and public affairs. We represent no stylistic or ideological coterie. The editors seek a balance between established writers and artists and promising new ones, and material of variety and vitality relevant to the intellectual and aesthetic life of our time. We aspire to have a broad appeal; our commitment, in part regional, is not provincial.

Our guidelines are as follows:

FICTION: We accept one short story per submission, usually between sixteen and twenty-two pages in length.

POETRY: A poetry submission may consist of up to six poems. There are no restrictions in terms of length, but generally our poems are less than one-hundred lines. Please write your name on every page.

ARTICLES: Reviews of breadth and depth are considered, as well as discussions of leading writers; of art, music, and drama; analyses of trends in literature, science, philosophy, and public affairs. "Inspired pages are not written to fill a space, but for inevitable utterance; and to such our journal is freely and solicitously open" (Emerson). We encourage queries as to subjects. No short reviews on single books.

Please submit poetry to "Poetry Editor," and, in a separate envelope, fiction to "Fiction Editor."

BE SURE TO ENCLOSE A SELF-ADDRESSED, STAMPED ENVELOPE FOR OUR REPLY. NO MS. CAN BE RETURNED NOR QUERY ANSWERED UNLESS ACCOMPANIED BY AN SASE. In addition: 1) Please type fiction manuscripts double-spaced.
2) We do not read during the summer months.
3) Please include name and address on your manuscript.

The Massachusetts Review is a non-profit journal. Because mailing and printing expenses are very high, it is impossible for us to acknowledge receipt of the many manuscripts we receive, or to honor the many requests that are made for sample copies of the magazine. You may order an issue for $4.00 plus $.50 postage and handling, or begin a subscription with this form.

Name:_____

Address:_____ Zip:_____

__ 1 year ($12)   __ 2 years ($24)   __ 3 years ($36)   __ Single Copy ($4.50)

Make check payable to The Massachusetts Review. $14.00 outside the U.S. (1 yr.)
Thank you for your interest.

—The Editors

Editorial Office: Memorial Hall, University of Massachusetts, Amherst, Mass. 01003

So You Want to Write for *Mature Years*

Mature Years is published quarterly by The United Methodist Publishing House. The audience is persons of retirement age and beyond, and the magazine's purpose is to help persons understand and use the resources of the Christian faith in dealing with specific opportunities and problems related to aging. Writers are not restricted to older adults.

Articles and Fiction Stories
When we review manuscripts we look for

Positive Approach—Articles and stories should be upbeat, describing older adults who are enjoying and finding fulfillment in their retirement years.

Active Subjects—Persons highlighted in articles and stories should be active; busy; and involved in their families, their communities, the nation, and the world.

Variety of Topics and Approaches—Articles and stories can be serious or humorous; they can be based on memories or on here-and-now experience. We especially need articles that deal with opportunities of older adults for service, for adventure, for fulfillment, and for fun. We do not generally accept free-lance articles that deal with the problems and concerns of the retirement years, since we contract articles of that nature.

Christian Orientation—Articles and stories should demonstrate faith in God as a resource for life regardless of circumstances. Persons highlighted should be older adults who are enjoying their retirement years, not just by traveling, but by being in ministry helping and serving in a variety of ways. Articles and stories should reflect the joy of living out one's Christian faith.

Absence of Stereotypes—We are not interested in articles or stories that portray any group of people in a negative light, that poke fun at persons, that assume that all older adults are alike, or that stereotype people by age, gender, nationality, or race.

Poetry
We are looking for short, pithy poems with interesting twists or unusual insights or memorable lines.

Manuscript Preparation
Confine length to 2,000 words (eight or nine typewritten pages).
Type double-spaced on a 36-character line length.
Include photocopies of the original of any material quoted from other sources and give us complete source information.
Include suggested subheads if you like.

Payment: 4 cents per word for prose
50 cents to $1 per line for poetry

Send the manuscript and a self-addressed, stamped envelope
along with your name, address, phone number, and social security number to:

Mature Years
P.O. Box 801
Nashville, TN 37202

Expect a reply in six to eight weeks.

What is the purpose of *Merlyn's Pen*?

The magazine benefits English instruction in two ways. Because it is written by students, it offers students a relevant reason to read its challenging literature. And it offers young writers a genuine reason to write and revise. With *Merlyn's Pen*, students can approach the "big" themes without the fear of tackling the big books. Student-written literature is an exciting supplement to traditional literature.

This is the first I've heard of *Merlyn's Pen*. Who's behind it?

After earning his MAT in English from The University of Chicago and teaching in Bethesda, Maryland, and Vienna, Austria, Jim Stahl founded *Merlyn's Pen*. He worked closely with Mary Jane Sorrentino, former assistant coordinator of public education programs at the National Archives. Many of the magazine's editors are teaching colleagues of Jim Stahl. The magazine is supported by revenue from classroom subscriptions and from education-related advertising. (*Merlyn's Pen* does not accept advertising from makers of cosmetics, hygiene products, clothing, or snack-foods.)

Why Grades 7 through 10?

Because forums for the writing of juniors and seniors already exist — school newspapers and literary magazines, yearbooks, and writing contests. These forums are usually closed to middle schoolers and too crowded for freshmen. Adolescent writers need a real audience. *Merlyn's Pen* offers one.

Does *Merlyn's Pen* accept anything and everything for publication?

No. Stories, essays, poems, and plays accepted for publication should be effective and good enough to be taught. Published manuscripts represent 2% of those contributed.

What happens when a piece is accepted?

Instead of monetary compensation, authors receive three complimentary copies of the issue that contains their work. They also receive Strunk and White's *The Elements of Style*. Subscriptions are not solicited from published authors.

Can any student in grades 7 through 10 contribute, even if the supervising teacher is not a subscriber?

Yes. And students may contribute as often as they wish. Every manuscript is read by two editors, and every contributor receives a personal response within twelve weeks, often sooner. (That's why our staff is so large!)

How should students prepare manuscripts for *Merlyn's Pen*?

1. Include a self-addressed, stamped envelope large enough to return the author's work.
2. Staple every manuscript together and place the author's name on every page of every manuscript.
3. Type, double-space, with very wide margins.
4. Include the following information, in this order, in ink, on a cover sheet:
   Author's Name, Complete School Name, School Address, Teacher's Name, Author's Grade and Age, Home Address, School Phone Number, Home Phone Number
5. Place all manuscripts (stapled together) by the same author in the same envelope. Do not send report covers.
6. Send manuscripts and return envelope addressed to student to:
   Merlyn's Pen
   P.O. Box 1058
   E. Greenwich, RI 02818
7. Please allow the editors 10 to 12 weeks to respond.

Where does *Merlyn's Pen* fit into my curriculum?

If you investigate *themes* in the literature you teach now, then the magazine can help you introduce and develop them. Teachers build thematic units around the magazine, or use it to add interest to units already developed. If you teach writing, then you know the importance of audience, purpose, and response. *Merlyn's Pen* easily offers all three. In addition, the magazine is fertile ground for spelling, vocabulary, and sentence-combining activities.

If I order a classroom set, how and when will I receive my order?

You will receive four issues during the school year. They will arrive on or before these dates: September 15, November 15, January 31, and April 1. Classroom magazines and the *Teacher's Guide* are shipped via second-class mail in one secure package.

Merlyn's Pen: A Great Reason to Read and Write

To receive a copy of *Merlyn's Pen* for review, please call toll free 1-800-247-2027 (in Rhode Island: 401-885-5175)

The Detroit News

615 LAFAYETTE BLVD. / DETROIT, MICHIGAN 48231

Dear Letter Writer:

Here are a few guidelines for stories for MICHIGAN magazine:

-- All stories (with the possible exception of fiction) must have some
   sort of Michigan angle or connection (even if it's a somewhat tenuous
   one). Subject matter may vary, but we're looking for things with
   broad appeal for the cover, in particular.

-- Cover stories tend to run 2,000 to 2,500 words; secondary stories 1,500
   to 2,000. That's flexible, of course. Cover stories pay $500 to $650;
   secondary stories, $200 to $450.

-- We'll consider any art submitted with a story. We prefer color slides
   or 4-by-5 transparencies. We pay $150 per color page, $350 for covers.
   If a story doesn't come with art, we'll arrange for it ourselves.

-- We're interested in fiction -- preferably by Michigan authors or set in
   the Midwest or Michigan itself.

That's about it. If you have more specific questions, you're welcome to
call (222-2620).

Sincerely,

Cynthia Boal-Janssens
Editor, Michigan Magazine

CBJ/jb

Military Lifestyle

WRITER'S GUIDELINES

DOWNEY COMMUNICATIONS, INC.
1732 WISCONSIN AVE., N.W.
WASHINGTON, D.C. 20007

Military Lifestyle is a privately owned magazine published 10 times a year (July/August and November/December issues are combined) in two editions--United States and Overseas. Lifestyle publishes articles about military marriages, parenting, personal and family finances, health, beauty and travel and leisure.

Lifestyle's readers are primarily between the ages of 18 and 38. Most have young children, travel extensively and move frequently. Freelancers should know in advance that any material submitted for publication must have a military families slant.

About 90 percent of the articles in Lifestyle are written by freelancers. Many of the contributors are military spouses or servicemembers who have an intimate knowledge of military life and can write from the special point of view we seek. However, a number of freelancers without military backgrounds who are willing to go the extra distance to tailor their material to our audience have done fine work for Lifestyle.

Payment ranges from $75 for light, humorous essays to $300-600 for articles about military life. The average article length is 1800 words. Lifestyle also publishes short fiction about personal aspects of military life. Payment for fiction is $200 per story. Payment is generally made on publication. If the article has to be held for more than six months, payment will be made on acceptance.

Interested freelancers should submit queries first, including either an outline or detailed description of the prospective topic. Queries are generally answered within eight weeks. The magazine's lead time is about six months. Articles submitted by first-time writers will be accepted on speculation only; after an article has been accepted, the editor will negotiate a fee with the writer.

All material submitted must be accompanied by a self-addressed, stamped envelope, otherwise it will not be returned. Address queries to:

Hope Daniels, Editor
Military Lifestyle
1732 Wisconsin Ave. NW
Washington, DC 20007

Manuscript Preparation

Style. Lifestyle follows the Associated Press Stylebook. Writers are expected to double-check the spelling of proper names, geographical names and military acronyms.

Individuals must be fully identified by first and last names, professional titles (if applicable) and city and state where they reside. Military members must be correctly identified by rank, duty title and military installation.

Length. Average length of feature articles is 1800 words; average length of department columns is 1200 words. A manuscript submitted to us that is excessively long will be returned to the author for cutting.

IDs. Material submitted should be accompanied by a 1-3 sentence biography of the writer, which will appear with the article to identify the writer to our readers. Connections with the military or with the subject matter should be included. Examples:

> Donna Harrington-Lueker fights   (article on fleas and
> fleas in San Francisco.   ticks)
>
> Judy Ford Hogan, an Air Force   (article on making
> wife for 24 years and author   fabric flowers)
> of Fabric Into Flowers (EMP
> Publications, Inc.), lives
> in Fairfax, Va.

Contacting Sources. In very few cases can active-duty personnel speak with writers for publication without clearance from military Public Affairs. Call Public Affairs offices at military installations first to arrange interviews. This is a formality, but it can speed contact with the individuals you want to interview.

We also permit sources to review quotes obtained in interviews with the writer. This makes people more comfortable and eliminates errors in fact and context. However, it is against Lifestyle policy for contributors to submit entire articles for review by anyone outside the magazine, including sources, Public Affairs personnel and others. Occasionally, however, such a requirement will be asked of the writer before the interview will be granted. Should this happen, please contact Lifestyle's editor for further guidelines.

It is not necessary to contact Public Affairs if you are interviewing family members unless they are connected with an installation function about which you are writing.

When in doubt about whether to contact Public Affairs, contact them. It fosters good relations.

Publishing Rights. Lifestyle buys First North American Serial
Rights to its articles. Contributors are free to resell their
material after publication, but not before.

Lifestyle often receives requests from various nonprofit organizations, asking permission to copy and distribute an article.
that has appeared in an issue. We give permission routinely
if the reprint will be used for educational or nonprofite purposes.
However, if the reprint would result in a resale for the writer, we
will contact that writer and put him in touch with the group
seeking reprint rights.

Expenses. On assignment, writers are usually reimbursed a portion
of their expenses, but terms must be agreed upon prior to the
writer's acceptance of the assignment. Persons writing on speculation should not expect to be reimbursed for expenses connected
with an article.

Copies. Each contributor to Lifestyle will automatically receive
two copies of the issue in which his article appears. Writers
may also submit a list of individuals mentioned in their article
whom they would like to receive a copy of that issue. Copies
will be mailed to these individuals on publication.

Extra copies of a current issue are available at $1.50 each.
Copies of back issues are $2. Send requests to:

                    Magazine Requests
                    Military Lifestyle
                    1732 Wisconsin Ave. NW
                    Washington, DC 20007

MILKWEED CHRONICLE / MILKWEED EDITIONS

P.O. Box 3226   Minneapolis, Minnesota 55403   (612) 332-3192

FICTION WRITERS' GUIDELINES FROM MILKWEED EDITIONS

We publish only a very few books of fiction each year. Please send query
letter before sending manuscript. The second round of the Milkweed Editions
National Fiction Award will be held in the autumn of 1987. Winning manuscript
will be selected by an American fiction writer. Author receives $3,000 in
prize money as an advance against royalties. Please send for guidelines in
August, 1987.

Emilie Buchwald/Editor
R.W. Scholes/Art Director
Milkweed Editions
P.O. Box 3226,
Minneapolis, Minnesota 55403
612-332-3192

Emilie Buchwald *Editor*
Deborah Keenan *Managing Editor*

R.W. Scholes *Art Director*
Steve Chase *Business Manager*

Milwaukee Magazine, Inc.
312 East Buffalo Street
Milwaukee, WI 53202
414·273·1101

Dear Writer:

Thank you for your interest in Milwaukee Magazine. Here is some information that may help you in getting material published in Milwaukee Magazine.

1) Get to know our publication by reading it. It's hard to write for a publication you don't read. Sample copies ($3.25, mailed) and subscriptions can be ordered through the Milwaukee Magazine circulation department.

2) Our readership is sophisticated and well-educated. We like timely ideas related to politics, current events, local personalities, local history, significant issues, etc. But don't submit ideas that don't have anything to do with Milwaukee or Wisconsin. We are a regional publication. Example: travelogues of trips to other states or countries (even though it was a Wisconsin traveler) would <u>not</u> be appropriate.

3) The Insider section (at the front of the magazine) is an excellent entry point for new writers. Stories submitted for this section should be no longer than 500 words.

4) Most of our columns are written by regular contributors (Politics, Restaurants, Fine Arts, etc.) and thus are not open to freelance submissions.

5) We usually do not make assignments to writers new to Milwaukee Magazine. Most material from new writers is accepted on a speculation basis.

6) Submissions for feature-length stories should be no longer than 5,000 words.

7) We will review completed manuscripts or queries. To make a query, send a detailed letter describing your idea(s). Sample paragraphs are helpful, as are an outline and information on sources to be used in a story. You should also send a resume and clips of your previously published work.

8) You can expect a response to your submission in six weeks.

Thanks again for your interest in Milwaukee Magazine.

                                        Sincerely,

                                        Judith Woodburn
                                        Managing Editor

WRITER'S GUIDELINES

GENERAL INFORMATION

MBM is a lifestyle magazine targeted primarily at black American professional men aged 25 to 54; a market of approximately 5 million, growing at a rate of about 11% a year. MBM is <u>not</u> a how-to-be-middle-class magazine. It <u>is</u> a middle class magazine which assumes a certain level of resources, sophistication and exposure that <u>already has been attained</u> by its readership. An MBM reader is <u>at least</u> middle class, meaning, a median household income of $32,000. Our readers are doctors, lawyers, managers, engineers, corporate business executives, entrepreneurs, executives of non-profit organizations, teachers and professional government workers. In short, our readers are well educated, well rounded, well traveled and curious about the world they live in.

DEPARTMENTS

Innovators (profiles of entrepreneurs); Discovery (best bets to see, do or buy); Ovations (profiles of entertainment personalities or events); Memorandum (general business or corporate profiles); Sports (about particular sports or persons involved in sports -- male or female); Health (mental or physical: could involve nutrition, medicine, drug therapy, new alternative treatments, surgery, etc.); Fitness and Grooming: The Good Life (food, wine, home entertaining, automotive); Destinations (travel inside or outside the USA); Horoscopes; Fashion; Watch Out (brief profiles of up-and-coming males or females in entertainment, politics or business); Arts and Culture (focusing on Jazz and Classical music, art sculpture, photography, dance); MBM Music (about popular music and artists who perform it).

<u>NONFICTION</u>   (1,200 to 2,500 words)

Pieces should be timely and topical, or, they should uncover and examine some aspect of a modern black man's life that has never been considered before. Subject matter should be well researched and documented, especially if it is of a technical nature. We are particularly interested in articles about successful black men who are involved in sports, entertainment, business, politics, education and related fields. We want to see black men portrayed in a positive way. We <u>are not</u> interested in articles about pimps, prostitutes, drug addicts, criminals, terrorists, revolutionaries, or malcontents of any kind.

The subject matter of personal profiles can be either male or female but they should be written from a <u>male perspective</u>. Persons profiled in MBM can be of any race, creed, color or national origin, but, given the fact that our readers are black, the article must deal with a subject that would be expecially interesting to them. (For example, we would consider an article about a white saxophone player who plays jazz, because our readers are heavy consumers of jazz records and attend jazz concerts.)

1123 Broadway, Suite 802, New York, N.Y. 10010   (212) 924-5480

FICTION (2,500 to 5,500 words)

MBM will consider a limited number of fiction manuscripts for publication -- about eight each year. Subject matter can range from mystery, humor, adventure, suspense, science fiction, to just about anything your mind can conjure up. But, <u>WE ARE NOT INTERESTED IN PORNOGRAPHY.</u> If there is any sexual aspect to your story it should develop as part of the plot. Sex should not be depicted in an overly graphic manner and should not deal with perversions or fetishes. Considering our target audience, your fiction should relate to black people in some way.

SHORT FILLERS (100 to 1,000 words)

We would like to see short pieces on career development, personal growth (positive thinking, spiritual development, religion, etc.), money management, financial planning, new trends, events or relations with the opposite sex. We will also consider book and record reviews, video reviews and "caught in the act" critiques of major events.

PHOTOGRAPHY ACCOMPANYING MANUSCRIPTS

If you can supply good color transparencies (35mm or larger) or crisp, sharp black & white prints, you stand a better chance of getting a good manuscript accepted. Persons depicted in photos should be identified on the back or on an accompanying sheet -- include captions. MAJOR PHOTO SPREADS IN MBM ARE INTERNALLY GENERATED. A FREELANCER HAS LITTLE OR NO CHANCE OF GETTING AN ASSIGNMENT.

MECHANICS

Manuscripts should be submitted on clean, letter sized paper. NO MORE THAN TWENTY LINES SHOULD APPEAR ON ANY ONE PAGE AND EACH LINE SHOULD BE NO LONGER THAN 45 CHARACTERS (INCLUDING SPACES). Double space throughout and indent each paragraph 5 spaces. Author's name, address and phone number should appear on first page along with an estimated word count. <u>A SAMPLE MANUSCRIPT PAGE IS ATTACHED FOR YOUR REFERENCE.</u>

STYLE

The Associated Press Stylebook is used for continuity throughout the magazine.

FEES

Rate of payment ranges from $15 to $200, depending on length and quality of the submission. Cover stories and other long features are negotiable.

OTHER INFORMATION

All correspondence with MBM should include a <u>self-addressed stamped envelope</u> (SASE). Send us complete manuscripts or send a query with clips of your previously published work. We try to report within four weeks or less. REMEMBER: OUR READERS ARE BLACK -- YOUR ARTICLE IDEAS SHOULD BE RELEVANT TO A BLACK AUDIENCE.

# # #

G. Codrington Dapp III
444 Seventh Avenue
New York, New York 10017
(800) 444-5678

Length: 2,000 words

S A M P L E   S A M P L E

HOLIDAY CHEER FOR EIGHTIES

10   20   30   40   45

1   While it is true that you can't please

2   all of the people all of the time, it is

3   quite possible to please most of the people

4   some of the time. If that sounds confusing,

5   imagine how confusing it is to put on a holi-

6   day event for a house full of guests with a

7   wide variety of tastes in alcoholic bever-

8   ages. For holiday entertaining the task

9   can be simplified by planning ahead and

10   giving some serious thought to the prefer-

11   ences of the invited guests.

12   Recently we've begun to hear a great

13   deal about the changing drinking habits

14   of today's young, affluent movers and

15   shakers. Even within the pages of this

16   issue, MBM notes that wine tasting has

17   become an acceptable way to imbibe and en-

18   joy the company of good friends. For small

19   groups, this is highly recommended, especi-

20   ally where the assembled guests share simi-

(more)

Modern Short Stories

500-B Bi-County Blvd.
Farmingdale, NY 11735
1-516-293-3751

Writer's Guide

Dear Author,

Modern Short Stories publishes a wide range of material; from popular fiction, to serious literature, to the absurd. If your short story lies in the realm of adventure, mystery, romance or science fiction, send it in. If your writing raises questions about the world we live in, the disappointments and frustrations experienced in everyday life, or looks critically at social relations, let me see it. And if your story is entertaining through humor, sarcasm, or cynicism; or if it makes the impossible seem possible, the absurd seem real, send it to me. If I like your short story I'll buy it and use it in an upcoming issue of Modern Short Stories.

General Suggestions

Do not submit unfinished manuscripts, outlines or concepts. Proof read carefully. Spelling and grammatical errors are signs of incompleteness and poor preparation.

Use standard 8-1/2 by 11-inch white bond paper. Double space between lines. Type on one side only. Letter-quality printing is best, but dot matrix is accepted. Letter-quality or dot-matrix, please use a new ribbon. No simultaneous or photocopied submissions accepted. Type your name and address in the top left corner of the first page; some authors use a rubber stamp to put their name and address on the back of each succeeding page or type their last name and the story title at the top left of each succeeding page. Also include the telephone number where you can be reached during the day should our editors have a question that requires immediate attention.

We accept short stories that range from 1,000 to 5,000 words. However, stories between 2,000 and 3,500 words are preferred. For the return of unaccepted manuscripts, include return postage. We cannot be responsible for manuscripts submitted without return postage.

Rates of Payment

Our rates for a story range from $25 to $75, depending on variables such as reader interest, originality of concept, and number of words. Payment is made on acceptance. Some stories may be sent back to the author for further revision while others will be accepted outright. Since we know every author is vitally interested in our evaluation of his story, we have established a manuscript acceptance procedure that is intended to give you our decision in two weeks.

Modern Short Stories is intended to give new and unpublished authors a chance to have their work published, but encourages submissions from established authors as well. I encourage submissions of all perspectives, approaches and subject matter and look forward to reviewing your manuscript soon.

Sincerely,

Glenn E. Steckler
Editor

MOMENT
MAGAZINE

MOMENT Magazine Fiction Writers Guidelines:

MOMENT is an independent Jewish monthly. We print cultural, historical, political, and "lifestyle-oriented" articles, and "think pieces." We also review books, cover the arts and print occasional poetry and short stories. Regarding the latter two categories, however, a word of caution: We rarely have more than one piece of poetry or fiction in an issue, and sometimes not even that.

All fiction should have Jewish content. Avoid over-sentimentalized writing, and use themes which are fresh. We look for liveliness of style and tight, clear writing.

Manuscripts should be double-spaced, computer printouts are acceptable but we prefer letter-quality, and photocopies are also allowable. All submissions must be accompanied by a self-addressed stamped envelope. The optimal length is around 2500 to 4000 words.

THE MOUNTAIN LAUREL

THE BLUE RIDGE DIGEST

LAUREL PUBLICATIONS, INC.

The Mountain Laurel is a monthly journal of mountain life. We print fiction and non fiction articles pertaining to the Blue Ridge mountains. Becoming familiar with our publication is the very best guideline you could follow. We will send a sample copy if you send us a 9 x 12 stamped envelope.

We are printed in a tabloid newspaper format and have a greater need for short stories (around a thousand words or less). These stories can be humorous and heart warming. We shun violence and print no off color stories or words. We also shun the stereotyped "hillbilly" image. Real mountain people are smart. They were downright ingenious in many instances, to be able to survive in an area of the country that was often harsh. Mountain people have a wry sense of humor also.

We will come closer to considering stories that deal with a specific incident than a story that is too general in its topic. We get too many stories about "I walked five miles to school" or "We grew all we ate on the farm".

Upon acceptance of stories, we will pay in contributor's copies, upon printing. There may be a waiting period before a particular story fits into an issue. Usually it takes longer to fit longer stories than shorter ones. We give a full byline and copyright each story to the writer. We ask only for a one time right to print and occasionally accept previously published works. We have printed many first time writer's stories. The most important thing to us is the content of the story. It must fit within some aspect of mountain life. We like simple down to earth stories that don't get so bogged down in descriptive adjectives.

It usually takes a month after receiving your manuscript for us to respond. Seasonal materials should be submitted at least three months in advance. We are always looking for good articles to fit in our December (Christmas) issue, in particular.

In the past we have printed excerpts from books by well known Appalachian writers such as James Still, Alice Kinder and John Parris. In 1987 we were awarded The Heritage Award from Ferrum College's Blue Ridge Institute, for contributing to the awareness of preserving Blue Ridge culture. We have subscribers in every state in America and a few foreign countries and are also distributed by wholesale distributors in Virginia, West Virginia, North Carolina and Tennessee. At present we have a monthly circulation of 22,000, which increases seasonally.

ROUTE 1, MEADOWS OF DAN, VIRGINIA 24120 - TELEPHONE 703-789-7193

Rhyme Time
Story Time/Mystery Time

Writer's Info
P.O. Box 2377

Linda Hutton, Editor
Coeur d'Alene, ID 83814

Mystery Time

Mystery Time is an annual collection of short stories with a
suspense/mystery theme only. This is not a contest; there is
no entry fee. Payment to authors for first rights is ¼¢ to
1¢ per word; payment is one copy for reprint rights. Submit
your short story (to 1500 words) typed double-spaced, and
enclose SASE. Photocopied, simultaneous and previously published work is welcome. Avoid present tense and do not
copyright your work. All rights revert to authors upon publication. Six authors are nominated annually for the Pushcart
Prize in Fiction. Mystery Time sells for $5 postpaid.
Editor: Linda Hutton

NEGATIVE CAPABILITY
SHORT FICTION COMPETITION

R.P. Adams $1,000⁰⁰ Award

Judge: Thomas York

Top Three Winners will be Published in <u>Negative Capability</u>
Deadline (postmarked) December 15, 1987

- Unpublished stories only.

- 1,500 - 3,500 words, typed, double-spaced

- Submit one copy with author's name, address and the title of story on a separate page.

- No limit on number of entries but each story should be accompanied by $10⁰⁰ reading fee. ($13⁰⁰ Canadian)

- No entries will be returned. Each entrant will receive a copy of the issue with the winning stories.

Mail American Entries to:

Negative Capability
Sue Walker
English Department
University of South Alabama
Mobile, Alabama 36688

Mail Canadian Entries to:

Thomas York
St. Paul's College
University of Waterloo
Waterloo, Ontario
N2L - 305

by

Eugene Walter

On Submission

I have worked with some ten or twelve literary magazines since 1947, and I'd like to point out some do's and don't's, in regard to the submission of manuscripts or typescripts.

1. Be sure the text you're submitting is the definitive one. Once, in Dickens' day, authors sent drafts to their type-setters and made correction on the proofs. Simple facts of economics make that impossible now.

2. Please don't send anything single-spaced. Editors blanch and tend to put such typescripts aside until later...later...later...

3. Use a fairly newish ribbon. I've received typescripts in ghostly blue which really were illegible.

4. Put your name AND address clearly on the first page of your typescript. Put your last name and the key work of your title on EVERY page. With all the best will in the world, there are always cases where things get shuffled. I have a trunkful of pages from who knows what works by who knows what writers. Out of genuine respect for the creative individual, even the would-be creative individual, even the village idiot, I always try to return what is not accepted, offer advice where not presumptuous, always a thank-you for submitting, but what can you do when you have a sheaf of untitled, unnamed typescripts?

5. Always send a SASE (self-addressed stamped envelopes.) Literary magazines are always over-enthusiastic and under-financed and while MOST magazines bravely return things even when no return postage has been sent, there comes a day when bookkeeping catches up. I now put typescripts which are to be returned and have no postage into my Time Capsule (a battered trunk of stuff which I'll ship some day to the Humanities Research Centre in Texas.)

6. Don't be impatient. The more serious the magazine, the more the editors will take time to read, even re-read, mull over. This does take time. Most editors of literary magazines make their living otherwise.

7. It is helpful to send a brief *curriculum vitae* but not obligatory. However, if you do, and your poem or story is accepted, then the editors need not write you to have such. Time and money saved, and on with the show.

8. Don't send "blind". Read a number of the magazine before submitting. Sometimes your work will be quite simply unsuitable for one reason or another. If you take the time to read one or two copies you'll get the picture.

9. Don't commit suicide if your work is returned. Sometimes the best work is returned because of countless irrelevant factors, such as length, the fact the review has just published a similar work, some editor has a blind spot or a real *tic* against your type of work, or your-subject, or your style. Grit your teeth; go on submitting.

10. If you think you can write, WRITE. Don't stop for anything at all. Write every day, even if just letters to Aunt Minnie. Be brave, pray to St. Rita, the saint of the impossible, think lofty thoughts, be kind to humans and animals, learn to speak, to read aloud with expression, never let the daily irritations of modern life get to you; don't be envious, jealous or small-minded (all writers tend, by their very nature of Special Conservationists, to fall into these unpleasant habits).

11. Read. Think. Listen to music. Keep a pet, whether animal, bird, reptile, or human.

12. Get drunk, as Baudelaire says, "On wine, on poetry, or on virtue, according to your whim."

NEGATIVE CAPABILITY
6116 Timberly Road North
Mobile, Alabama 36609

Sue Walker, Editor
Pete Davis, Managing Editor

❄ *NER/BLQ*

New England Review and Bread Loaf Quarterly

Middlebury College
Middlebury VT 05753

Guidelines for Writers

New England Review and Bread Loaf Quarterly has a few requirements and suggestions:

1. Enclose an SASE that is large enough and carries enough U.S. postage to return your manuscript and our reply. If you don't need your ms. returned, just enclose a letter-size SASE or stamped postcard. Overseas contributors should enclose international reply-paid coupons. Please enclose an SASE with any query.

2. Our reading period is September 1 through May 31. Any submissions that arrive during the summer will be returned unread.

3. We suggest that you look at at least one sample issue (available from us for $4.00 each, post paid to U.S.) to see what our standards and preferences are. We publish short fiction--novellas, shorts, short-shorts, self-contained extracts from novels; long and short poems; general and literary, but not scholarly, essays; book reviews; screenplays; graphics; and translations.

4. With very few exceptions, we print only work that has not been published previously elsewhere.

5. For book reviews , we prefer reviews that discuss several books, and ask that each book be the first or second written in that genre by that author. This is in keeping with our commitment to younger and less established writers.

6. We have found it impractible to consider submissions that have been offered simultaneously to other publications, so please do not send us work that is also under consideration elsewhere.

7. It takes about 6-8 weeks for us to respond to your submission.

8. A contract is sent on acceptance, and payment is $5.00 per page, $10.00 minimum, plus two free copies and a free subscription. Authors proof the galleys. Copyright reverts to the author on publication. *NER/BLQ* retains the right under Copyright Law to reprint your work only as part of a whole volume--as for example, in a re-issue--or in publicity materials.

9. Manuscripts that are crisply and carefully typed in standard type on one side only of heavy white 8"x 11" bond paper, and with generous margins, are of course easier for us to read, but good photocopies, dot-matrix, or laser-printed materials are acceptable. Brief cover letters are useful.

10. We follow the Chicago Manual of Style and Webster's Dictionary, when appropriate.

NEW ENGLAND
SAMPLER

P.O. Box 306   Belfast ME 04915-0306

WRITER'S GUIDELINES

The Sampler is a labor of love, published for those who share our affection for New England and its heritage. As with many small presses, our staff works on a volunteer basis. Contributors are paid in copies and receive by-line credits with all published work. We acquire one-time rights only, so all manuscripts, photographs and art work remain the property of the author/artist and may be resubmitted elsewhere at any time. Send fiction, articles, artwork and photographs to VIRGINIA M. RIMM, EDITOR at address above. See "POETRY" (next page) for poetry submissions.

Our first issue appeared in August, 1980. Our goals were to build the finest New England regional we could within our budgetary constraints, and promote quality writing for the family audience. We select for publication those manuscripts of professional caliber that best portray the New England spirit. Since 1983 we've been ranked annually by Writer's Digest among the top ten U.S. markets for fiction in our class of non-paying magazines. We're proud of that rating. In 1984 we founded our Annual Creative Writing Contest with $500 in prizes for poetry and fiction (entry deadline is June 15; send LSASE for entry form and details).

WHAT KIND OF MATERIAL DO WE WANT?

We solicit optimistic, upbeat stories that reflect the traditional moral and spirtual values of New England. Problems or hardships must be resolved in a positive, constructive manner that respects the rights of others. Articles or stories glamorizing drugs, alcohol, affairs, etc. are innapropriate.

Our subscribers like to read about self-reliant, resourceful New Englanders who live creatively, not as despairing drop-outs but as giving members of an admittedly troubled society. We feature people from the past who helped shape this historic corner of America and exemplify the qualities associated with it, and their modern-day counterparts - people of vision who care little about material gain but accomplish much on a personal or spiritual level, who confront life with humor and courage, are compassionate, or surmount obstacles or hardships through inner strength or faith.

But don't be maudlin or syrupy. Our subscribers include teachers, doctors, psychologists, lawyers, farmers, housewives, craftspeople and blue collar workers. They have strong ties to rural New England but are discerning readers who want credible, realistic characters and situations.

SUBJECT MATTER

Our Yankee forebears were a breed apart - rugged individualists who fended for themselves without benefit of government dole. We believe that our survival as a nation hinges on reviving their kind of resourcefulness and adaptability. We need material aimed at the over-30 reader which focuses on these qualities or evokes respect for our New England heritage. Articles and fiction must be tightly written and well-paced with strong general interest and a distinct New England flavor, but while we tend toward the homespun and folksy we avoid a too-colloquial style which talks down to our readers. Above all keep in mind that we're a NEW ENGLAND regional - we don't use material set elsewhere.

We print one or two short stories per issue, but our greatest need (and your best chance of breaking in) is NON-fiction. We want personality sketches on unique individuals (past and present); regional lore; features on historic places and events, unusual family traditions, rural or small-town living; articles on old-time craftsmen; tales of neighbor helping neighbor; humor (subtle, not slapstick); holistic living. Our nature articles are staff-written.

We try to preserve the old-time knowledge of folk medicines, wild edible foods, energy conservation and other basic survival skills. But we want this material woven into the background of anecdotal or nostalgic stories such as "An Old-Time Log Cabin Raising", "The Day Grandpa Brought Home The Bees", "Before Aspirin There Was Chamomile", etc. Such lore should be presented as an integral part of a people-oriented story, not as factual, how-to pieces.

Beyond this, though, we seek to preserve our heritage of personal ingenuity. We want no stories on government-funded or government-initiated projects. "Big Brother" has no place on our pages. We're interested only in old-fashioned grass roots gumption long associated with crusty, independent New England country-folk.

SPECIAL DEPARTMENTS

OFF THE BEATEN PATH: 500-1000 word upbeat photo-essays on lesser known points of interest in New England, preferably rural or small city, written from the reader's perspective rather than as a personal experience item. Include ample selection of black & white photos (see PHOTOGRAPHS for specific requirements).

OF THINGS THAT GO BUMP: true first-person accounts (200-1500 words) of mysterious or paranormal happenings in New England: pre-cognitive dreams, telepathy, clairvoyance, hauntings, etc. Must be presented in a solid, low-key manner. Names witheld upon request but must be included on m/s along with address and telephone number for verification if needed.

LIFE BACK THEN: excerpts from old New England journals or diaries, true tales based on such diaries, or first-person accounts of growing up in New England forty or more years ago. Maximum length 1500 words, snapshot-type photos welcome. Writing here does NOT have to be on a professional level; our primary interest here is to convey the flavor of rural living in earlier times.

OTHER NEEDS

POETRY: 3-6 poems per month for our Poetry Nook, edited by Arnold Perrin. We want readable, understandable poetry of professional quality in either traditional or modern forms. We seldom use avant-garde which we feel must be hauntingly moving to carry, and poetry too obscure in meaning is not used. We occasionally publish inspirational poetry but do not accept sermons in verse or ideological poems. Poetry should relate to New England, nature, family relationships or friendship (no erotic or romantic poems). Maximum length 30 lines, shorter preferred. Send all poetry submissions to: ARNOLD PERRIN, NES POETRY EDITOR, RFD 1 Box 390, Warren, ME 04864. (Sample copy or guideline requests should be sent to our Belfast address.)

FICTION: We use 1 or 2 quality short stories per issue. They must be plausible and tightly plotted (or have a coherent theme), with carefully drawn characters who display a realistic mix of strengths and flaws and have some dimension. Sexual themes, erotica, pointless violence, profanity etc. are taboo. Mystery, suspense, humor, adventure, historical and nature stories are welcome, also an occasional light romance or fantasy (but these must be outstanding). Preferred length 2000-3500 words; outstanding longer works are sometimes serialized.

NON-FICTION: This is your best chance at breaking in. We can't get enough quality non-fiction manuscripts. So write about rural or small-town New England in sparkling, down-to-earth style and your chance of acceptance is excellent; add a few black & white photos and it is virtually assured. Concentrate on the human interest angle and give insights into lesser-known aspects of New England's history and culture. Nostalgia, historical pieces, travel, interesting people (past or present), gardening, our seafaring heritage, outdoor activities, personal experience with strong general interest. Maximum 3500 words, no essays or "think" pieces.

ART: We use pen and ink drawings for fillers and feature illustrations. Typical fillers include rural or farm scenes, flowers, animals, landscapes, trees, etc. Features appear on our front cover or illustrate specific articles. The latter are by assignment unless submitted with the article itself. Before we give assignments we need photocopied samples of your work for our files and an indication of the type of illustrating you prefer, e.g. cartoons, faces, people, landscapes. Submit line drawings proportionally reduceable to a 6" x 9" page or a 2 1/2" wide single column; photocopies preferred for initial submission to protect you from possible loss of or damage to your originals.

PHOTOGRAPHS: We need professional quality black & white glossy photos up to 5x7" size with good contrast for feature and filler illustrations. Photos must be simple and uncluttered with strong visual impact and appeal: New England scenics, humorous shots, human interest pix, animals, children, farm or rural scenes, etc. Photos must be well composed and razor-sharp with descriptive cutlines. We use vertical and horizontal pix (more vertical than horizontal) and like to see a good mix of close-up and distance photos taken at interesting angles.

LITERATURE AND FINE ARTS

Wright State University
006 University Center
Dayton, Ohio 45435
513/873-2031

Guidelines for All Submissions

Nexus is Wright State University's student-run magazine of the creative arts. Now in its 23rd year, *Nexus* publishes three quarterly issues. Submission deadlines are in October, February, and April. The author/artist of each accepted work receives five copies of the magazine. All rights revert to the author/artist upon publication. Submissions should be titled, and separate envelopes should be used for work of different categories.

The name and address of the author/artist should be typed or legibly printed on the back of each page or piece of artwork. A two- to five-line biography should be included. Wright State students should list an Allyn Hall student mailbox number and a home phone number.

Each submission should include a stamped, self-addressed envelope of sufficient size and with sufficient postage to allow the work to be returned. Wright State student fiction, plays, and poetry will be returned via Allyn Hall mailboxes (no postage is required).

Nexus sponsors a contest in the spring issue which is open to current Wright State students. Other works may also be printed in that issue. Winners are chosen from student work that is published throughout the academic year. To enter, Wright State student status must be specified, and the social security number must be provided. *Nexus* staff members and their families are ineligible. All decisions are final.

Guidelines for Fiction, Plays, and Poetry

All fiction, plays, and poetry must be neatly typed. Dot matrix, photocopied, and simultaneous submissions are acceptable. Please submit no more than one short story, one play, *or* six poems per envelope. Each poem should be on a separate page. Fiction and plays of about 1,500 words are preferred, but longer and shorter works will be considered.

Guidelines for Photography and Artwork

All work should be suitable for black-and-white printing. Subjects of full tonal range are preferred for best reproduction. Slides and negatives will not be considered. Please submit no more than four pieces of work at a time. The title of the work and a description of the medium (for example, ink drawing, intaglio, photo composite, etc.) should be typed or legibly printed on the back of each item with an arrow to indicate the top edge.

Sample Copies

To receive a sample copy of the most recent issue of *Nexus*, visit the office or send a self-addressed, 9x12-inch envelope with five first-class stamps for each copy. Some back issues are also available. Mailed requests should include a $2 handling fee for the first copy and a $1 fee for each additional copy. Make checks payable to WSU Foundation. *Nexus* is available to any little magazine or small press on an exchange basis.

Nimrod

is an international fiction and poetry journal, now in its 30th year of publication. From its inception, *Nimrod* has been dedicated to discovering new and dynamic voices, voices that stimulate new insights in readers.

For the past decade, *Nimrod* has annually sponsored the Katherine Anne Porter Prize for Fiction: a $1,000 cash prize for the first-place winner and a $500 cash prize for second place.

This is our invitation to you to enter *Nimrod's* annual literary prize competition, and to join writers like Tess Gallagher, Denise Levertov, Pablo Neruda, and Isaac Bashevis Singer, all of whom have contributed to *Nimrod* throughout the past 30 years.

CONTEST RULES

1. DEADLINE: Submissions must be postmarked NO LATER THAN APRIL 1.

2. Only one submission per author.

*3. No minimum length; 7500 words maximum.

4. No previously published works, works accepted for publication, or dual submissions are eligible.

4. AUTHOR'S NAME MUST **NOT** APPEAR ON THE MANUSCRIPT! Submissions should be accompanied by a cover sheet containing the title of the work and the author's name and address. The title of the work should also appear on the first page of the manuscript.

5. "CONTEST ENTRY" should be clearly indicated on both the outer envelope and the cover sheet.

6. Manuscripts should be typed and double spaced.

7. MANUSCRIPTS WILL **NOT** BE RETURNED. Author should submit **TWO** PHOTOCOPIES of the manuscript for judging. Include a self-addressed, stamped envelope for notification of acceptance or rejection. (If you want to be notified of receipt of manuscript, also include a self-addressed, stamped post card.)

8. **NIMROD requires first refusal rights on all submissions.** All entries not officially accepted for publication will be released to their authors within six weeks after the contest results are announced. Contest winners will be announced in June.

9. Winning entries will be published in either the Fall/Winter or the Spring/Summer issue of *Nimrod*. Winners will be brought to Tulsa for a reading and the presentation of the prize; domestic airfare will be paid by *Nimrod*.

10. **ENTRY FEE:** $10.00, for which you will receive a copy of NIMROD to familiarize yourself with our magazine.

SUBSCRIPTIONS to NIMROD — $10/one yr., $18/two yr., $26/three yr., 2 issues per year — are eagerly accepted, or you may, of course, become a contributor to NIMROD for $25 or more. (See subscription form)

13. **Be sure to follow our rules; submissions which do not meet all requirements will not be considered for the competition.**

* *NIMROD reserves the right to withhold the prize in any one year.*

PAST WINNERS

Past prize winners include Carolyne Wright of Seattle, Washington; Regina deCormier-Shekerjian of New Paltz, New York; Don Welch of Kearney, Nebraska; Jane Vandenburgh of San Francisco, California; John Hildebidle of Boston, Massachusetts; Merna Summers of Edmonton, Canada; Carol Haralson of Tulsa, Oklahoma; Kathleen Lignell of Orono, Maine; and Anne Forer of New York City.

KATHERINE ANNE PORTER PRIZE FOR FICTION
First Prize $1000, Second Prize $500

NIMROD
International Journal of Fiction & Poetry
A Publication of the Arts and Humanities Council of Tulsa.
Published twice a year. Founded in 1956.

Send manuscripts to:
NIMROD
Literary Contest—Fiction or Poetry
Arts & Humanities Council of Tulsa
2210 S. Main Street
Tulsa, Oklahoma 74114

*T*he National Novella Award is an annual award of $2,500 plus publication for the best novella-length manuscript. Cosponsored by the Arts and Humanities Council of Tulsa (publisher of *Nimrod* literary magazine) and Council Oak Books, the National Novella Award has been established in recognition of the novella's increasing importance in contemporary literature. The Award winner will be published in quality trade paperback by Council Oak Books and distributed and promoted nationally. The winning writer will be the guest of the Arts and Humanities Council of Tulsa for a reception and reading in the spring of 1989 when the book is published. Council Oak will facilitate an author's tour to promote sales of the book.

The author will receive a $2,500 cash prize and a standard royalty on book sales.

Contest Rules:

1. DEADLINE: Submissions must be postmarked no later than December 31.

2. Each entry must be a single work of fiction, 18,000 to 40,000 words in length. No previously published work or works already accepted for publication may be submitted.

3. If the novella is accepted for publication elsewhere, the author must notify the National Novella Award committee immediately.

4. Author's name must not appear on the manuscript. Submissions should be accompanied by a cover sheet containing the title of the work and the author's name and address. The title of the work should also appear on the first page of the novella.

5. "Novella Contest Entry" should be clearly indicated on both the outer envelope and the cover sheet.

6. Manuscripts should be typed and double-spaced. Author should submit two photocopies of the novella for judging.

7. Manuscripts will be returned only if a self-addressed envelope with sufficient postage is enclosed. (If you want to be notified of receipt of manuscript, also include a self-addressed, stamped postcard.)

8. The Contest winner will be announced in May. Non-winning entries will be released to their authors within six weeks of announcement of the Contest winner.*

9. The winning entry will be published in the spring and at that time the author will be brought to Tulsa for a reading and reception in conjunction with the publication.

10. Entry Fee: $10 per submission.

* The National Novella Award committee reserves the right to withhold the prize in any one year.

Send manuscripts to:

The National Novella Award
Arts and Humanities Council of Tulsa
2210 South Main
Tulsa, Oklahoma 74114

```
NORTH DAKOTA QUARTERLY
Box 8237
University of North Dakota
Grand Forks, ND 58202
```

Quality fiction, any style, up to 7500 words but preferably under 5000 words.

Simultaneous submissions OK.

NORTHWEST REVIEW

WRITERS' GUIDELINES

NORTHWEST REVIEW is published tri-annually, and invites submissions of previously unpublished poetry, fiction, essays, interviews, book reviews and artwork. Artists and authors of reviews are encouraged to query before sending their work. Manuscripts are considered year-round.

1. The only criterion for acceptance of material for publication in Northwest Review is that of excellence.

2. No simultaneous submissions will be considered.

3. A self-addressed, stamped envelope (SASE) must accompany every submission. If submitting both poetry and fiction, please send in separate envelopes, with separate SASE's.

4. There are no length restrictions, but fiction in excess of 30 pages will be at a disadvantage.

5. The author's name and address should appear on each poem, and on the cover page of each story submitted. The author's name should appear on each page of his or her story.

6. We try to respond within six to eight weeks. Payment (unless grant money comes available for this purpose) is in contributor's copies. Potential contributors are encouraged to subscribe to any magazine that they respect enough to want to have their work appear therein. Magazines such as Northwest Review have no institutional funding, and depend for their survival on their subscribers.

7. We encourage you to study a recent issue of Northwest Review. These are made available to authors at the discounted price of $2.50.

396 PLC, University of Oregon, Eugene, OR 97403 (503) 686-3957

PUBLISHERS SYNDICATION INT'L.

1377 K STREET N.W. SUITE 856 ■ WASHINGTON, D.C. 20005

Novelettes

GUIDELINES

EDITOR: A. P. Samuels

Pays on acceptance plus royalty...Byline given...Reports in 4 to 6 weeks...SASE required for return.

Will buy first time manuscripts if good enough. Photocopies okay. No simultaneous submissions please. We prefer letter quality printing.

NOVELETTES

ROMANCE: 30,000 words...buy 12 a year.

MYSTERY: 30,000 words...12 a year.

MISCELLANEOUS SUBJECTS: 30,000 words...submit manuscript...12 a year.

RATE: 3/4 to 3 cents per word on acceptance.

Show word count on your submissions.

COMPUTER: If you use a computer please specify kind, disk size, density and the name of the word processing program you are using. In some cases we may request disk copy of your story.

EDITORS NOTE: The type of mystery we are looking for is devoid of references which might offend. (Sherlock Holmes would be a good example of the type of stories we require.)

Romances should not include explicit sex. Remember you are writing for a general audience.
10/13/87

DUGENT PUBLISHING CORP.
2355 Salzedo St., Coral Gables, Florida 33134/(305) 443-2378

Nugget   GUIDELINES FOR WRITERS

DUGENT PUBLISHING CORP. publishes three magazines, Cavalier, Gent and Nugget. We buy all fiction and articles from freelance writers. Each magazine has its own editorial slant and a description of each magazine's special needs follows:

CAVALIER is a sophisticated men's magazine aimed at the 18 to 35 year old male. We feature beautiful girls and entertaining fiction and articles. Stories must be professionally written and presented (first-timers welcome) and articles must be carefully researched and documented, if necessary. Subject matter for both stories and articles can vary from serious to sex to humor, keeping our readership in mind.

FICTION: We buy all types of fiction -- all kinds of plots, but they must be well-plotted and exceptionally well written. We are looking for good, solid stories...no intellectual or obtuse exercises and no poetry. We prefer at least one very graphic and erotic sexual encounter in each story and we are also interested in scenes of girl/girl fighting, or boy/girl fighting within the context of a story whether it is murder, science fiction, sex, horror or whatever. Length: 1,500 to 3,500 words. Pay from $200 to $300.

ARTICLES: Also cover a wide range but within the restriction that it must be a subject of interest to our readers, not dated material (since we have a four month lead time) and, preferably, that it be on a subject that is somewhat off-beat and not something that will be extensively covered by the media nationally. Please query first with a brief but comprehensive outline. First time writers may be asked to submit the finished article on speculation, but we give firm assignments to regular contributors. Where necessary, material must be carefully researched and documented. We are not interested in expose type articles, politics, historical figures or current events unless different and off-beat. Pay is similar to fiction but we pay additional for photos if submitted with article (and if professional and appropriate) and length is the same as for fiction. Our most urgent need is for non-fiction and we welcome beginners.

GENT: Specializes pictorially in large D-cup cheesecake and prefers both fiction and non-fiction articles gauged to the subject of breasts, bras, fat women, lactation, etc. Fictional female characters should be described as extremely large busted with detailed descriptions of breasts. Fiction length can vary from 2,500 to 3,500 words. Articles from 1,500 to 3,000 words. Payment is from $125 to $150 (with more for specialized material and articles with photos) upon publication. Query first on non-fiction articles, with brief comprehensive outline.

NUGGET: This magazine is primarily concerned with offbeat, fetish oriented material (sado-masochism, TV, TS, B&D,WS, amputees, fetishism, etc) and we prefer both fiction and articles slanted to this variety of subjects. Payment, length, etc., same as GENT magazine. Query first on articles.

WE DO NOT PUBLISH material on minors, religious subjects or on characters or subjects that might be considered libelous. Interviews (query first) must be accompanied by permission of the interviewee and supporting documentation. ALWAYS enclose self addressed stamped envelope for returns.

Oak Square
THE SHORT FICTION QUARTERLY

Guidelines

About Oak Square

We publish short fiction, non-political essays, interviews, photographs and illustrations. Imagine your reader as someone who'd like to finish a story during the course of a subway ride. Imagine also that s/he'd rather read your story than *People* magazine. Distribution is through subscriptions and bookstores, mostly in the Boston area.

General Guidelines

Be sure your submission includes your name, address, and telephone number on the first page. Your name should appear on subsequent pages. Include a self-addressed stamped envelope if you want your work returned. We will consider work without a SASE, but we will not return it. If you are submitting the same work to someone else, or if the work has appeared in another publication, let us know so we can avoid conflicts.

Fiction and Poetry

We specialize in short fiction. Submissions must be under 4000 words; preferred length is 2500 words. Manuscripts should be typed, doubled spaced. Place name, address, telephone number and **word count** on first page; name on succeeding pages. Dot matrix and clean copies are OK.

We publish a small amount of poetry.

Photographs & Illustrations

We publish black and white photographs and illustrations. We handle all material with reasonable care, but we cannot be responsible for material damaged in the mail. Be sure you protect your work with stiff cardboard and mark the package "Do Not Bend." Be sure the packing material can be used to return your work.

Essays

We are interested in literate, well-informed essays. Suggested topics include fiction and literary themes, modern life, the impact of technology. We are not interested in "How To" articles or political essays.

Interviews

Interviews can be about anyone interesting. Artists and writers are obvious choices, but don't restrict yourself to them. We will accept unsolicited interviews, but we prefer that you query first. There is no kill fee.

Payment

We pay contributors in copies. Number of copies varies with the kind of work.

Rights

We "buy" first and second serial rights. All rights revert to you upon publication. We do not buy the copyright to your work, merely the right to publish it. This right and any other rights revert to you upon publication.

Reporting time

We generally report within three months.

Contacts

Publisher: Philip Borenstein / Fiction: Anne E. Pluto / Poetry & Art: Scott Getchell
Oak Square Publications
Box 1238
Allston, MA 02134

BOX 1238 · ALLSTON MA · 02134

OMNI

OMNI PUBLICATIONS INTERNATIONAL LTD., 1965 BROADWAY, NEW YORK, NY 10023-5965. 212-496-6100

WRITERS' GUIDELINES: FICTION

We want to intrigue our readers with mind-broadening, thought-provoking stories that will excite their sense of wonder. We are looking, therefore, for literate, strongly plotted science fiction stories on a variety of subjects and themes. However, since many of our readers are not familiar with technical jargon, the stories must be written in clear, understandable prose. And characterization, moreover, is crucial.

Our minimum story length is 2,000 words, maximum 10,000. Payment: $1250-2,000.

Keep in mind that we do not publish sword and sorcery, space opera, supernatural stories, or poetry. For an idea of the kinds of stories we do publish, read some recent issues.

We will read dot-matrix computer printouts only if they are readable and do not tax the eyes. If you choose to submit photocopies they, too, must be clear and readable. Be sure to include an appropriately-sized self-addressed, stamped envelope (SASE) with your submission. (Contributors residing outside the United States should use international response coupons.) Manuscripts without an SASE will not be returned.

It's impossible for us to judge a story's quality based on a proposal. We need to see the complete manuscript. If you have a story you think fits our requirements, submit it for our consideration. But, please, do not send more than one story at a time; wait for a response on one before submitting another. And do not send us simultaneous submissions; we will not even read a story under consideration elsewhere.

If you have a self-contained short story that may later be developed into a novel, or a part of a novel, you may submit that, as well. Full-length novel manuscripts for serialization or excerpt consideration, however, should be submitted by the author's publisher or agent.

We usually respond within three to five weeks after we receive a submission, occasionally sooner. Depending on numerous variables, however, it can sometimes take longer. Please give us ample time before you begin writing or calling to inquire about a submission's status.

Ellen Datlow
Fiction Editor

General Guidelines

Manuscripts must be typewritten on 8 ½ × 11 white paper, double-spaced on one side of the sheet only. (Computer printout also acceptable.) Enter your name and address in the upper left-hand corner, and the approximate number of words (and character count, if known) in the upper right-hand corner. All manuscripts must be accompanied by a self-addressed stamped envelope (SASE). Seasonal material should be submitted six months in advance. Book reviews are to follow the guidelines and form provided for their report.

Manuscripts will be read as promptly as possible and returned or purchased upon acceptance. We purchase one-time rights only.

We seek to treat each manuscript carefully, but urge that the author keep a copy for personal reference. While we respect the writer's style and purpose, we reserve the right to edit the copy to fit our literary standards. If major content changes are necessary, the editor will send a revised manuscript to the author for approval.

Rates of payment vary among the magazines. The quality of the material and the relative need for it also affect the rate. Contact editor about specific questions. Generally payment is made upon acceptance of manuscript. Payment for a book review is the book reviewed. Maximum rates for one-time use, $50.00 per thousand words. Payment for reprints is one half of one-time rights.

On the Line

Editor: Virginia A. Hostetler
Audience: children, ages 10-14—copublished with the General Conference Mennonite Church
Focus: story paper that reinforces Christian values
Frequency: monthly in weekly parts

The goal of *On the Line* is to help juniors grow in their understanding and appreciation of God, the created world, themselves, and other people. *On the Line* uses materials that

- Help readers feel they are persons of worth
- Help juniors in handling problem areas of life
- Encourage children to live up to their potential
- Introduce juniors to the wonders of God's world—nature, art, music, poetry, and human relationships
- Help juniors accept people of other races and cultures as their equals
- Nurture in readers a desire for world peace and provide tools for practicing peaceful living
- Make the message of the Bible attractive to juniors
- Help children grow toward a personal commitment to Christ and the church
- Help Mennonite juniors appreciate both their Christian heritage and Mennonite traditions and current activities of the church

Needed are articles and stories 500-1,000 words in length. Also puzzles, quizzes, appropriate verse from 3 to 24 lines, and professional quality 8 × 10 photos.

WHEN YOU WRITE

For the personal reading and leadership magazines of the Mennonite Publishing House

Mennonite Publishing House
616 Walnut Avenue
Scottdale, PA 15683-1999
Telephone 412-887-8500

GUIDELINES FOR CONTRIBUTING TO "ORBEN'S CURRENT COMEDY"

We are looking for material that can be used by speakers and
toastmasters. Lines for beginning a speech, ending a speech,
acknowledging an introduction, introducing specific occupations,
special occasions, roasts, responding to a roast, retirement
dinners -- anything that would be of use to a person making
a speech.

We also use material that would be of interest to the business
speaker and to those in advertising, public relations and
communications. Such material could be lines to be used at sales
meetings, presentations, conventions, seminars and conferences.
Short, sharp comment on business trends, management problems,
sales tactics and approaches, is also desirable.

We are also a market for funny, performable one-liners, short
jokes and stories that are related to happenings in the news,
fads, trends, topical and seasonal subjects. The accent is on
laugh-out-loud comedy. Ask yourself: "Will this line get a
laugh if performed in public -- and if you were a speaker, would
you have enough confidence in it to perform it?" Material should
be written in a conversational style and if the joke permits it,
the inclusion of dialogue is a plus.

Please DO NOT send us material that is primarily written to be
read rather than spoken. We do not want definitions, epigrams,
puns or poems. Please do not send us sexist or stereotype jokes.
We prefer material with an upbeat point of view.

Most important of all - the submissions MUST be original. One
old joke makes the rest of the material suspect. If items are
sent to us that we find to be copied or rewritten from newspaper
columns, jokebooks, magazines, TV or radio shows, comedy acts, etc.
-- or any source other than the contributor's own talent and
creativity -- we will no longer consider further material from
him or her.

If you enclose a stamped, self-addressed #10 size envelope,
unused material will be returned to you within a few days.
WE DO NOT SEND REJECTION SLIPS. All other material will be
destroyed after being considered, except for items to be purchased
and used in our services.

We pay $8.00 for all rights to each item used. Payment is made
at the end of each month for material used in issues published
that month.

Material should be typed and submitted in legible form. You need
not double-space, make neat corrections, or worry about how pretty
it is -- but please leave a few spaces between each joke.

Material should be sent to: Robert Orben
                             1200 North Nash Street   #1122
                             Arlington, Virginia 22209

Now that you've come this far, PLEASE go back and reread the
specific instructions relating to what type of material we are
looking for. Please save time, effort and postage for all
concerned by only sending us material that is ORIGINAL and PERFORMABLE.

other voices

820 RIDGE ROAD · HIGHLAND PARK, ILLINOIS 60035 · 312/831-4684

FICTION WRITERS' GUIDELINES

1. Short Stories and self-contained novel excerpts only. 5000 wd. maximum preferred, but not mandatory.

2. Manuscripts must be typed clearly, double-spaced, 1½" margins. Last name in upper rt. hand corner, if possible.

3. No multiple submissions, please. We try to reply in 10-12 weeks.

4. No taboos, except ineptitude and murkiness.

5. SASE, of course.

SEND US YOUR BEST VOICE, YOUR BEST WORK, YOUR BEST BEST. At present, payment is in copies plus a modest cash gratutity.

OUR FAMILY

Box 249, Battleford, SK Canada S0M 0E0

FICTION REQUIREMENT GUIDE

Please send fiction submissions
to Fiction Editor,
John Patrick Gillese
10450 - 144 Street
Edmonton AB
T5N 2V4 Canada

We are actively in search of good fiction that will appeal particularly to the average family man and woman — 18-40 — of high school and early college education. Of course, both younger and older people read our publication. We have a diversified readership. But our "target" group is the 18-40 bracket.

There is no sure-fire formula for selling *Our Family* a story.

We can not say exactly what stories we are in search of until we see them. But we are interested in seeing more short fiction that honestly reflects the lives, problems and preoccupations of our readers.

However, our readership is composed of people who are interested in subjects other than themselves. And so we also want stories that will introduce them sympathetically to characters and cultures different from their own. We will use stories with a wide range of settings and characters — anything true to human nature.

We especially welcome stories that are hard-hitting and fast-moving, with a real "woven-in", not "tacked-on", Christian message. (No sentimentality or blatant moralizing.) We want honest observation, pace and emotional impact.

We do welcome stories which bring to life — even painfully to life — real human problems. However, since the Christian point of view presupposes that life has meaning and that no situation, no matter how bad, is without hope, we look especially for those two uplifting qualities in the stories submitted to us.

This does not mean that stories necessarily need a "happy ending." (In fact, we do not like stereotyped "happy-ending" stories.) It does mean that characters should be developed so as to portray the necessity of living with faith, hope and courage.

We also want stories that tell of a happy life. This is a difficult task for a writer to accomplish. Often, when a writer attempts to write about the sunny side of our life, the results are sentimental and untrue — told through the sugary smile of a Pollyanna or the jolly, jolly laugh of a Santa Claus that is as far from reality as the macabre horror of Frankenstein.

No subject is taboo — the good writer can treat "touchy" topics in an acceptable way. However, we will not accept stories which promote values contrary to the general Christian outlook; nor will we accept stories that would be offensive to the majority of people.

We do not want "true romance" stories, he-man adventure and spy stories, detective stories or science fiction. Nor do we want highly oblique or symbolic stories that reach no conclusion and have obviously contrived plots.

Since most of the material in our magazine has a present-day, modern-living orientation, we find it difficult to integrate the historical fiction form with the general content of the magazine. This same difficulty is experienced with regard to Biblical fiction. Therefore, historical fiction and Biblical fiction are rarely, if ever, used.

Generally, we prefer stories which are 2,500-3,000 words in length. Shorter stories of about 1,000 words are quite welcome. We will occasionally publish stories up to 5,000 words in length, but these are exceptions. Any length over 3,000 words begins to weigh against a manuscript.

We will give each manuscript submitted our honest consideration. We will make suggestions for revisions when we think there is a good chance such revisions will make the story suitable to our needs. However, we don't offer any general type of editorial guidance or evaluative reading service. We do not have the staff and time for this.

We ask writers not to be discouraged by a rejection from us. It simply means that that particular story was not suited to our needs. We have in fact bought stories from writers who had several previous rejections.

We try to return unacceptable manuscripts within four weeks. If two months have passed since a story was sent to us, the author may well inquire into its whereabouts. We keep a record of manuscripts submitted and will do our best to help you locate manuscripts which may have gone astray in the mail.

Authors with credits should list them, but no other covering letter is necessary. We appreciate neatly, double-spaced manuscripts. We will return a handwritten manuscript unread. We prefer a completed manuscript to a query letter. We pay 7-10 cents a word for original stories. (See payment rate on Writer's Guide.)

Attention U.S. and other non-Canadian authors: We suggest that you send your story in an envelope marked at First Class mail rates to expedite delivery. Manuscripts sent at Third and Fourth Class rates sometimes take several weeks to reach us.

Include a stamped, self-addressed envelope for return of unaccepted manuscripts.

NB: Canadian postage must be used on envelopes mailed in Canada. If you do not have Canadian stamps, you may enclose International Reply Coupon(s) or American currency or some other form of payment for return postage.

Envelopes with the wrong stamps or with insufficient payment for postage will be held until postage is provided. It is prohibitive for us to supply return postage for the many manuscripts with wrong stamps or insufficient postage.

A sample copy of *Our Family* is available for $2.50. (Covers cost of magazine & postage.)

OUTERBRIDGE

Charlotte Alexander, Editor

OUTERBRIDGE publishes poetry and short fiction. We look for craft and originality. Mini-features (themes within general issues) to date are: urban, rural, Southern, war, outsider feeling, childhood. Annual. Payment, two copies. $5.00.

The College of Staten Island   715 Ocean Terrace   Room A-324   Staten Island, New York 10301

Millea Kenin, Editor
1025 55th St., Oakland, CA 94608

UNIQUE GRAPHICS, Publisher
(415) 655-3024

GUIDELINES

We never use seasonal material due to our long lead time to publication. We read all year round; however, we are often overstocked with stories of certain lengths or themes. Query with a Self-Addressed Stamped Envelope (SASE) to find out what we are open for, and be sure to let us know you already have this guideline. If you have a specific story in mind, *don't* describe it in detail in your query—just mention its approximate length and whether it is science fiction, fantasy or fantastic horror.

SAMPLE COPY: $2.50 (back issue, $4.00 (current), postpaid, check or m.o. payable to Unique Graphics.

All material considered for publication must be science fiction or fantasy. We are interested in diversity of style and theme, from new-wave to sociological to high-tech sf, from surreal fantasy to sword-and-sorcery to supernatural horror to far-out humor. We're particularly looking for works that fall within the genre but outside the parameters of the commercial markets. Unless there is no conceivable commercial market, however, this should not be the first place a work is submitted; most of the stories published in **OWLFLIGHT** (whether by new writers or medium-sized "names") were rejected by commercial markets for reasons we and the authors felt were unrelated to their quality. *We are not a testing ground for those who feel unready for the pros.*

We are NOT interested in anything that promotes racism, sexism or any other form of bigotry, or that glorifies war, genocide or ecocide. Sex is welcome if intrinsic to the work; so is violence, but if the intention is erotic they should not be linked. We are also uninterested in material using characters or settings copyright by someone other than the submitter without the copyright holder's permission—in particular, no Star Trek or other media sf. If the intent is to parody, the work parodied should be familiar to most sf/fantasy readers, and the names, etc., should be changed, as should be names of any living persons referred to for parodistic reasons. Characters on which the copyright has lapsed are o.k. The same basic rules apply to visual representations of copyright characters.

Previously unpublished work is preferred, but material published outside the genre, outside North America, more than five years before submission and /or in an edition of 200 or less will be considered. Any previously published material must be accompanied by a statement of publication history and copyright date, as well as written permission from the copyright holder if other than the author, or a statement in good faith by the author that only one-time rights were sold to the copyright holder (since the latter may be a defunct and unreachable small press, for example).

Submissions may include originals or legible photocopies of manuscripts (please, no crude dot-matrix printouts—dots should be invisible to the average naked eye) and photocopies of black and white art or halftone (including photos). *Do not submit unsolicited original artwork or slides!!!* Except for poems with unusual formats, writing should be typed double-spaced. Author's name and address should appear on the first page of each work, and name and keyword from title on succeeding pages. With all photocopies, include a statement as to whether the submission is simultaneous; with art submissions, indicate whether they are samples for assignment or available for publication, and if the latter, whether you are interested in illustration assignments. One set of samples, to be retained in our files, is sufficient to have an artist considered for assignments illustrating any or all Unique Graphics publications.

If you wish your art or mss. returned, include a large enough SASE (Self-Addressed Stamped Envelope) with enough postage; if not, please enclosed a business size SASE for our reply. Be sure your name and return address appears on the ms. or art itself, not just the envelopes and cover letter. While cover letters are not necessary except to give information we have requested elsewhere in this guideline, brief ones are always welcome, including information about yourself or the information about yourself or the submissions that we should know; lengthy credit sheets or descriptions of an enclosed story are not. Unless the story you wish to submit is over 10,000 words or is a graphic story, when you query to find out if we are open in a given length or theme category, do not give specific details about the story.

(Canadian writers, please note: if you can't get U.S. stamps, enclose detached Canadian ones, which will be traded for U.S. stamps with U.S. writers needing SASES for submissions to Canada. International Reply Coupons are a ripoff. Overseas contributors will have to use them, unfortunately.)

TERMS

We report within a day or two on queries, within a month or less on submissions, though the report may be a request to let us hold the submission longer before deciding. If this is the case, we try hard to specify a date by which the decision will be made and to stick to it.

OWLFLIGHT is copyright and all rights revert to the creator on publication. Payment is as follows: for writing, one cent per word, $1.00 minimum; for art, $5 to $15 depending on reproduction size. The full amount or $10, whichever is smaller, will be paid on acceptance, balance on publication, along with one to three copies of the issue in which the work appears. If a work is not published within the period specified in the letter of acceptance or contract (which may be as long as two years), the creator may withdraw it at any time thereafter on two months' written notice, keeping the payment received as a kill fee. Contributors may also order additional copies of any issue in which their work appears at cost, and/or take any part of the money owed them in the form of double its value in credit on Unique Graphics publications, on acceptance or at any time thereafter prior to cash payment.

WRITING NEEDS

OWLFLIGHT consists mainly of fiction and some poetry that fit the general guidelines above. Preferred length for fiction is 3,000 to 8,000 words; longer and shorter work can be considered when we aren't overstocked with it. Preferred length for poems is 8 to 100 lines; groups of shorter works such as haiku or quatrains are also considered. All forms and styles are welcome. Longer poems are more likely to be accepted if they tell a story, and narrative poems are particularly welcome at any length.

We'd also like very much to see plays (same lengths as fiction) and songs, including original camera-ready sheet music, with sf and fantasy themes. We use occasional speculative science articles and humorous "non-fact" articles, but not reviews, letters or criticism. We also use graphic stories with sf/fantasy themes (see "art needs" below, as they must be submitted in camera-ready format), especially ones that fall outside comics publishers' formats; however, our space for these is limited.

ART NEEDS

Black and white art (can include black areas and/or fine detail) or halftones (e.g. wash, pencil, art photos), black & white collages, etc. Samples for assignments or freelance submissions of spot illos. Cartoons. Graphic stories of one to six pages with 7x10" image areas. See general guidelines for themes, submission procedures.

PANDORA AUTHOR GUIDELINES

Dear PANDORA Contributor,

PANDORA is a science fiction and speculative fantasy magazine, and is role-expanding. This means that we try to be non-sexist, non-racist, and non-stereotyped. Like all magazines, we are looking for fresh, well-written stories.

PANDORA is published twice a year and has a constant need for stories under 5000 words long. We print stories up to twice that long, especially for the "Only PANDORA Can Print" feature, but you will increase your chances of both sales and early publication if your story is shorter. We do not print stories that exist only for the sake of a pun, nor do we print x-rated material, or retellings of the Adam and Eve story.

Stories should be typed in standard manuscript format, and accompanied by a self-addressed stamped envelope. Staff will read dot-matrix printed manuscript on 8 1/2" x 11" white paper if matrix is easily read by the human eye. Please avoid matrices designed for machine scanning, where "g" and "y" have no tails, etc. They are very difficult to read. Also please use double-strike, emphasized, NLQ, or whatever way your printer has of making the print easier to read.

We buy three or four poems for each issue, and are currently (Fall, 1986) able to say we are not overstocked. That situation never lasts long. Please send no more than three poems at one time. We cannot use epic-length or even story-length poems. Be sure to enclose a stamped, self-addressed envelope.

If you still have questions, feel free to write and ask, but staff cannot judge a story from a plot-synopsis, a telephone call, or a sample page. Send the whole thing.

Send fiction to Susan Ross Moore
            1115 North Indiana Avenue
            Kokomo, IN   46901

Send poetry to Ruth Berman
            2809 Drew Ave. S.
            Minneapolis, MN   55416

Allow four weeks for response. If we keep your story longer it is under serious consideration. If you remembered to enclose a SASE and it's not back in your hands or you have had no other response from us in three months, please query.

For a sample copy of PANDORA, please send $3.50 to Empire Books
                                    PO Box 625
                                    Murray, KY   42071

SEND SUBSCRIPTIONS, ADDRESS CHANGES, AND ORDERS FOR BACK ISSUES OR SAMPLE COPIES TO THE EMPIRE BOOKS ADDRESS IN KENTUCKY.

© 1987 by Pandora Magazine

PANGLOSS PAPERS
Box 18917
Los Angeles, Calif.90018

The reason for little mags to exist
is to stretch convention and bend it
into new forms. Stale authority,
wornout words, and self-promoting
showmanship are the proper targets
for the independent writer.

Our freedom hangs on not having to
make a profit. In fact, we give our
mag away, depending on other financing
to continue. We also eschew grants,
prizes, and other threats to indepen-
dence.

We add one more ingredient by asking
that writing be grounded in reality,
commenting on the terms of our existence.
If the choice has to be between muckraking and literary acrobatics, we
prefer muckraking.

THE PARIS REVIEW

541 EAST 72 STREET

NEW YORK, N. Y. 10021

UN. 1-0016

SUBMISSION OF MANUSCRIPTS

Fiction manuscripts should be submitted to George Plimpton; poetry to Jonathan Galassi c/o The Paris Review, 541 East 72nd Street, New York, NY, 10021. We regret that we are not responsible for manuscripts not accompanied by stamped, self-addressed envelopes. Material must be in English and previously unpublished. Translations are acceptable and should be accompanied by a copy of the original text. A cover letter is not necessary. We suggest to all who submit that they read through several issues of The Paris Review to acquaint themselves with the material that we publish.

Copies of The Paris Review are available in many public libraries. Sample copies may be ordered from the Flushing office (45-39 171 Place, Flushing, NY, 11358) for $6.50 per copy, including postage and handling, or $16.00 for a one year subscription (four issues).

THE AGA KHAN PRIZE FOR FICTION

The Aga Khan Prize for Fiction is awarded annually by the editors of The Paris Review for the best previously unpublished short story submitted. Manuscripts must be a minimum of 1,000 words and a maximum of 10,000 words. All work should be submitted between May 1st and June 1st. The winning selection will be announced in the fall issue. The winning manuscript, awarded $1,000, will be published in the following issue of The Paris Review. Please address to Aga Khan Prize for Fiction c/o The Paris Review, 541 East 72nd Street, New York, NY, 10021. No formal application form is required; regular submission guidelines apply. Submissions should be limited to one per envelope.

THE BERNARD F. CONNERS PRIZE FOR POETRY

The Bernard F. Conners Prize for Poetry is awarded annually by the editors of The Paris Review for the finest unpublished poem over 200 lines submitted. All work should be submitted between April 1st and May 1st. The winning selection will be announced in the fall issue. The winning manuscript, awarded $1,000, will be published in the following issue of The Paris Review. Please address to the Poetry Editor/B. F. Connors Prize c/o The Paris Review, 541 East 72nd Street, New York, NY, 10021. No formal application form is required; regular submission guidelines apply. Submissions should be limited to one per envelope.

THE JOHN TRAIN HUMOR PRIZE

The John Train Humor Prize is awarded annually for the best previously unpublished work of humorous fiction, nonfiction, or poetry. Manuscripts must be less than 10,000 words and should be received by March 31st. The winning manuscript, awarded $1,500, will be published in The Paris Review. Please address to The John Train Humor Prize c/o The Paris Review, 541 East 72nd Street, New York, NY, 10021. No formal application form is required; regular submission guidelines apply. Submissions should be limited to one per envelope.

141 Bay State Road
Boston, Massachusetts 02215
(617) 353-4260

WRITERS GUIDELINES FOR UNSOLICITED MANUSCRIPTS

As we have no specific editorial requirements, we suggest
you read some past issues of the magazine to get a sense
of our style and subject matter.

We read all unsolicited submissions of poetry, fiction,
and essays as long as they are accompanied by a self-
addressed stamped envelope. Photocopies are acceptable.
Fiction generally runs twenty-five manuscript pages or
less. Poetry of any length. We do not print art work
of any kind. Name and address of author should appear
on each page of manuscript. PLEASE ALLOW THREE TO FOUR
MONTHS REPORTING TIME before making inquiries regarding
the status of your manuscript. Manuscripts will not
be returned unless accompanied by a SASE.

Our policy is only to publish work which has not appeared
elsewhere. We reserve the right to reject an accepted
manuscript if it should be published elsewhere prior to
our publication date.

Sample copies are available by request for $5.00.
Write to: Partisan Review Subscriptions
           Norman Wells
           Office of Publications
           Boston University
           985 Commonwealth Avenue
           Boston, MA 02215

passages north

William Bonifas Fine Arts Center
7th Street and 1st Avenue South
Escanaba, Michigan 49829
Phone (906) 786-3833

GUIDELINES FOR WRITERS

The purpose of *Passages North* is two-fold:

* to stimulate and recognize writing of high quality in the Northern Michigan and Upper Midwestern region

* to bring to the same region writing of high quality from other parts of the state and nation.

The Bay Arts Writers' Guild, composed of experienced writers and instructors, serves as an editorial panel for submissions. Individual tastes of our members vary, but high quality is a common goal. "High quality," of course, may seem a matter of opinion. By this phrase *Passages North* means writing that aspires to be good literature, rather than purely popular or commercial reading. Contributors should be aware of what is happening in contemporary poetry and fiction. They should strive for writing that makes readers see, imagine, and experience.

MANUSCRIPTS

Passages North uses primarily poetry and short fiction. Fiction under 5,000 words is preferred. Occasionally, a short sketch or informal essay may be used. Submit all prose typed double-spaced with ample margins and your name and address on the top lefthand corner of the first page. Please use paper clips, not staples. Photocopied submissions are acceptable, but please let us know at time of submission if they have been simultaneously submitted. Notify us at once if they are accepted elsewhere. A cover note about previous publications or other background is interesting but not necessary. Notification of acceptance or return of manuscript could come anytime from a week to several months after submission, depending on the manuscript load and cycle of production. The panel reviews work continuously for publication in spring and fall. Please don't forget to enclose a self-addressed, stamped envelope (SASE) with adequate postage with all communications requiring a reply. Payment is in three copies. Occasionally prizes and honoraria are available.

BLACK AND WHITE PHOTOGRAPHY AND ART

Passages North uses black and white photography and graphic arts, usually a portfolio of a single artist or other related work. Inquire first, with a description and sample of what you propose.

SAMPLE COPY $1.50
including postage

SUBSCRIPTIONS $2 a year

SPECIAL 3-YEAR RATE $5

PEN Syndicated Fiction Project

P.O. Box 6303 • Washington, D.C. 20015 • (301) 656-7484

FYI: SYNDICATION FOR QUALITY SHORT FICTION

PEN SYNDICATED FICTION, Box 6303, Washington, D.C. 20015. (301) 656-7484.
Director: Caroline Marshall. Invites short story submissions once a year;
stories are then read by a distinguished panel of writers. Those chosen are
sent in groups of five/eight each month to participating newspapers for
possible syndication. Established in 1982 by the National Endowment for the
Arts. Audience: Five million.

Needs: Tight, well-plotted short stories of high quality, unpublished or
previously published in publications with less than 2,000 circulation. No
obscenities. Receives approximately 1,800 unsolicited mss. per reading
period. Length: 2,500 words or less, preferably less.

How to contact: Submissions invited in December, 1987, for seventh reading
period. Send two copies mss., brief bio and SASE for return of mss. and a
list of writers whose work was selected. Decisions announced in March 1988.
Please note: Neither mss nor announcement will be sent without SASE.

Payment: $500 for selected story; $100 per publication by participating
newspapers. Realistic possible potential: $1000.

Terms   Pays $500 on return of contract; $100 within 60 days of newspaper
publication. Provides tearsheet or copy.

Tips: Newspapers prefer short pieces of general or family interest.
Submitters are encouraged to imagine their work in a Sunday magazine with
accompanying illustration to judge a story's suitability.

Pen Syndicated Fiction Project is a cooperative project
of PEN American Center and the
National Endowment for the Arts Literature Program

University of Pittsburgh English Dept./526 C.L. Pittsburgh, PA 15260

WRITERS GUIDLINES for submissions to THE PENNSYLVANIA REVIEW

1. Writers are invited to submit fiction, poetry, nonfiction (essays, reviews, criticism, interviews) drama and illustrations.

2. All manuscripts must be typed. Prose must be double spaced.

3. A self-addressed stamped envelope must accompany all submissions.

4. Writer's name and address should appear in upper right-hand corner of each page.

5. Photocopies of good quality are acceptable.

6. Submission deadlines: November 1, April 1.

7. We suggest you read a sample copy of THE PENNSYLVANIA REVIEW before submitting. (You may order a sample copy for $5.00.)

Additional information

Submissions are usually returned 6-8 weeks after receipt.

Payment is $5 per page and one copy of the magazine.

Copyright automatically reverts to the author after our first use.

Only two issues are published a year (in March and September). We do not read submissions in the summer.

Thank you for your interset in THE PENNSYLVANIA REVIEW.

Pennywhistle Press®

Freelance Guidelines

We are primarily looking for fiction pieces -- 450-word fiction for
5 to 7 year olds and 850-word fiction for older children. We rarely
accept non-fiction, as our non-fiction needs are met through member
Gannett newspapers. No multiple submissions will be accepted.

We will also consider puzzles, poetry and craft ideas. Please,
no inquiries on these or the fiction -- we can consider finished
manuscripts only. Subject matter can vary, though stories with
religious overtones, talking animals, and fairy tales have virtually
no chance of acceptance.

Manuscripts are welcome, but neither publication nor return are
guaranteed though a self-addressed, stamped envelope usually results
in a return. Payment is on publication, and varies according to
length and quality, among other factors.

Pennywhistle Press is a news and feature supplement for children
published by the Gannett Company and distributed through approximately 40 newspapers around the country. The charge for mail and handling
of a sample copy is 75 cents. Make checks payable to Pennywhistle
Press.

Manuscripts should be sent to   ANITA SAMA, Editor
                                        Pennywhistle Press
                                        P.O. Box 500-P
                                        Washington, D.C. 20044

Thank you for your cooperation.

GANNETT

P.O. Box 500-P, Washington, D.C. 20044

PENTHOUSE

PENTHOUSE INTERNATIONAL LTD., 1965 BROADWAY, NEW YORK, NY 10023-5965. 212-496-6100

Writer's Guidlines

1. The best way to discern the material Penthouse might be interested
in is to look at the magazine. Articles are usually related to
current affairs or topics which would appeal to our readers (predominately
male, ages 18-49). Subjects might include celebrity/athlete profiles,
exposes on goverment or corporate affairs, and analyses of trends in
lifestyle or sexuality. Interviews should be exclusive queries on
personalities who are obviously of interest to a wide-ranging audience.

2. Queries should include a detailed description of your article,
who or what your sources will be, and how you plan on presenting the
subject. Queries should demonstrate an in-depth knowledge of the
subject. Proposals for photo essays should be accompanied by slides
or suggestions for sources of art.

3. Please submit any credits, clips or other examples of your published
writings, if available. A stamped, self-addressed envelope is essential
for any response.

4. Features run 3,500 to 5,000 words and shorter articles for our 'View
From the Top' section are 500-750 words.

5. Writers fees and expenses are negiotiated when an assignment is made.
Features pay form $2,500 to $5,000 depending on length and complexity
of the subject. Shorter pieces pay $500. Payment is made on acceptance.
There is a 25% kill fee on assigned articles.

PIEDMONT LITERARY REVIEW   PIEDMONT LITERARY SOCIETY
                                            P.O. BOX 3656
                                            DANVILLE, VA 24543

Gail White, Poetry Editor, 724 Bartholomew Street, New Orleans,LA
Barbara McCoy, Haiku and Oriental Editor, 861 Wimbleton Drive,
                                            Raleigh, N.C. 27609
Don Conner,Sec'y., Treasurer, Membership Chm'n.
                                            c/o PLS, P.O. Box3656
                                            Danville, VA 24543
William R. (Bill) Smith, President / Newsletter Editor
                                            3750 Woodside Ave.
                                            Lynchburg, VA 24503

The Piedmont Literary Society is a non-profit organization
dedicated to the appreciation of poetry and other creative
writing. The society was formed in 1976 as a regional group
in Virginia's Piedmont Region. It quickly spread throughout
the state and the nation, and we are now international in
scope. There are now about 120 members, and our normal membership is even higher. There is one active membership "chapter",
in Lynchburg, VA. Membership is open to all who are interested
in writing or literature. $10.00 annual dues entitles a member
to a subscription to the quarterly Piedmont Literary Review,
the PLS Newsletter, and other activities including periodic
competitions for the membership and others.

The Piedmont Literary Review is a quarterly publication
containing the creative efforts of members and others whose
contributions are deemed of high quality. It ranges in size
from 32 to 44 pages,about 60 poems, 2 to 3 short stories,
and is published in April, June, October, and January. Contributors include established writers and poets, as well as students
and previously unpublished writers and poets. Quality is
the key factor in selection. Previous publishing credits,
or academic positions of the authors are not considered.
A sample copy of a recent issue may be obtained for $2.00.

In addition to poetry, the PLR uses short prose fiction,
critical essays, book reviews, informative articles, and other
features. Please limit poetry submissions to a maximum of
5 poems per submittal. Shorter prose items, (1500 to 2000 words
max.). Contributors should include name and address on each
sheet of material sent, and include a self-addressed stamped
envelope with -all submissions.

Deadlines for quarterly issues are March 15, (June issue), June 15,(Sept.),
September 15, (January), and December 15, (March). Allow 90 days for report
or return of material. Submissions received after a deadline must be held
for the next following issue if accepted. Payment is free contributor's
copy.

SEND SUBMISSIONS TO:

All poetry (except oriental forms), chapbooks for review to

Gail S. White, Poetry Ed., 724 Bartholomew Street, New Orleans, LA 70117

Oriental Verse (Haiku, Tanka, Senryu) and reviews to

Barbara McCoy, All Oriental Verse, 861 Wimbleton Drive, Raleigh,
NC, 27609.

Newsletter Editor; William R. Smith, 3750 Woodside Ave.,
Lynchburg, VA 24503.
All Short Fiction;

DAVID CRAIG
201 HIGHLAND CT
DANVILLE, VA 24543

Membership Information, Dues Submission: Don Conner, Membership Chairman/ Secretary/ Treasurer.P.O.Box 3656, Danville,
VA24543

_____

MEMBERSHIP SUBSCRIPTION APPLICATION

To: Piedmont Literary Society

P.O. Box 3656

Danville, VA 24543   Date_____   Sponsor (if any)_____

NAME_____ ENCLOSED IS $____ to cover __ member-
ships (at $10. 00 per membership).

ADDRESS_____

CITY_____STATE_____ZIP_____

MAKE ALL CHECKS PAYABLE TO THE PIEDMONT LITERARY SOCIETY.

PIG IRON PRESS

Post Office Box 237
Youngstown, Ohio 44501

(216) 783-1269

PIG IRON

◀GUIDELINES▶
for Writers,
Artists
& Photographers

THE PIG IRON GALLERY

○ WOMAN (Pig Iron No. 7; 1980) $3.00
○ THE NEW BEATS (No. 8; 1980) $3.00
○ BASEBALL (No. 9; 1981) $4.00
○ SCIENCE FICTION (No. 10; 1982) $5.00
○ THE NEW SURREALISTS (No. 11; 1983) $4.00
○ VIET NAM FLASHBACKS (No. 12; 1984) $5.00
○ PSYCHOLOGICAL (No. 13; 1985) $4.00

○ Kenneth Patchen, STILL ANOTHER PELICAN
   IN THE BREADBOX (1981) $4.00
○ Jack Remick, THE STOLEN HOUSE
   (1980) $2.00
○ George Peffer & Terry Murcko, ORPHAN
   TREES (1980) $2.00
○ T-Shirt (white on blue)
   M, L, XL $5.00

No. Copies_____ Total Enclosed_____

Name _____

Address _____ Apt. No. _____

City _____ State _____ Zip Code _____

PIG IRON PRESS
Post Office Box 237, Youngstown, Ohio 44501

POPULAR CULTURE ANTHOLOGIES

Pig Iron Press welcomes unsolicited
manuscripts, art and photography for consideration for publication in Pig Iron
Literary Magazine. The content of Pig Iron
includes fiction, poetry, non-fiction and
art in both traditional and experimental
forms. Published annually. Themes only.
Send SASE for current list of themes. Pig
Iron is distributed by mail order to
libraries and individual patrons.

FORMAT: Paperback; 8.5 x 11 inches;
Perfect bind; 60 lb. text; 120 line screen;
96 pages; 1,000 copies. Retail Price: $5.95

CONTRIBUTORS: Includes new writers and
professionals. Previous publication not
necessary. Interested in experimental
writers and new talent.

CONTENT: Primarily publishes new material, but will consider previously published works of special merit.

NEEDS: Pig Iron buys 20-50 poems, 10-30 stories and 20-50 drawings and photographs per year.

MECHANICAL REQUIREMENTS

Material must not be under consideration by another publisher.

Literary submissions should be typewritten on 8 1/2 X 11 in. white paper. The author's name and address should appear on the first page of each individual work, with the number of words for prose and the number of lines for poetry. Dry photocopies only. The author's complete name and address should appear on the envelope.

Include a self-addressed, stamped envelope if you want your work returned. Postal regulations prohibit the use of metered return envelopes.

Quantities of poems more than ten or prose submissions exceeding 10,000 words will not be considered. Pig Iron is not currently reading booklength manuscripts.

Art submissions are limited to black and white ink drawings, pencil drawings, block or screen prints, collages, charcoal drawings and washes. Submit original art or PMT print. For drawings with shaded areas submit original art.

Black and white photographs only. Submit any size photograph. Semi-gloss paper preferred, but matte acceptable. Submit finished prints.

Submit any number of graphics or photographs. We will examine slide portfolios.

THEMES

Since 1980 Pig Iron has published thematic anthologies only. Both popular and literary themes have appeared in this series.

A wide variety of viewpoints, styles and media are included in each edition. Unusual viewpoints and interpretations are encouraged. Themes are announced one to two years in advance of publication. Send SASE for current list. See the back of this brochure for a list of previously published themes and information about ordering sample copies.

TERMS

Pig Iron purchases First North American Serial Rights, or One-time Reprint Rights.

Payment is $2.00 per poem or $2.00 per published page, whichever is greater. $2.00 per published page for fiction. Contributors receive two free copies; additional copies at 40% list.

The editors reserve the right to edit or revise literary submissions, and to alter or crop art and photography as long as such changes are reasonable and do not alter the creator's intent.

Reports in six months; publication within eighteen months.

Pig Iron will not assume responsibility for submissions not containing sufficient return postage or packaging, or for materials lost in the mail.

Deliver by mail to P.O. Box 237, Youngstown, Ohio 44501. UPS materials to 3306 Hillman St., Youngstown, Ohio 44507. Phone: (216) 783-1269.

EDITORS: Rose Sayre and Jim Villani.

ASSOCIATE EDITORS: George Peffer, Nate Leslie, Sheri Matascik.

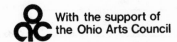
With the support of the Ohio Arts Council

PIG IRON
GALLERY

Edited by Rose Sayre & Jim Villani

From the ridiculous to the sublime. A potpourri of funny, amusing, and comical literature: satire, parody, light verse, the absurd, black humor, cartoons. We guarantee you will be entertained and delighted. Over 80 of today's best writers and artists demonstrate their talents as humorists.

HUMOR   **$6.95**
Pig Iron No. 14
1987. Pb. 8.5x11 in. 96 pp. ISBN 917530-22-5

▽

Landscapes of the Mind
PSYCHOLOGICAL LITERATURE

Explores and articulates a vast variety of psychological states: personality, the past, dreams, reflections, depression, paranoia, black humor. Intensely personal and provocative.

LANDSCAPES of the MIND   **$5.95**
Pig Iron No. 13
1985. Pb. 8.5x11 in. 96 pp. ISBN 917530-21-7

▽

Viet Nam Flashbacks
VIETNAM ERA LITERATURE

Captures the glory, frustration, and horror of America's longest war. Raging battle stories, human interest stories, and personal reflections on the role of the U.S. military in Southeast Asia. Candid photographs reveal the human dimension of the GI presence, the Vietnamese countryside, and its strife-torn people. Work by 36 Vietnam veterans.

VIET NAM FLASHBACKS   **$7.95**
Pig Iron No. 12
1984. Pb. 8.5x11 in. 96 pp. ISBN 917530-20-9

"Newcomers to print, eloquently telling their stories. . .conveys just what being in Vietnam felt like."
         Merritt Clifton. *Samisdat*

THE NEW SURREALISTS

The brave new vista of 20th century art and literature; the metaphysical zone of the aesthetic experience; and the highest form of liberation and revelation — a world of *surreality*. Interview with Lawrence Ferlinghetti.

THE NEW SURREALISTS   **$5.95**
Pig Iron No. 11
1983. Pb. 8.5x11 in. 96 pp. ISBN 917530-19-5

"Energetic and original. . .skillfully blends emerging talents with established artists. Ferlinghetti comments on a variety of political and literary issues."
         Fred F. Paulenich, *Ohioana Quarterly*

▽

SCIENCE FICTION

Filled with speculation, wonder, and the fantastic: dystopian panoramas, chemical and spiritual migration of consciousness, and humanistic reviviscence. Interview with Frederick Pohl.

SCIENCE FICTION   **$5.95**
Pig Iron No. 10
1982. Pb. 8.5x11 in. 96 pp. ISBN 917530-18-7

"Exceptional quality and originality. . .a collector's item."
         Fred. F. Paulenich, *The Warren Tribune*

▽

KENNETH PATCHEN
Still Another Pelican in the Breadbox
Richard Morgan, Editor

Kenneth Patchen rose from a town of soot and steel to stand before the world. These poems, stories, and critical essays were written over a span of thirty years, but were either unpublished or published in obscure places. With a chronology and a portrait of Patchen's literary triumphs and personal agonies. Also, photographs and a forward by Patchen's wife, Miriam.

STILL ANOTHER PELICAN   **$5.95**
IN THE BREADBOX
1981. Pb. 5.5x8.5 in. 96 pp. ISBN 917530-14-4

"A valuable addition to the Patchen canon."
         George Myers Jr., *Harrisburg Patriot-News*

BASEBALL

Mythic, heroic, and reflective — an unusual collection of Baseball fiction, poetry, photographs, art, memorabilia, and commentary. A delight for fans and collectors. Big and beautiful for reading or browsing.

BASEBALL   **$5.95**
Pig Iron No. 9
1981. Pb. 8.5x11 in. 96 pp. ISBN 917530-17-9

"Delves into the psyche of the game."
Stephen Sawicki, *Cleveland Magazine*

▽

THE NEW BEATS

Comedy, rebellion, and subjective analysis in an absurd universe. The Beat movement didn't end in 1960, or in 1965. It continues today, a strong and dominating force in literature, its troubadours alive and well and thumping the land, spreading its message.

THE NEW BEATS   **$4.95**
Pig Iron No. 8
1980. Pb. 8.5x11 in. 96 pp. ISBN 917530-16-0

▽

WOMAN

It is not so much a question of writing about woman as it is reconstructing man. At the mythical level, woman is a new future revealed. Within a sociological framework, woman is all that man must become to save himself, woman, and the planet Earth itself.

WOMAN   **$4.95**
Pig Iron No. 7
1980. Pb. 8.5x11 in. 96 pp. ISBN 917530-15-2

▽

THE STOLEN HOUSE
A Human Story About A House
Jack Remick

Guiph loves his house. If it was a doughnut, he'd eat it, but since it is a house, he steals it. A tender and zany novel about a young writer and the house he lives in.

THE STOLEN HOUSE   **$4.95**
1980. Pb. 5.5x8.5 in. 168 pp. ISBN 917530-13-6

ORPHAN TREES
George Peffer & Terry Murcko

Poems of insight and imagination by two Youngstown poets. Two unusual, complimentary styles combine to explore a variety of contemporary themes.

ORPHAN TREES   **$3.00**
1980. Pb. 5.5x8.5 in. 80 pp. ISBN 917530-08-X

T-Shirt $6.00
White on black: M, L, XL

ORDER FROM
Pig Iron Press
P.O. Box 237
Youngstown, Ohio 44501

Qty.	Title	Price
	Humor	
	Landscapes of the Mind	
	Viet Nam Flashbacks	
	The New Surrealists	
	Science Fiction	
	Baseball	
	The New Beats	
	Woman	
	Still Another Pelican in the Breadbox	
	The Stolen House	
	Orphan Trees	
	T-Shirt M L XL	
		Total

Name _____

Address _____ Apt. No. ____

City _____ State _____ Zip Code _____

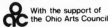 With the support of the Ohio Arts Council

For Your Personal Cultural Evolution

Plainswoman

P.O. Box 8027
Grand Forks, ND 58202
(701) 777-8043

Guidelines for Contributors

Plainswoman is published in Grand Forks, North Dakota, ten times a year (once a month excluding July and August). Our main interest is the interpretation of historical and contemporary issues related to women in the Plains region; however, we look for strong, clear writing on a variety of subjects regardless of region. We print articles, essays, poetry, fiction and graphics, and we like to work with writers as their contributions develop.

Submissions should be typed double space on one side of the page, with author's name and address at the top of the first page. (Please note if your submission is being considered elsewhere.)

Poetry should be typed one poem to a page with author's name and address on each sheet.

Plainswoman will pay $5 to each contributor whose work is published, and more as funds allow.

Please enclose self-addressed, stamped envelope with all correspondence.

Thank you for your interest in **Plainswoman**. Write if you have further questions, and best wishes with your work.   The editors..

PLAYBOY

Thank you for your recent inquiry regarding submission of your story to PLAYBOY.

PLAYBOY is considered to be one of the top fiction markets. It pays to take a close look at the magazine before submitting material. We look for well-written, well-constructed stories. We aren't doctrinaire about subjects, but writers should remember that the magazine's appeal is chiefly to a well-informed, young male audience.

We publish serious contemporary stories, mystery, suspense, humor, science fiction and sports stories. We often reject stories of high quality simply because they are inappropriate to our publication. Fairy tales, extremely experimental fiction and out-right pornography all have their place, but it is not in PLAYBOY. In addition, we do not consider poetry, plays, story outlines or novel-length manuscripts.

The average length of PLAYBOY fiction is 1000 - 6000 words and payment is usually $2000; very short pieces are paid $1000.

Manuscripts should be addressed to the Fiction Department. They should be typed, double-spaced, on paper of letter or legal size. Hand-written submissions will be returned unread. All properly submitted stories are given careful consideration by our staff.

All submissions should be accompanied by a self-addressed, stamped return envelope. We strongly suggest a brief cover letter, listing publishing credits or other relevant information. The response time is approximately 4 - 6 weeks.

A little advice for the new writer: Please don't telephone the editor to ask how to submit a story or to explain a story. Don't write a letter requesting sample copies, a statement of editorial policy, or reaction to an idea for a story.

We appreciate your interest in our magazine, and hope you will submit material you feel is suited to PLAYBOY's high standards.

PLAYGIRL

801 SECOND AVENUE, NEW YORK, N.Y. 10017 (212) 986-5100   Telex 6711779 DRAKEUW

FICTION GUIDELINES

Playgirl usually publishes 12 short stories each year. We look for the offbeat story that might not appear anywhere else. Preferably, the story will be about relationships between people.

Our fiction is not limited to romance. The relationships we like to explore may be between men and women, mothers and daughters, sisters, friends, grandparents and grandchildren... The story should be a commentary on the human condition, made in a fresh, insightful way.

We don't want violence, graphic sex, murder, suspense, science fiction, adventure, mystery, Westerns, children's stories or male fantasies. We will not buy a story that is tasteless or portrays physical brutality.

We prefer that submissions be made one at a time and limited to 24 typed pages. Shorter pieces are much in demand. Simultaneous submissions are accepted. A self-addressed, stamped envelope is necessary for return of the manuscript.

Rates vary, but start at $500. Payment is made within 30 days of our receipt of your signed contract. We buy one-time magazine rights in the English language.

The magazine's editorial offices are in New York but fiction only should be submittted to Fiction Editor, Playgirl, 311 S. Spring St., Los Angeles, CA 90013.

Mary Ellen Strote
Fiction Editor

POCKETS

A DEVOTIONAL MAGAZINE FOR CHILDREN

Published by The Upper Room

The purpose of *Pockets* is to open up the fullness of the gospel of Jesus Christ to children. It is written and produced for children and designed to help children pray and be in relationship to God. The magazine emphasizes that we are loved by God and that God's grace calls us into community. It is through the community of God's people that we experience that love in our daily lives.

General Guidelines

Each issue is built around several themes with material which can be used by children in a variety of ways. Scripture stories, fiction, poetry, prayers, art, graphics, puzzles, and activities are included. Submissions do not need to be overtly religious. They should help children experience a Christian lifestyle that is not always a neatly wrapped moral package, but is open to the continuing revelation of God's will. Seasonal material, both secular and liturgical, is desired. Material submitted by children is also desired.

Age Group

The magazine is for children six through twelve, with a target reading age of eight through eleven. Though some may share it with their families, it is designed primarily for the personal use of children.

Format and Length

The magazine is published monthly except January and includes a wide variety of materials.

Fiction and scripture stories should be 600 to 1500 words. Occasional two-part stories are used and can be up to 2500 words. Our primary interest is in stories that can help children deal with real-life situations, that can help in any setting—realistic or fantastic—and can be communicated through adventure, legend, history, present day, etc. Fictional characters and some elaboration can be included in scripture stories, but the writer must remain faithful to the story. Both Old and New Testament stories can be used.

Poems should be short, never more than one page.

Non-fiction articles should be 400 to 600 words. These should be related to a particular theme which has been projected (a list of themes and due dates is available from the editorial office). We are interested in articles about the Bible, church history, the liturgical year, etc. We also seek biographical sketches of persons, famous or unknown, whose lives reflect their Christian commitments and values. These may be either short vignettes (a single incident) or longer and more complete biographies. Articles about various holidays and about other cultures are included.

Cartoons should be no more than two to four pages and may be as brief as one frame.

Style

Contributions should be typed, double-spaced, on 8½" × 11" paper and should be accompanied by a self-addressed, stamped envelope for return. Writers should include their Social Security number.

The target reading age for this publication is eight through eleven years. Stories should contain lots of action, use believable dialogue, be simply written, and be relevant to the problems faced by this age group in everyday life. It is important that they not be "preachy" or didactic. Use short sentences and paragraphs. When possible, use concrete words instead of abstractions. However, do not "write down" to these children.

It is no longer common practice to use such terms as "man," "mankind," "men," in the familiar generic sense. Substitute non-sexist terms that are inclusive of everyone (e.g., "humankind," "persons," "human beings," "everyone").

The publication is ecumenical and our readers include persons of many cultures and ethnic backgrounds. These differences should be reflected in the references which are made to lifestyles, living environments (suburban, urban, rural, reservation), families (extended families, single-parent homes), and individual names (Juaquin, Mai Ling, and Horacio should also appear in our stories).

Children need to be able to see themselves in the pages of the magazine. Show appreciation of cultural differences, and do not leave the impression that one way is better than another.

Payment

Payment will be made at the time of purchase. We will report within two months after receiving the manuscript. We purchase first periodical rights and accept previously published material and multiple submissions.

• Stories and articles: 7¢ and up a word. (An honorarium will be paid for a manuscript that needs little or no editing.)
• Poetry: $25.00 to $50.00
• Activities, etc.: $10.00 to $25.00
• Cartoons: $15.00

Writers' Guidelines and list of themes will be sent free upon receipt of SASE.

Mail manuscripts to:
Willie S. Teague, Editor
1908 Grand Ave.
Box 189
Nashville, TN 37202-0189

PUBLISHERS SYNDICATION INT'L.
1377 K STREET N.W. SUITE 856 ■ WASHINGTON, D.C. 20005

The Post

GUIDELINES

EDITOR: A. P. Samuels

Pays on acceptance plus royalty...Byline given...Reports in 4 to 6 weeks...SASE required for return.

Will buy first time manuscripts if good enough. Photocopies okay. No simultaneous submissions please. We prefer letter quality printing.

THE POST

MYSTERY/SUSPENSE: 10,000 words (approx.)...buy 12 a year

ROMANCE: 10,000 word...12 a year.

No explicit sex...gore...sadism or horror. Manuscripts must be for a general audience. Just good plain story telling with unique plot.

RATE: 1 to 4 cents per word on acceptance plus royalty.

University of
Nebraska
Lincoln

Prairie Schooner
201 Andrews Hall
Lincoln, NE 68588-0334
Telephone: (402) 472-1800

Thanks for your interest in our magazine. Prairie Schooner publishes short stories, poems, interviews, imaginative essays of general interest, and reviews of current books of poetry and fiction. Scholarly articles requiring footnote references should be submitted to journals of literary scholarship.

Prairie Schooner's intention is to publish the best writing available, both from beginning and established writers. In our sixty-one years of continuous publication, we have printed the work of Eudora Welty, Mari Sandoz, Jessamyn West, Randall Jarrell, Loren Eiseley, Diane Wakoski and others.

All submissions to Prairie Schooner should be typed double-spaced on one side of the paper only. Number pages consecutively and use margins of at least one inch. A self-addressed envelope, with adequate return postage enclosed, must accompany the submission.

We encourage you to read Prairie Schooner. Sample copies of previous issues are available for one dollar, and subscription prices are as follows: $11 for one year, $20 for two years, and $29 for three years (Nebraska residents add 5% sales tax).

the Editors

Name_____

Address_____

City_____ State_____ Zip_____

PRIMAVERA
1212 East 59th Street
Chicago, Illinois 60637

        PRIMAVERA is interested in submissions of poetry
and short fiction reflecting the experiences of women. All
submissions should be typed, double-spaced and accompanied
by a self-addressed stamped envelope. Short stories should
be no more than thirty pages. Please send no more than six
poems at a time. Contributors receive two copies of the
magazine.

PUERTO DEL SOL

Writing Center
New Mexico State University
Box 3E/Las Cruces, New Mexico 88003
Telephone (505) 646-3931

SUBMISSION INFORMATION

Fiction Editor: Kevin McIlvoy
Poetry Editor: Joe Somoza

Semi-annual publication
Established 1961
Circulation 1000

Send complete manuscript with SASE. We accept simultaneous and photocopied submissions. We report in *six to eight weeks*.

Payment: *three contributor's copies*. One-time rights (revert to author). Publication copyrighted.

Accept about *sixty poems/yr.; twelve to fifteen stories/yr.*

Manuscripts may be submitted from *September 1 to May 1.*

Need: contemporary, ethnic, experimental, literary, mainstream, prose poem, excerpted novel, translations.

Poetry: *We like all types of authentic poetry -- not formula poems (including MFA-workshop formulas). We like poems that stretch the language but that are more than mere exercises.*

Fiction: *We are open to all forms of work, from the conventional to the wildly experimental, as long as they have integrity and are well-written. Too often we receive very impressively polished manuscripts that will dazzle the reader with their sheen but offer no character/reader experience of lasting value.*

Sample copy: $3

THE SMITH
5 BEEKMAN STREET   NYC 10038   RE 2-4821

PULPSMITH
<u>EDITORIAL GUIDELINES</u>:

PULPSMITH publishes poetry, fiction, and articles. We are interested in a wide

variety of subject matter--as our mottos says, "anything goes as long as it's good."

We publish lyric poetry, epic poetry, and have a special interest in ballads.

Fiction ranges from short-shorts to long stories. We're interested in fiction that

deals seriously with formal considerations, as well as stories with gripping plot

and character. We publish satire, science fiction, mysteries, surreal stories

that border interestingly on the edges of reality, and stories with conventional

structure. Articles/essays concern the edge between science and speculation, law,

literature ... anything that brings creativity to its subject.

Payment is modest, beginning with $10 for a very short poem to $25 for a longer

poem, and ranging from $35 to $100 for essays, stories and very long poems. The

author receives two copies of the issue in which his/her work appears. Rights are

returned to the author, on request, after publication. Reply on manuscripts is made

between four and eight weeks. A self-addressed, stamped envelope is required with

any submission.

Sample copies are available at $3 each, with PULPSMITH paying the postage. A one

year subscription (four issues) is $10.

PULPSMITH is published by The Generalist Association, a non-profit literary

foundation. Gifts are tax deductible.

General Guidelines

Manuscripts must be typewritten on 8½ × 11 white paper, double-spaced on one side of the sheet only. (Computer printout also acceptable.) Enter your name and address in the upper left-hand corner, and the approximate number of words (and character count, if known) in the upper right-hand corner. All manuscripts must be accompanied by a self-addressed stamped envelope (SASE). Seasonal material should be submitted six months in advance. Book reviews are to follow the guidelines and form provided for their report.

Manuscripts will be read as promptly as possible and returned or purchased upon acceptance. We purchase one-time rights only.

We seek to treat each manuscript carefully, but urge that the author keep a copy for personal reference. While we respect the writer's style and purpose, we reserve the right to edit the copy to fit our literary standards. If major content changes are necessary, the editor will send a revised manuscript to the author for approval.

Rates of payment vary among the magazines. The quality of the material and the relative need for it also affect the rate. Contact editor about specific questions. Generally payment is made upon acceptance of manuscript. Payment for a book review is the book reviewed. Maximum rates for one-time use, $50.00 per thousand words. Payment for reprints is one half of one-time rights.

Purpose

Editor: James E. Horsch
Audience: adults of all ages
Focus: action oriented, discipleship living
Frequency: monthly in weekly parts

Purpose is in the market for fillers (up to 350 words), articles (350-1,200 words), and short stories (up to 1,200 words). The material must be clearly written in terse, fast-moving style. *Purpose* is a Christian periodical which focuses on the resolution of human problems.

Purpose is also interested in articles and stories that
• Show Christians putting their faith to work
• Help readers in their beliefs and decision-making
• Stress church loyalty and community duties
• Inspire interest in other peoples and cultures
• Highlight biographical and historical information of Christian persons, places, and events
• Emphasize hobbies, nature, travel, art, science, and seasonal topics from a Christian perspective

Purpose buys appropriate poetry up to 12 lines. Rates on art and photographs vary according to quality.

WHEN YOU WRITE

For the personal reading and leadership magazines of the Mennonite Publishing House

Mennonite Publishing House
616 Walnut Avenue
Scottdale, PA 15683-1999
Telephone 412-887-8500

The pages which follow describe the manuscript needs of the personal reading and leadership magazines published by the Mennonite Publishing House. Writers are invited to contact the editor(s) of the publication(s) of their interest.

<u>Quarry West</u>, Kenneth Weisner, Editor; Thad Nodine, Kathryn Chetkovich, Fiction Editors; Porter College, University of California, Santa Cruz, CA 95064, 408-429-2155. Past contributors: Joyce Carol Oates, Raymond Carver, J. B. Hall. Gary Ligi, Steven Dixon, Gary Soto, George Hitchcock, James Houston, Jerry Stahl. Circulation 750. 2/year. Reporting time: 2 months. Payment: 2 issues.

6,000 word maximum. One manuscript per SASE. Traditional and experimental stories read with interest. We look for stories that work on their own terms. We encourage new and unknown as well as established writers.

RAMBUNCTIOUS REVIEW

Rambunctious Press, Inc.

1221 West Pratt Blvd.
Chicago, Illinois 60626

WRITERS' GUIDELINES

RAMBUNCTIOUS REVIEW SEEKS CONTRIBUTORS

Rambunctious Review, Chicago's newest literary arts magazine, is
seeking contributors. Poetry, fiction, arts-related essays, and short dramatic
works are welcome. Black-and-white graphics and photography are also
sought. All literary submissions should be typed, double-spaced. Fiction
should be no more than 15 pages. Submissions are not accepted June 1
through August 31. Successful contributors will receive two copies of
Rambunctious Review, fame and glory.

Submissions should be sent to the following address:

Rambunctious Review

1221 West Pratt Boulevard
Chicago Illinois 60626

For more information, please contact:

Mary Dellutri   864-8234
Richard Goldman 973-3529
Nancy Lennon   338-2439

Working for the Nature of Tomorrow™

NATIONAL WILDLIFE FEDERATION

1412 Sixteenth Street, N.W., Washington, D.C. 20036-2266   (202) 797-6800

RANGER RICK WRITERS' GUIDELINES

SUBJECT SELECTION

o Our audience ranges from ages six to twelve, though we aim the reading level of most materials at nine-year-olds or fourth graders.

o Fiction and non-fiction articles may be written on any aspect of nature, outdoor adventure and discovery, pets, science, conservation, or related subjects. To find out what subjects have been covered recently, consult our annual indexes. These are available in many libraries or are free upon request from our editorial offices.

o The National Wildlife Federation (NWF) discourages the keeping of wildlife as pets, so the keeping of such pets should not be featured in your copy.

o Human qualities may be attributed to animals only in fantasy stories, where it will be obvious to readers that you're not writing about real animals.

o Avoid the stereotyping of any group. For instance, girls can enjoy nature and the outdoors as much as boys can, and mothers can be just as knowledgeable as fathers.

o The only way you can successfully write for Ranger Rick is to know the kinds of subjects and approaches we like. And the only way you can do that is to read the magazine. Recent issues can be found in most libraries or are available free upon request.

SUBMITTING MATERIALS

o Send us a query describing your intended subject, along with a lead or sample paragraph. Any special qualifications you may have to write on that subject would be worth mentioning. Please do not query by phone.

o List all your reference sources when submitting your finished work, unless of course you are an expert in the field. We strongly recommend that you consult with experts in the field when developing your material and that one of them read the finished manuscript for accuracy before you submit it to us.

o All submissions are made on speculation unless other arrangements have been made. Manuscripts are considered carefully and will be returned or accepted within one to two months. Our planning schedule is 10 months prior to cover date. Please do not submit your manuscript to other magazines simultaneously.

(continued on back)

PAYMENTS

o Payments range up to $350 for a full-length feature (about 900
   words), depending on quality. Poetry is paid for at about $3
   a line.

o Upon acceptance of a manuscript, a transfer of rights form will be
   sent to you. The NWF prefers to buy all world rights. However, in
   some cases rights are negotiable. Payment checks will be processed
   after we receive the signed transfer of rights form.

o It is not necessary that illustrations or photographs accompany your
   material. If we do use photographs you've included with your copy,
   these will be paid for separately at current market rates.

The NWF can take no responsibility for unsolicited submissions. However,
we make every effort to return such materials if accompanied by a self-
addressed, stamped envelope.

Direct all correspondence to The Editors, RANGER RICK, 1412 16th St., NW,
Washington, DC 20036-2266. We appreciate your interest.

                              The Editors
                              RANGER RICK

REDBOOK

224 WEST 57TH ST.,
NEW YORK, N.Y. 10019

(212) 262-8250

FICTION GUIDELINES

Thank you for your interest in REDBOOK. We publish approximately 40 short stories a year, and we welcome unsolicited short story manuscripts. Our fiction has received such prestigious honors as the National Magazine Award for Fiction and inclusion in PRIZE STORIES/THE O. HENRY AWARDS and THE BEST AMERICAN SHORT STORIES.

REDBOOK'S target reader is a woman between the ages of 25 and 45 who is or was married, has children, and generally is employed outside the home. Because she's a bright, well-informed individual with varied interests, she's not solely concerned with fiction that reflects her own life--although most of our stories deal with topics of specific interest to women: relationships, marriage, parenthood, relatives, friendships, career situations, financial problems, and so forth. But our reader also enjoys off-beat, ground-breaking stories; there is also room in our pages for humor and, occasionally, mystery and thrillers. (Highly oblique or symbolic stories that come to no conclusion and stories with obviously contrived plots are not right for REDBOOK.)

No cover letter is necessary--your story will be judged on its own merits. (If you do wish to send a letter, please include only your fiction credits.) All submissions should be typed and double-spaced and accompanied by a self-addressed stamped envelope large enough for the manuscript. (If you do not send an SASE, you will not hear from us unless we are interested in buying the story.) Our reply time is usually 8 to 10 weeks. We receive approximately thirty-five thousand submissions a year and take every care in handling them, but we cannot be responsible for the receipt or the condition of the manuscript. (In the interest of protecting the original manuscript, you may submit a legible photocopy.) Please note that we do not consider simultaneous submissions: Any story submitted to REDBOOK should not be offered to another magazine for consideration until after we have declined on it.

The two categories of stories published by REDBOOK include short-shorts (9 manuscript pages or fewer) and short stories (25 manuscript pages or fewer; the average length is 15 pages). Payment for a short-short begins at $750. Payment for a short story begins between $1,000 and $1,500, depending on various factors. REDBOOK buys First North American Serial Rights and pays on acceptance. Most stories are scheduled within a year of purchase, and prior to publication, short story galleys are sent to the author. (Our contract gives us final say on all editing decisions, but we make every effort to accommodate an author's wishes.) Please note that we do not consider unsolicited poetry and novels (condensed novels are no longer a regular feature in the magazine).

To submit your story, please address it to:

Fiction Department
REDBOOK Magazine
224 West 57th St.
New York, NY 10019

THE HEARST CORPORATION

REFLECT

W.S. Kennedy, ed.
3306 Argonne Ave.,
Norfolk, Va. 23509

REFLECT__Literary/variety quarterly. $8.00 yearly subscription.
$2.00 per copy. Page size: 5½ X 8½". 48 pages. Xerox.

REFLECT POLICY: A magazine of thought-inspiring fiction, essays, poetry,
REFLECT'S editorial policy and direction might be described by
saying it suggests the question: "Did you ever think of that, or
look at it that way?" Following the truth where it may lead takes
us into diverse fields including science, philosophy, the occult.

We have become a vehicle for the presentation of poetry and prose
representing the 1980's Spiral Mode, the mystical, euphony-in-writing
school showing "an inner-directed concern with sound"—termed "The
Back-to-Beauty Movement" by some of its adherents.

REFLECT GUIDELINES: We use three or four short stories each issue, mostly
short-shorts—Spiral Fiction (see REFLECT for the four rules of this
fiction mode). Maximum length of fiction, twenty-five hundred words.
Essays average fifteen hundred words. Up to sixty-five poems are
used each issue, none longer than can be printed on a 5½ X 8½" page.
One or two cartoons are used each issue. We feature a regular column
on antique collecting.

Obscene material or anything considered here to be objectionable
or in bad taste will be rejected.

Work submitted is understood to be the contributor's own original,
unpublished work. No simultaneous submissions are needed—in this
connection, we do not accept photo copies. Any re-use of material
published in REFLECT by anyone other than the author must have the
author's consent. Upon publication in REFLECT, ownership rights
revert to author.

Always include a stamped, self-addressed envelope (SASE) with submissions. Poetry submissions that are single-spaced are preferred
since they are to be published single-spaced. Payment is one copy.

REFLECT AD RATES: $5.00 for one-third of a page; classified: 10¢ a word.

PLEASE MAKE ALL CHECKS AND MONEY ORDERS, NOT TO "REFLECT," but to
W.S. Kennedy.

River Styx

Magazine

14 South Euclid

St. Louis, Missouri

63108

314.361.0043

16 July 1987

Fiction Guidelines for <u>River Styx</u> magazine:

<u>River Styx</u> publishes serious fiction, with a preference
for ethnic, translations, and experimental works. Two to
twenty pages, clean copy, double-spaced, SASE. Editors
read in September and October only.

To the Aspiring Writer:

RIVERSIDE QUARTERLY

RQ issues no guidelines but just asks each would-be con- tributor to inspect a copy or two of the magazine to see the <u>type</u> of story it prints. Fred Pohl once remarked that <u>IF</u> received 2,000 manuscripts per year that never would have been submitted had the writer bothered to read the magazine-- and a similar statement applies to RQ.

Not every number of RQ contains fiction, so relevant issues and titles are listed here:

#2-Kris Neville, "The Outcasts"
#3-Algis Budrys, "Balloon, Oh, Balloon"
#7-Janet Fox, "Just for Kicks" R. Bretnor, "The Other Way"
#10-Janet Fox, "The Taste of Eternity"
#13-Odean Cusack, "Schadenfraude"

#15-George Thompson, "Method"
#16-Steven Saffer, "Room 402"
#18-Lance Lee, "Mr. Smith Resolves a Crisis"
#19-Diane Luty, "The Angel of Fire Was Called Arel"
#29-David Goldknopf, "Cogito Ergo Sum"

Also noteworthy are Works in Progress by Arthur Cox and Kris Neville in issues #5 and #9, respectively; William Fagan's essay-story, "On Breaking the Linear Barrier" in #2; Derek Carter's fictional history, "The Saskatoon Explorer Project" in #15; and parables by Julian Brown and Patrick Welch in #7 and #12.

Preferred length is under 3,500 words, although longer stories are occasionally accepted. Send manuscripts directly to the fiction editor, Redd Boggs, Box 1111, Berkeley, CA 94701

Although RQ is not sold at news-stands, you should have no trouble in finding copies, since it's taken by virtually all major American university and public libraries. Instead of listing the nearly 200 domestic libraries that <u>do</u> subscribe, we find it easier to list the dozen that do <u>not</u>:

Universities	Cities
Brown	Atlanta
Columbia	Chicago
Dartmouth	Cleveland
Minnesota	Detroit
Pennsylvania	Miami
Texas	San Francisco

Concerning the above-listed cities--Atlanta or Chicago residents can inspect the RQ at Georgia State University or the University of Illinois (Chicago Circle), while those of Miami or San Francisco can follow the Tamiami Trail to Florida International University or cross the Bay to the University of California, Berkeley. Inhabitants of Detroit can look at <u>one</u> issue--after requesting a sample copy, the city public library failed to subscribe--but Cleveland readers and writers are simply out of luck.

Finally, if the editor takes time to write criticism of your story, try to <u>learn</u> something from it: do not waste your time composing a letter proving that the editor rejected your story because he is too young, too stupid, or too neurotic.

Sincerely,

Leland Sapiro (editor)

Leland Sapiro

St. Anthony Messenger   1615 Republic Street   Cincinnati, Ohio 45210

INFORMATION SHEET FOR FREE-LANCE WRITERS

ST. ANTHONY MESSENGER is a general-interest, family-oriented Catholic magazine. It is written and edited largely for people living in families or the family-like situations of Church and community. We want to help our readers better understand the teachings of the gospel and Catholic Church, and how they apply to life and the full range of problems confronting us as members of families, the Church and society.

The articles we publish usually fall under one of seven categories:

1. <u>Church and religion</u>: e.g., "What It's Like to Be a Deacon's Wife," "Ethics in the Trenches: Profile of a Hospital Ethicist," "The Synod: Holding to the Vatican II Course." Under this heading fall articles on the Scripture, Catholic doctrine and theology.
2. <u>Marriage, Family and Parenting</u>: "Coming in From the Cold: Healing Long-term Family Rifts," "I'd Like to Say: Divorce Stinks," "Teach Quarreling Children How to Make Peace." This includes husband-wife and parent-child relationships.
3. <u>Social</u>: "Opening Church Doors to the Handicapped," "Senior Gleaners: Helping to Feed the Poor," "Throwaway Kids," "Sanctuary in the Rio Grande Valley."
4. <u>Inspiration and Practical Spirituality</u>: "Prayer for Sunset Years," "Saying 'Yes' to the Cross," "Unthinkable That He Should Die Now."
5. <u>Psychology</u>: "Rediscovering the Child Within You," "Guilt: A Tool for Christian Growth."
6. <u>Profiles</u>: "Ann Jillian," "The Many Sides of Colman McCarthy," "Cardinal Jaime Sin," "Nat Hentoff."
7. <u>Fiction</u>: "Eagles," "Diamonds Are for Never." Stories should provoke thought, make the reader reexamine values and attitudes. Characters suggest how 'believing people' react and deal with the same problems readers face. Make a statement. Must not be sentimental or preachy. No children's fiction.

Query in advance. State subject, sources, authorities and your qualifications to do the article proposed. Library research does not suffice. Firsthand sources and authorities in the field should be consulted and interviewed. Reporting articles are needed more than opinion pieces.

Articles and stories should not exceed 3,000 words. Style and vocabulary should be simple and readable; suited to high-school graduates. Use an interest-grabbing opening, state why the subject is important to readers, use examples, quotes, anecdotes, make practical applications and end strongly.

We do not consider articles submitted to other magazines at the same time.

Manuscripts should contain your name, address and <u>Social Security</u> number. They must be typewritten--double or triple spaced. They will not be returned unless accompanied by a self-addressed, stamped envelope.

Photographs should be protected to prevent cracking. We pay $20 for each photo submitted with an article and used in the magazine.

Please allow six to eight weeks for return of manuscripts. Do not phone to ask if the manuscript has been received. <u>We assume no responsibility for material damaged or lost.</u> Authors should keep a carbon or xerox of any manuscript submitted.

Payment is 12¢ a published word on acceptance. Your Social Security number is necessary to issue the check.

THE BEST WAY TO KNOW WHAT WE PUBLISH IS TO READ AND STUDY SEVERAL ISSUES OF <u>ST. ANTHONY MESSENGER</u>.

SOME RECENT ARTICLES IN ST. ANTHONY MESSENGER

Mary Remembers Jesus Growing Up
How Should We Control Our Borders? An Interview With Congressman Romano Mazzoli
Sanctuary on Trial: Sister Darlene Nicgorski's Story
Acting Like Saints
'If I Had a Son, I Wouldn't Want Him to Be a Priest': Readers Respond
David Toma: Crusader Against Drug Abuse
A Firsthand Report From a Salvadoran Refugee Camp
Are You Called to Be a Lay Minister?
Senior Gleaners: Helping to Feed the Poor
What Trappists and Families Can Learn From Each Other
I'd Like to Say: 'If I Had a Son, I Wouldn't Want Him to Be a Priest!'
Opening Church Doors to Handicapped Catholics
The Many Sides of Colman McCarthy
Cardinal Jaime Sin: Spiritual Leader of the Philippine Revolution
Prayer for Sunset Years
Archbishop Roger M. Mahony: Taking Stands, Making Waves
The Wife of a Deacon: Sharing in Ministry
Hollywood Entertainers Share Their Faith
A Time to Live--One Teenager's Story of Recovery From Alcohol, Drugs and Attempted Suicide
Is Straight a Cult?
Builder of Bridges, Seeker for Justice: Bishop Emerson J. Moore
'Unthinkable That He Should Die Now!': The Death of a Husband
Coming In From the Cold: Healing Long-term Family Rifts
The Gift of a Daddy
Throwaway Kids: An American Tragedy
Ethics in the Trenches: Profile of a Hospital Ethicist
Boys Hope: Turning Lives Around
DRE's: Parish Bridge-Builders
'I'm Lucky to Be Your Daughter'
Rediscovering the Child Within
Sanctuary in the Rio Grande Valley
Living the Spiritual Life: An Interview With Henri Nouwen
Feeding Ethiopia's Hungry: A Firsthand Account
Called at Any Age: Second-Career Priests and Brothers
Post-Abortion Reconciliation: What Is the Church's Role?
Death and Damage in the Ring: The Case Against Boxing
The Synod: Hearing From the Third World
From Egypt to the Empty Tomb: An Exodus-to-Easter Meditation in Pictures
Saying 'Yes' to the Cross
Guilt: A Tool for Christian Growth
What the People of Papua New Guinea Taught Me About Life--and Death
The Three C's of Reconciliation
The Synod: Holding to the Vatican II Course
I'd Like to Say: 'Divorce Stinks!'
Teaching Your Children to Resolve Conflicts
Nat Hentoff: The Church's Unexpected Defender
The Church and the Farm Crisis
Rebuilding Trust: Life With a Recovering Alcoholic
The Bible, the Church and Fundamentalism: An On-the-Run Talk With Raymond Brown
The Vatican's Arizona Astronomers: Blending Science and Faith
Joy to You, Mary! Five Modern Advent Meditations
The Christmas We'll Always Remember
St. Vincent de Paul Society: Commitment to Compassion
The Christophers: 40 Years of Lighting Candles
The World Synod: Will Charisma Survive?

Salmagundi

Skidmore College • Saratoga Springs, New York 12866-0851 (518) 584-5000

Guidelines for Fiction Submissions

We publish very little fiction, unfortunately (sometimes only one story a year)Some of the authors we
have published are Nadine Gordimer, Cynthia Ozick,
Jeff Lipkis, William Gass, Guillermo Cabrera Infante,
Barry Targan,George Konrad and Jorge Semprun.

All manuscripts should be accompanied by a self-
addressed stamped envelope.

Salmagundi
Robert Boyers and Peggy Boyers, Editors

SCRIVENER

McGill University 853 Sherbrooke St.W. Montreal, PQ H3A 2T6

SUBMISSION GUIDELINES

Scrivener accepts submissions of poetry, short fiction, essays, articles, freelance reviews, freelance interviews and black and white graphics and photography. The name and address of the submitter should be on each page of work and graphics and photography should be in well marked envelopes.

Scrivener does not accept previously published poetry or fiction, however, simultaneous submissions of poetry are accepted. All submissions must be neatly typed, (dot-matrix accepted), on white 8½ x 11" paper and accompanied by a cover letter and a SASE with Canadian postage. I.R.C.'s are also accepted.

Length guidelines are as follows:

Poetry	5-15 poems
Fiction	20p max.
Freelance Reviews	5p max.
Freelance Interviews	3000w max.
Essays/ Articles	10p max.
Graphics/ Photography	no limit

The subscription price for Scrivener is $3.00 for 1 year, (1 issue), and $5.00 for 2 years, (2 issues).

creative journal

SECOND COMING, INC
PO BOX 31249
SAN FRANCISCO, CA 94131

WRITER GUIDELINES

The only criteria for publication in SECOND COMING is literary
excellence. We do confess to favoring POST BEAT prose. The
only REAL guideline is to read past issues of our magazine and
book line. We have carefully selected a sample package of
two fiction issues, a novella, and two short story collections,
for the serious writer who hopes to break into print with us.
The retail value, including postage and handling, is over $25.00.

Writers may obtain this sample package for only $10.00, including
postage and handling, but must mention the source of this special
writer guidelines offer.

guidelines for our contributors . . .

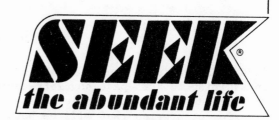

a publication of STANDARD PUBLISHING COMPANY
8121 hamilton avenue • cincinnati, ohio 45231

For Your Information . . .

SEEK is a colorful, illustrated weekly take-home or pass-along paper designed to appeal to modern adults and older teens. SEEK first appeared in its present form in 1970, expanding a four-page Sunday school lesson leaflet, which was published for ninety-five years, into a new concept for personal spiritual enrichment. Its use ranges from the classroom of the Sunday morning Bible class to group discussion and light inspirational reading for individuals and the family.

Materials Accepted for Publication . . .

ARTICLES—400 to 1200 words in length. Usual rate of payment is about 3¢ per word. Articles for publication in SEEK should be in one of the following categories:

1. Inspirational, devotional, personal, or human interest stories.
2. Controversial subject matter, timely religious issues of moral or ethical nature.
3. First-person testimonies of Christian life or experiences, true-to-life happenings, vignettes, emotional situations or problems, examples of answered prayer.

Articles should not be preachy or patronizing. They must be wholesome, alive, vibrant, current, relevant for today's reader, and have a title that demands the article be read. No poetry, please!

Articles are purchased for SEEK as early as one year before the date of publication. Complimentary copies of articles are mailed to writers immediately following publication.

PHOTOGRAPHS—Good human interest pictures of professional quality to accompany articles. We prefer 8 x 10-inch glossy photos with sharp black-and-white contrast. Rate of payment is about $15.

May We Suggest . . .

Please type manuscripts on 8½ x 11-inch paper (not erasable), one side of sheet only. Double space—leave generous margins, write name, address, and social security number in upper left-hand corner of the first page. Also indicate approximate number of words in the manuscript at the upper right-hand corner of the first page. Number all pages in center top.

Enclose self-addressed stamped envelope with manuscript.

Because of the large volume of correspondence involved, we are unable to critique or offer suggestions in regard to contributions that are not acceptable. You may best determine our needs by a careful study of issues of the magazine. Write for free copies. Self-addressed stamped envelope appreciated.

MAGAZINE 850 THIRD AVENUE, NEW YORK, N.Y. 10022 (212) 759-8100

FICTION GUIDELINES

SEVENTEEN publishes one 1,000- to 3,000-word story each month, in addition to a 25-page novelette every June. The editors welcome submissions of stories that focus on the female teenage experience; stories that will be both accessible and appealing to the young readers of SEVENTEEN, while at the same time providing them with inspiration and challenge, stories that have the quality and integrity of today's best literary short fiction.

All submissions must be typed double-spaced and accompanied by a self-addressed, stamped envelope (SASE) large enough to accommodate the manuscript. Manuscripts without SASEs will not be returned. Address all submissions to Sara London, SEVENTEEN, 850 Third Avenue, New York, N.Y. 10022.

We read all submissions and try to respond within six to eight weeks. We regret that we cannot offer individual comments or criticism.

While we do not accept fiction by writers under 21, we do run an annual teen fiction contest. Rules for the contest are published each year in our October issue.

SEVENTEEN pays $500 to $1000 on acceptance for first rights.

We strongly recommend reading the magazine before submitting your work.

TRIANGLE COMMUNICATIONS INC.

The Sewanee Review   *Sewanee, Tennessee, 37375*   615-598-5142

This form responds to your query. ¶For matters of usage consult the Chicago Manual of Style, Webster's Third, and the New Collegiate Dictionary. Unsolicited manuscripts should be original typescripts accompanied by self-addressed envelopes; rejected mss without sufficient return postage will be held. Only unpublished work can be read. ¶Queries are suitable for essays (7500 words or less) and reviews (unassigned reviews are rarely accepted). Send fiction and poetry without writing in advance. Poems (40 lines or less) should not exceed 6 per submission; stories (7500 words or less) should be sent individually. Roughly 250 poems are considered here for each published; 150 stories, for each published. Average time to decide on a submission: 3 to 5 weeks. ¶For information about literary magazines see the latest editions of International Directory of Little Magazines and Small Presses, Literary Market Place, Magazine Industry Market Place, and Ulrich's International Periodicals Directory. ¶Thank you for your interest in the Sewanee Review.

GEORGE CORE
Editor

MARY LUCIA CORNELIUS
Managing Editor

Shofar

SHOFAR, Senior Publications Ltd., 43 Northcote Drive, Melville, New York 11747. October-May. Executive Editor: Alan A. Kay, Ed.D. For Jewish children 8-13. Reports in 6-8 weeks. Complete manuscripts preferred. SASE. Queries welcome. Pays on publication: 7¢/word plus five copies. Black/white, color prints purchased with mss. at additional fee.

Nonfiction, fiction (500-750 words), poetry, photos, puzzles, games, cartoons. (Artwork on assignment only.) All material must be on a Jewish theme. Special holiday issues. (Submit holiday theme pieces at least 4 months in advance.) Will consider photocopied and simultaneous submissions. Buys First North American Serial Rights or First Serial Rights. Free sample copy.

Short Story
REVIEW

P.O. Box 882108   San Francisco, CA 94188   (415) 753-2228

Payment: Five author's copies and a one year subscription.

Length: 500 - 3,500 words. Longer works will be rejected.

Practical Notes:

  a) Manuscripts must be typed and double-spaced.
  b) Name and address should appear on page one.
  c) Photocopied submissions are acceptable.
  d) Writers may submit only one story at a time.
  e) Send a self-addressed stamped envelope with submission.
  f) Simultaneous submissions are acceptable. Please notify
     us if the story has been accepted elsewhere.
  g) Publication acquires first North American serial rights
     when it accepts a story.
  h) Publication replies within twelve weeks, and usually
     quicker.

Guidelines:

We welcome all kinds of stories, both conventional and experimental, serious, humorous, bittersweet, as long as they are well-crafted, convincing, and, in some way, needing to be told. Though we keep an open mind, we tend to prefer short stories of literary merit with a strong narrative line and focus. In addition, we seek stories of character development and psychological insight in which the themes more often than not evolve from the characters themselves. We are not much given to stories based on a clever idea, a trick ending, or elaborate plotting if the other elements of short story writing are neglected. We would prefer not to see science fiction, mystery, romance or journalism.

Editorial Profile:

The Short Story Review, which appears quarterly, is devoted to the short story. Through interviews with prominent writers and editors, reviews of collections, and the publication of stories, it explores aspects and developments in contemporary short fiction. The format is four columns across in an eleven by fifteen inch tabloid. The paper is a hard-surfaced newsprint called electrabrite. Circulation varies from twenty-five hundred to three thousand, of which eight hundred are subscribers, the rest going on a controlled basis to magazine editors, book publishers and publicists, literary agents, reviewers and writers. Subscriptions for one year in the United States and Canada are $9.

Essays • Reviews • Interviews • Short Stories

S I D E W I N D E R

Division of Arts & Humanities, College of the Mainland
8001 Palmer Highway, Texas City, Texas 77591 (409) 938-1211, Ext. 317 or 218

GUIDELINES FOR SUBMISSION

All submissions must be accompanied by a stamped, self-addressed envelope.
We accept only fiction and poetry, require first North American Serial
rights, and pay in copies. Only complete manuscripts should be submitted,
no queries. We will reply within eight weeks of the reception of the
manuscript.

FICTION - We are interested in any length or style of fiction. If
a selection from a novel is submitted, it should be relatively self-
contained. Our main concern is with the originality and skill in
presentation, so we are not interested in genre or formula stories.
The fiction we are looking for is exciting because it takes risks,
and takes them successfully.

POETRY - Any length or form is acceptable. We are not looking for
poetry which is imitative, unsophisticated, or sentimental. Poems in
series or unusual format are welcome.

SING HEAVENLY MUSE!
women's poetry and prose

P.O. Box 13299   Minneapolis, Minnesota 55414

Sing Heavenly Muse! was founded in 1977 to foster the work of women poets, fiction writers, and artists. The magazine is feminist in a broad, generous sense: we encourage women to range freely, honestly, and imaginatively over all subjects, philosophies, and styles. We do not wish to confine women to "women's subjects," whether these are defined traditionally, in terms of femininity and domesticity, or modernly, from a sometimes narrow polemical perspective. We look for explorations, questions that do not come with ready-made answers, emotionally or intellectually. We seek out new writers, many before unpublished, and we welcome men's work that shows an awareness of women's consciousness.

The editors try to reduce to a minimum the common bureaucratic distance between a magazine and its readers and contributors. Although our staff is small, we encourage writers by discussing their work, and we solicit comments from our readers. This relationship makes *Sing Heavenly Muse!* a community where women with widely varying interests and ideas may meet and learn from one another.

The Editors

Query for information on themes and
schedule of upcoming issues.

Sinister Wisdom
P.O. Box 3252
Berkeley, CA 94703

GUIDELINES FOR SUBMISSION

SINISTER WISDOM explores and develops lesbian imagination in the arts and politics. Sinister Wisdom is a place where disagreements stimulate, ideas engage and visions encourage us; a place to find beautiful, original work which expresses a serious and joyful radicalism.

We are particularly interested in work that reflects the diversity of our experiences: as women of color, ethnic women, Third World, Jewish, old, young, working class, poor, disabled, fat. We will not print anything that is oppressive or demeaning to lesbians or women, or which perpetuates negative stereotypes. We do intend to keep an open and critical dialogue on all the issues that effect our work, joy and survival.

ALL WRITTEN WORK SHOULD BE SUBMITTED IN DUPLICATE. Submissions may be in any style or form, or combination of forms. Experimental, accessible work welcome. We prefer you type your work*, and put your name on each page. We will accept handwritten manuscript if legible. SASE MUST BE ENCLOSED. Selection may take up to nine months. If you want to know if we received your manuscript right away, enclose a separate, stamped postcard.

We encourage graphic and visual artists to submit work. Reproduction will be in black and white. Send B&W or work with strong contrast. PLEASE DO NOT SEND US THE ORIGINAL – SEND STATS, COPIES, OR DUPLICATES. Let us know if artwork can be cropped. Let us know if we can put your artwork on file for possible future use if we can't use it right away. ENCLOSE SASE, and stamped postcard for immediate acknowledgement.

Themes for 1988-90 may include: Passing, Revenge, Surviving Therapy and Institutionalization, Addiction, Taboo, Disabled Women, His/Herstory, Upward Mobility, Size, Friendship, Boundaries & Borderlines

Current Editor: Elana Dykewomon. Published quarterly, 128-144pp.
Subscription: $17.00 per year, $6.00 for sample (current) issue.

---

* If you have a Macintosh, you may submit your work on single sided disks – we'll copy from that and return your disk to you in your SASE.

PUBLISHERS SYNDICATION INT'L.

1377 K STREET N.W. SUITE 856 ■ WASHINGTON, D.C. 20005 ■

GUIDELINES

EDITOR: A. P. Samuels

Pays on acceptance plus royalty...Byline given...Reports in 4 to 6 weeks...SASE required for return.

Will buy first time manuscripts if good enough. Photocopies okay. No simultaneous submissions please. We prefer letter quality printing.

Sleuth

EDITOR: Mary Staub

    Sleuth requires mysteries which involve the reader. A story with one or two pencil diagrams..ex: street map with placement of figures pertinent to the story...floor plans...seating arrangements...et cetera. The reader must solve the mystery. Your solution to the mystery and reasoning should be on a separate page. Remember you need multiple obvious suspects.

Submit entire manuscript

We prefer letter quality print but will accept dot matrix

REPORTS: In 4 to 8 weeks

By-line given

SASE required for return

Pays on acceptance

LENGTH: 10,000 words

RATE: 3/4 to 3 cents per word

QUANTITY: 18 a year (will go to 36 in 1989)

Will consider first time manuscripts

Photocopies okay

No simultaneous submissions please

Show word count on your submission

P.S. We are not looking for blood and gore; we are looking for good mysteries which convert the reader into a detective.

the SMALL POND magazine
of literature

The <u>Small</u> <u>Pond</u> <u>Magazine</u> <u>of</u> <u>Literature</u>, aka <u>Small</u> <u>Pond</u>.

FICTION: To 2500 words. Max. <u>is</u> adhered to. Any subject, any
style, but...no syrupy lovelorn material, nor Cosmo-type formula
stories. Originality a big factor. Poor grammar, poor spelling,
poor quality dot matrix mss. don't get finished being read. No
handwritten mss. Name and add. on title page, pages numbered, and
key word from title at top of subsequent pp. Double spaced.

No previously published and/or copyrighted material. Accepted work
not returned, goes to Fairfield Univ. archives in permanent collection with scholar access. Keep all rights, reprint permit given
upon written request. Self-addressed, stamped env. a <u>must</u> for return
of work not accepted. Seeing a sample useful but not essential. Way
back issue, $1.50; back issue, $2.00; current $2.50. Any of these
provide adequate sample. Sample sent will try to focus on your
interest, prose.

The Southern Review

Contribution Policy

Poems and fiction are selected with careful attention to craftsmanship and technique and to the seriousness of the subject matter. Although willing to publish experimental writing that appears to have a valid artistic purpose, The Southern Review avoids extremism and sensationalism. Critical essays and book reviews exhibit a thoughtful and sometimes severe awareness of the necessity of literary standards in our time.

The Southern Review publishes fiction, poetry, critical essays, book reviews, and excerpts from novels in progress, with emphasis on contemporary literature in the United States and abroad, and with special interest in Southern culture and history. Minimum rates to contributors are twelve dollars a printed page for prose and twenty dollars a page for poetry. Payment is made on publication. Two complimentary copies of the issue in which his work appears are sent to each contributor; no reprints are available. Manuscripts must be typewritten, double-spaced, and accompanied by self-addressed, stamped envelopes with sufficient postage to cover return. Manuscripts will not be returned without adequate return postage. Only previously unpublished works will be considered. Allow at least two months for editorial decisions.

Poetry lengths preferred are one to four pages; fiction, four to eight thousand words; essays, four to ten thousand words. All book reviews are on a commissioned basis. Do not send fillers, jokes, plays, feature articles, or artwork. Queries are not necessary. First American serial rights only are purchased.

Sample copies are $5.00 payable in advance. For style information, see A Manual of Style, published by the University of Chicago Press. Use a minimum of footnotes. The Southern Review and Louisiana State University do not assume responsibility for views expressed by contributors. Address manuscripts to the Editors, The Southern Review, 43 Allen Hall, Louisiana State University, Baton Rouge, Louisiana 70803.

SOUTHWEST REVIEW

• 6410 Airline Road
Southern Methodist University
Dallas, Texas 75275
(214) 373-7440

GUIDELINES FOR SUBMISSION OF SHORT STORIES

In each issue the Southwest Review publishes two
or three stories, which must be of high literary
quality. We have published fiction in widely
varying styles. We prefer stories of character
development, of psychological penetration, to
those depending chiefly on plot. We have no
specific requirements as to subject matter.
Some of our stories have a southwestern
background, but even more are not regional.
We prefer, however, that stories not be too
strongly regional if the region with which they
deal is not our own.

The preferred length of our stories is 3,000 to
5,000 words. All submissions should be typed
neatly on white paper and accompanied by a
stamped, self-addressed envelope. The
Southwest Review does not consider simultaneous
submissions or work that has been published.

We also send the author three gratis contributor's
copies of the issue in which the story appears
as well as nominal payment. We publish quarterly.

SOUTHWEST REVIEW AWARDS

The JOHN H. McGINNIS MEMORIAL AWARD is
given each year for material--alternately
fiction and nonfiction--that has been published
in the Southwest Review in the previous two
years. Thus, stories or articles are not
submitted directly for the award, but simply
for publication in the magazine. From among
those published in each two-year period, then,
the judges select what they feel to be the best
story or article for the McGinnis award...$1000.

Likewise, poems are not submitted directly
for the ELIZABETH MATCHETT STOVER AWARD. This
annual prize of $100 is awarded to the author
of the best poem published in the magazine
during the preceding year.

STARWIND
BOX 98
RIPLEY, OH 45167

WRITER'S GUIDELINES

STARWIND is a quarterly publication for the young adult (approx. ages 16-25) who has an interest in science and technology, and who also enjoys reading well-crafted science fiction and fantasy. Rights are negotiable, payment ranges from 1¢ to 4¢ per word.

NON-FICTION: Articles of scientific and technological interest. Possible topics might include: reviews of places you can visit and be struck by a gee-whiz sense of awe and wonder about how far man can go if he puts his mind to it! (i.e. museums, NASA installations, Oak Ridge, etc.); "did you know" articles dealing with development of current technology, medical or scientific advances; interviews with or profiles of the unsung heroes of science, engineering and technology. A good model would be a short article from *High Technology* or *Discover*. Or, take a tip from TV and watch "Nova" to get a feel for the type of stuff we like to see. Use your imagination! We also publish book reviews, both on books of a scientific or technological nature, and science fiction. Word length for non-fiction: 1000-7000 words (approx.). Sketches, Charts and Pictures are encouraged! No query necessary.

CURRENT NON-FICTION NEEDS: Geriatric reseach / Human Life Extension; SDI or SDI-related research; Current research in Veterinary medicine; Chemistry of Paint / Science of Color; Robotics; Computer Security systems; How "Anytime" Bank machines work; Methods of Communicating besides speech, Educational Systems (U.S. and Abroad); Artificial Intelligence; the Tech of the Olympics; Martial Arts; and Lumbering (that is, the felling of trees)

FICTION: Both hard and soft science fiction and fantasy. We like to see positive, plausible SF and fantasy, with strong characters who interact with their environment, rather than letting themselves be controlled by it. Although we aren't interested in blatantly feminist fiction, we do like to see stories with strong female protagonists. We especially look for SF which depicts hope for the future. Word length for fiction: 2000-10,000 words (approx.). No query necessary. We don't publish novel excerpts or serializations, nor are we interested in poetry or vignettes.

INFORMATION ON SUBMITTING: Send SASE with proper postage for the manuscript's return or for a reply (postage stamps or *undated* meter postmarks, please - the USPS Domestic Mail Manual states that *the date must not be shown* on meter postmarks used to prepay reply postage).

If you're out of the country, send US postage or International Postal Reply Coupons (an IRC is currently redeemable for 37¢ US postage). We're sorry, but we cannot accept manuscripts that arrive postage-due, return manuscripts with no SASE, or be responsible for material that gets lost in the mail (please keep a copy for your files).

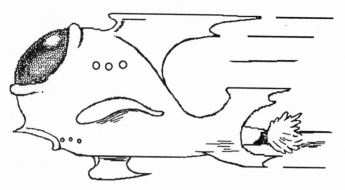

We appreciate non-simultaneous submissions, with one manuscript per mailing. Photocopies, computer printouts and electronic disk submissions are fine with us (IBM-PC or PC-compatible, and Macintosh, in Multimate, MacWrite or ASCII format). Please include your name, address, story title and word count on the story's first page.

Guidelines for SASE; STARWIND #2, #3 or #4 available for $2.50; STARWIND #7 (Spring 1987) to be available soon for $3.50.

Stephen Wright's
Mystery Notebook
BOOKS NEWS INFORMATION℠

<u>Stephen Wright's Mystery Notebook</u> is a limited circulation publication for mystery readers and writers.

Our main contents are articles on the mystery, in various aspects, but occasionally we have published fiction, short shorts or novel excerpts. It is most difficult to get any piece accepted for publication in the <u>Mystery Notebook</u>, as our standards are high. In this kind of journal, we cannot afford to pay our contributors. Besides publication, the accepted writer receives free copies of the issue containing his or her piece.

Formerly a quarterly publication, the <u>Notebook</u> is now issued twice a year, so there is even more difficulty in gaining acceptance. I'm afraid I cannot encourage the beginning or new writer at all, as we are only interested in a highly professional product. However, depending on many factors, even if the product is professional, it is does not necessarily mean an acceptance. Furthermore, we insist on a query letter always before giving our permission for submission.

These may serve as general guidelines, but we refuse to be limited by them.

P. O. BOX 1341 • F.D.R. STATION • NEW YORK, N.Y. 10150

STORIES

GUIDELINES FOR WRITERS

STORIES is a quarterly magazine devoted exclusively to the short story. It is designed to encourage the writing of stories that evoke emotional response. We publish new stories primarily and also consider advance publication of fiction to be released by other publishers. For First North American Serial Rights we pay a minimum of $150, upon publication.

We look for a simple, universal style and avoid subjects that are fashionable. The caliber and variety of our material can best be appreciated by reading an issue, which we will supply to authors for $3.00 upon request.

MANUSCRIPT PREPARATION: Please send a photocopy of the typed manuscript (dot-matrix discouraged). Your name, current address, and telephone number should appear on the first page. We will assume you have retained the original; we cannot be responsible for loss or damage of manuscripts. In the event your story is declined, we will return it if you will provide the traditional self-addressed, stamped envelope—or, if you prefer, you may instruct us to destroy the photocopy and to notify you in the s.a.s.e.

MAILING: Manuscripts may be sent "fourth class, special," and these words should appear on the envelope to avoid "postage due" charges. If you wish receipt confirmed, kindly enclose a postcard that we can drop in the mail. International reply coupons should be sufficient for the weight of the overseas package.

NOTIFICATION: Please allow 8-10 weeks for notification. If you feel this period is too long and wish to send your work to other magazines, please indicate on the manuscript that it is a simultaneous submission.

Thank you for the opportunity to consider your work for STORIES.

Single copies are mailed under separate cover;
please allow several weeks for delivery

All stories published in this magazine
are automatically submitted to "The Best American
Short Stories" and "O. Henry Prize Awards" anthologies

STORY CARDS

P.O. Box 11575, Washington, D.C. 20008-0775, (202) 462-3263

Story Cards Writers' Guidelines

Story Cards is a unique, literary publication. Inside each Story Card is a short story relating to an occasion, such as birthdays, anniversaries, Valentine's Day, or April Fool's day. On the front of each Story Card is an original illustration based on that story. The biographies of the writer and artist are printed on the back of each Card.

Story Cards was conceived as a way of getting quality, short fiction to people who haven't read a short story since English 101. It was also designed as a vehicle for writers and artists to have their works seen by the public.

A Tradition Revived

Story Cards continues the tradition of giving stories as gifts, a custom popular in America during the 1700s and 1800s. We believe that short fiction is exciting, and can convey superb images and ideas through its strong prose and concise form. We hope you enjoy reading and sending Story Cards.

What to Write

Short stories about holidays. The stories do not have to focus on the occasion, as long as they pertain to it. For example, a tale that involved a father and daughter could be a Father's Day story. Friendship is also an occasion. What matters is that the reader can tell that your story is about a particular occasion: The card form is the means to encourage people to read short stories. The stories must be superbly written, interesting, and neatly typed. Please, no overly religious or sentimental themes. The best hint we can offer is to write for the story, not for the occasion. Story Cards is aimed at an educated audience -- people who may have once enjoyed reading short fiction, but who haven't come across short stories for a while. Wit and surprise are appreciated qualities. No more than 2000 words -- the shorter the better.

Only the highest quality fiction is accepted. We can't emphasize that enough. Send only one story at a time.

Madison Bell's thesis in "Less is Less" in the April 1986 issue of Harper's describes the kind of story we enjoy reading.

Please include a stamped, return envelope along with your manuscript. Simultaneous submissions are okay, as long as you let us know. Indicate which occasion your story is tied to, and tell us something about yourself in a short letter. We will respond as quickly as possible.

Story Cards is copyrighted, and pays $100 to $900 a story plus 5 Cards. (For illustrations, too.)

Sample copies are $5.

Publishers: Bill Adler, Jr. and Katharine McKenna

STORY CARDS

P.O. BOX 11575, WASHINGTON, D.C. 20008-0775, (202) 462-3263

What Is Story Cards?

Story Cards^{tm} is a new, exciting literary form published by Story Cards, Inc.

Inside each Story Card is a 200 to 2500 word short story; on the front of every Card is an original illustration based on that story. Story Cards contain the best contemporary fiction and art in North America.

Story Cards is a literary journal in the disguise of a greeting card. We use the greeting card shape to entice people to read short fiction, especially individuals who haven't read a short story since English 101. Because content follows form, all Story Cards stories relate --however loosely-- to an occasion, such as birthdays, bon voyage, Halloween, or friendship.

Story Cards continues a tradition of giving stories as gifts, a custom popular in America during the 1700s and 1800s. Story Cards' publishers believe that short fiction is moving and provocative, and can convey superb images and ideas through its strong prose and concise form. We think that stories make wonderful gifts.

Story Cards, Inc.'s second goal is to provide a valuable outlet for writers and artists. We pay writers and illustrators top fees for their work. On the back of Story Cards are printed the biographies of the story's author and illustrator.

The Story Behind Story Cards

Story Cards was conceived by Bill Adler, Jr., a Washington, D.C. writer and Katharine L. McKenna, a New York City artist -- the publishers. Adler frequently gave short stories to friends as birth-day presents, and at the same time, wrote stories for literary magazines. But he noticed that while his friends always read (and liked) the stories he gave them, few purchased fiction journals. Soon Bill Adler realized that the best way to inspire people to read short fiction was simply to present it to them. After he wrote a story for Katharine for her 28th birthday, they decided to create Story Cards, Inc.

Bill Adler received his B.A. from Wesleyan University and M.A. from Columbia University's School of International Affairs. Katharine McKenna also graduated from Wesleyan; she received her M.I.A. from Pratt University.

Some Technical Information

Story Cards were designed by Watermark Design in Alexandria, Virginia. Story Cards are printed in Times Roman type on 100 pound, Mowhawk superfine paper -- paper that holds ink so well that it is able to preserve the fine detail in Story Cards' illustrations. The actual stories are printed on the inside panels of the Cards, which unfold like accordions. Each panel contains about 400 words: The largest Story Cards are 30 inches long. Story Cards are sold by mail and in stores around the United States and Canada. Retail prices range from $1 to $3 a Card.

Finally, Story Cards Is or Story Cards Are?

Story Cards is an _is_ when referring to the company, the art form or a particular Card. Story Cards is an _are_ when talking about more than one Card. But as long as you spell our name right, we're happy.

WHEN YOU WRITE

For the personal reading and leadership magazines of the Mennonite Publishing House

Story Friends

Editor: Marjorie Waybill
Audience: children, ages 4-9
Focus: story paper that reinforces Christian values
Frequency: monthly in weekly issues

Story Friends needs stories (300 to 800 words), poems, and activities that speak to the needs of all children.

Stories should
- Provide positive ways to express love and caring
- Introduce readers to children from many cultures
- Reinforce the values taught by the church family (at home or in the gathered group)
- Focus on God's creation and how to care for it
- Acquaint children with a wide age range of friends
- Portray Jesus as their friend and helper—a friend who cares about their happy and sad experiences
- Mirror the joys, fears, temptations, and successes of the readers in the story characters
- Emphasize that each one is unique and important

General Guidelines

Manuscripts must be typewritten on 8½ × 11 white paper, double-spaced on one side of the sheet only. (Computer printout also acceptable.) Enter your name and address in the upper left-hand corner, and the approximate number of words (and character count, if known) in the upper right-hand corner. All manuscripts must be accompanied by a self-addressed stamped envelope (SASE). Seasonal material should be submitted six months in advance. Book reviews are to follow the guidelines and form provided for their report.

Manuscripts will be read as promptly as possible and returned or purchased upon acceptance. We purchase one-time rights only.

We seek to treat each manuscript carefully, but urge that the author keep a copy for personal reference. While we respect the writer's style and purpose, we reserve the right to edit the copy to fit our literary standards. If major content changes are necessary, the editor will send a revised manuscript to the author for approval.

Rates of payment vary among the magazines. The quality of the material and the relative need for it also affect the rate. Contact editor about specific questions. Generally payment is made upon acceptance of manuscript. Payment for a book review is the book reviewed. Maximum rates for one-time use, $50.00 per thousand words. Payment for reprints is one half of one-time rights.

Mennonite Publishing House
616 Walnut Avenue
Scottdale, PA 15683-1999
Telephone 412-887-8500

The pages which follow describe the manuscript needs of the personal reading and leadership magazines published by the Mennonite Publishing House. Writers are invited to contact the editor(s) of the publication(s) of their interest.

WRITING FOR

STRAIGHT

A publication of Standard Publishing, 8121 Hamilton Avenue, **Cincinnati, OH 45231**

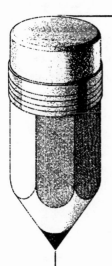

Before you submit...

. . . please get to know us. Sample issues are available on request (enclose SASE, please).

Manuscripts are submitted on speculation. Please type on 8½ x 11, nonerasable paper, one side of the sheet only. Double space and leave generous margins. Type your name, address, and Social Security number on the first sheet, as well as the approximate word count.

Package photos carefully and enclose a self-addressed mailing label, postage, and return packing.

All submissions must be accompanied by a self-addressed stamped envelope, or your submission will not be returned. Expect to wait 4-8 weeks to hear from us.

Send your work to:

> Editor, *Straight*
> Standard Publishing
> 8121 Hamilton Avenue
> Cincinnati, OH 45231

These clues will help you

To avoid a rejection, keep these things in mind:

- Teenagers today are different from the way they were when you were a teen, even if you are a young person. Get to know teens before you begin to write for them. Many manuscripts are rejected simply because the plot or vocabulary is outdated for modern teens.

- Some teenagers read no higher than sixth grade level. Don't write down to kids, but keep this in mind as you write. Words should be simple. Stories should be short and direct.

- A tacked-on moral does not make a religious story. Make your **characters** Christian, and the religious slant will take care of itself.

- We look for material to correlate with Bible-school lessons, so each quarter we are considering specific topics. If you request it, we will put you on our mailing list to receive quarterly themes.

- We produce *Straight* long before its publication date. Send seasonal material 9-12 months in advance.

We're Always Looking for IDEAS!

... and maybe you have just the one we're looking for!

Straight is a weekly magazine for Christian teenagers, published quarterly by the Standard Publishing Company, 8121 Hamilton Avenue, Cincinnati, OH 45231.

Straight is distributed through churches in the United States and other English-speaking countries. It's designed to correlate with Standard Publishing's Young Teen and Youth Bible-school lessons. We emphasize the victorious, fulfilling Christian life. We want what we print to be positive and uplifting.

Fiction must appeal to teenagers and have an interesting, well-constructed plot. The main characters should be contemporary teens who cope with modern-day problems using Christian principles. Stories should be character-building, but not preachy. Conflicts must be resolved realistically, with thought-provoking and honest endings. Accepted length is 1100 to 1500 words.

Non-fiction is accepted. We use devotional pieces, articles on current issues from a Christian point of view, and humor. Non-fiction pieces should concern topics of interest to teens, including school, family life, recreation, friends, part-time jobs, dating, and music. Occasionally we handle heavier topics like serious social or personal problems, but not often. You're more likely to make a sale if you stick to positive subjects.

Photos of professional quality are appreciated. Submit only high-contrast black and white glossies. We use photos of teens and teen activities, and those which accompany or illustrate articles. All photos should feature teens who are conservative in appearance, with no revealing clothing or outrageous hairstyles. Teens should have a natural, expressive appearance, not an artificial, posed, "too perfect" look.

Puzzles and Art are done by assignment only. If you'd like to be considered for an assignment, please let us know.

Poetry is accepted from teens only. The author's birthdate must accompany all poetry submitted.

What you can expect in payment

Payment is on acceptance. *Straight* pays 2¢ per word for first rights, and 1-1½¢ per word for reprint rights. Photos bring $15-$25 for first use, and $10-$15 for reuse.

Rates for teen submissions vary.

You will hear from us as soon as we accept your work. A check will be mailed to you about 2 weeks later.

Your **Social Security number** is required for payment if you live in the United States. Your birthdate is required if you are under 20 years of age. Please include this information with all submissions.

StreamLines
Minnesota Journal of Creative Writing

207 Lind Hall   207 Church Street S.E.   Minneapolis, MN 55455

Submission Guidelines

StreamLines: Minnesota Journal of Creative Writing, *a non-profit literary magazine, publishes a wide range of fiction, non-fiction, and poetry. Two issues are published each year, one in the spring and one in the fall. We accept short stories, memoirs, plays, creative essays (excluding scholarly or research essays), interviews, long poems, and excerpts from longer works.* **StreamLines** *especially encourages submissions from new or unpublished writers.*

Manuscripts should be no longer than 3,000 words. Please submit your manuscript typed and double-spaces, and include the page number and abbreviated title at the top of each page. Your name should not be written on the submission, but on your cover letter only, along with the title(s) of your submission, a short biography, and your phone number. You should also include a self-addressed stamped envelope. Submittors can expect a response from the editors within three months. Upon publication, authors will be paid with three complimentary magazines. The copyright on each submission returns to the author.

StreamLines *also publishes artwork and photography. Please submit original black and white ink drawings, sketches, graphics, or photographs with a short biography, your phone number, and a self-addressed stamped envelope. Artists are also paid with three complimentary magazines.*

Student Lawyer is a monthly legal affairs magazine published by the Law Student Division of the American Bar Association. It has a circulation of approximately 40,000, most of whom are law students.

Student Lawyer is not a legal journal. It is a features magazine, competing for a share of law students' limited spare time--so the articles we publish must be informative, lively "good reads." We have no interest whatsoever in anything that resembles a footnoted, academic article.

Student Lawyer has between four and six feature articles in each issue, ranging from 2,500 to 4,000 words apiece. We try to avoid imposing limits; writers should write according to the amount of their material and not beyond. We are interested in professional and legal education issues, sociolegal phenomena, legal career features, profiles of lawyers who are making an impact on the profession, and the (very) occasional piece of fiction. We do not accept poetry. We pay $450-$650 for features, depending on the story.

Student Lawyer's departments offer a shot at other kinds of writing as well. Our news section, **Briefly** is composed of 100- to 150-word items on matters of public policy, the press, personalities, and government that have an impact on legal education, the law, and the legal profession. These items should be submitted on speculation; we pay $25-$100, depending on length. **Pro Se** is an opinion column in which an author may wax eloquent for 1,000 to 1,500 words on a pet topic involving a legal issue or legal education. **Esq.** profiles lawyers who are doing something novel or out of the ordinary with their careers. **Legal Aids** is a forum for pieces about unusual people, programs, and approaches connected to the teaching, learning, or practicing of the law. **Ethics** is devoted to the discussion of moral/legal dilemmas and peccadilloes. **End Note** is our humor department, and Et Al. is for stories that fit none of the above categories. All of these departments run about 1,000 to 1,500 words; we pay from $125 to $250.

We want what a good writer can provide--fresh reporting, lively writing, and insightful analysis. Writers should expect to work with the magazine's editors to provide missing or additional information, to clear up the unclear, and to polish any rough edges. When you look good, we look good.

We do not make assignments to writers with whose work we are not familiar. If you're interested in writing for us, we suggest you send in either an actual story or a detailed, thought-out query with a good selection of previously published clips. We are always willing to look at material on spec.

But this is just talk. The best way to find out what Student Lawyer is all about is to read an issue. We'll gladly send one. Just forward $2 for postage and handling to the address below.

THE MAGAZINE OF THE LAW STUDENT DIVISION • AMERICAN BAR ASSOCIATION
750 NORTH LAKE SHORE DRIVE • CHICAGO, ILLINOIS 60611 • 312/988-6048

A MAGAZINE OF IDEAS

We're interested in all writing that makes sense and enriches our common space — articles, essays, interviews, fiction, poetry as well as photographs, cartoons, and drawings. The ostensible subject isn't as important as the writer's passion for it, the language, the love of truth.

We rarely run anything longer than 10,000 words. There's no minimum word length.

Payment is in copies and a six-month subscription to THE SUN. Because of a grant from the North Carolina Arts Council and the National Endowment for the Arts in Washington, D.C., a federal agency, we also pay modestly for published work — from $5 to $25 for poems, photographs and drawings, and up to $50 for longer stories and essays.

Submissions should be typed and double-spaced, unless that's impossible, in which case please print neatly. Include a stamped, self-addressed envelope, with the correct amount of postage for the weight of your manuscript. We usually reply within six weeks, often much sooner.

Sy Safransky
Editor, **THE SUN**

412 West Rosemary St., Chapel Hill, NC 27514

(919) 942-5282

Editorial Offices
Sunshine Magazine
Good Reading Magazine

SUNSHINE PRESS

Litchfield, Illinois 62056
Telephone: (217) 324-3425

House of Sunshine

Sunshine Magazine
Editorial Guidelines and Suggestions for Writers

Manuscripts are carefully reviewed by members of the editorial staff. Queries are not necessary and are, therefore, discouraged. Use of previously published material is quite selective. Authors must assume responsibility for originality. Articles and stories over 1,250 words in length will not be considered.

Manuscripts, including poetry, submitted without a self-addressed, stamped envelope (SASE) will NOT be returned. Such material is kept on file for one year only and authors are invited to send sufficient postage for their manuscripts' return within that time.

Return of a manuscript does not necessarily imply lack of merit, and limited time makes comment on individual submissions impossible.

Please allow six to eight weeks for our response to your submission.

Purchasing Policy

Payment is made on acceptance of a manuscript and we purchase first North American serial rights with the privilege of reprinting the manuscript in any of our other SUNSHINE PRESS publications. Authors retain all other rights to their material. Payment is based on the quality of writing, with consideration for the amount of editorial work required to prepare it for publication. However, acceptance and purchase of a manuscript does not guarantee its publication.

We strongly urge all interested writers to carefully examine our magazines. Pay particular attention to length limits and the types of articles used in the magazines. If your manuscript differs greatly in style and content from the examples in a sample copy, it is unlikely that the manuscript would be accepted for publication in one of our magazines.

Sample copies of SUNSHINE MAGAZINE and GOOD READING MAGAZINE are available on request at 50¢ each (please include a SASE).

Authors receive a complimentary copy when their manuscripts are published. Extra copies at half the cover price may be ordered at that time, subject to availability.

The quantity of manuscripts received requires us to be very selective. Manuscripts must be neatly typed, double-spaced on standard size paper. Please put your name and complete address on your manuscript.

Careful manuscript preparation is very important. Correct grammar, spelling and puncuation are the responsibilty of the author and weaknesses in these areas will affect our purchase decision.

We do not purchase clippings and cannot use material that is not attributed to an author.

Sunshine Magazine

Primarily human interest and inspirational in its appeal, SUNSHINE MAGAZINE provides worthwhile reading for the family and is fictional to a large degree. We do not accept material of a specifically religious or depressing nature (for example, divorce, gambling, drug abuse, alcohol, deathbed, violence, child abuse or juvenile delinquency). Humorous material or that with a surprise ending is especially welcome. To be valuable to the reader, stories should have a constructive, dynamic climax. Conversation within a story should be grammatically correct but not stilted, comfortable but not improper.

$40-$100 for *fiction* of maximum length (1,250 words) used on pages 3 and 16 of each issue. **$25-$60** for secondary stories (900 words or less) of the same nature.

$25 for *My Most Extraordinary Experience: Yes, It Happened to ME:* on page 5A, first-person, non-fiction accounts of an unusual or spectacular true event or circumstance (300 to 500 words maximum). The event or circumstance can be a once-in-a-lifetime occurence (piloting the blimp or meeting the president, for example) or a situation that helped influence a life (a miraculous escape, for instance, or advice from a respected person that continues to inspire).

$20 for *The Editor's Favorite Meditation* on page 2 and *The Gem of the Month* on page 22. Items should not exceed 200 words and should be inspirational, uplifting essays about nature, human nature, seasons, etc. Examples are: "Thoughts for a Busy Mother," "Golden Memories," "What is an Anniversary?" or "Sunrise . . . Sunset."

$15 for **The Editor's Favorite Poem** on page 15. Length should not exceed 16 lines. Read our Poetry Policy *carefully* for more explanation.

We also purchase juvenile stores for *Calling All Young People*, limited to 400 words and directed at ages four to fourteen. Acceptable material includes, story-type poetry, humor, true-to-life experiences or how-to articles.

Jokes and quotations should NOT be submitted. We do use short items and letters, and these submissions are very welcome. However, we do not purchase this material.

Good Reading Magazine

$20-100 for *non-fiction* articles (maximum 1,000 words). Articles and stories are generally based on a wide range of current or factual subjects that appeal to readers in the busy, modern world. Subjects preferred include business, success and personal achievement, humorous, lively articles, nature, inventions and crafts, travel (foreign and domestic) and biography (current and historical). Seasonal material is very welcome. Some recent topics published in GOOD READING MAGAZINE are: The Gateway Arch in St. Louis, Missouri, winter scuba diving, pets in the White House, England's mysterious Stone Henge, Virginia's Garden Week, the first personal computer, the giant panda, baseball's Tommy Lasorda and Harry Truman.

Good quality, **black and white glossy photographs** illustrating an article are desirable and should be submitted with the article since this can affect our purchase decision. The number of photographs required varies with the type of article, a biography may not need as many photos to be illustrated as a travel article, for example. Credit lines are given. Color photographs and slides are NOT acceptable for use in GOOD READING MAGAZINE. Please include sufficient postage for the return of photographs after publication.

Cartoons—We welcome cartoons as submissions for GOOD READING MAGAZINE only. We are very selective when purchasing cartoons and prefer those done in good taste about everyday life. Cartoon strips are not acceptable. Simple artwork that lends itself to reduction is most acceptable; please refrain from using shading or tinting. Payment is $10 for a single cartoon and a complimentary copy of GOOD READING MAGAZINE will be sent to the artist upon publication.

Quizzes and Puzzles—One quiz is used in each issue of GOOD READING MAGAZINE, payment is $10. Short quizzes are preferred and word search or maze puzzles are not acceptable.

Poetry Policy

We use some poetry in both magazines, but the greater amount is in SUNSHINE MAGAZINE. We do not pay for poetry we use, with the exception of *The Editor's Favorite Poem* or a feature poem. Accepted submissions are filed and used as needed.

The poetry we prefer is easy to read and pleasantly rhythmic; of general interest, uplifting and purposeful. Length should not exceed 12 to 16 lines. Short, humorous or seasonal poetry is used regularly.

Any poetry submitted without a self-addressed, stamped envelope (SASE) cannot be returned. A complimentary copy will be sent when an author's poem is published.

Fillers

We occasionally purchase short articles for use as fillers in both SUNSHINE MAGAZINE and GOOD READING MAGAZINE. We pay $10 for such material.

The Editorial Staff

SWANK MAGAZINE EDITORIAL GUIDELINES

As a response to all readers who have submitted fiction or have
requested editorial guidelines, here's an idea of what goes into
Swank:

(1) <u>Non-Sex Piece</u>. Every issue has a non-sex article accompanied
by photographs. The photographs must be clear and action oriented.
Recent examples are:
Feb. issue "Games of Death" about survival games
March issue "So You Want To Be A Mercenary"
April issue "Living on the Edge" (Men who work at dangerous jobs)
others include a piece on the "One Man SWAT Team Against Terrorists"
        (a man who rescues people held in foreign jails)
        and "The Stuntmens' Rodeo"
        We also ran a piece on the new breed of race car drivers.
The quality and abundance of photos determine whether or not the
piece will be accepted.

(2) <u>Sex Articles</u>. Recent articles have been on "Past Lives Sex
Therapy", where people get regressed to a former life experience to
explore how their sexuality developed. And then there is "Programming
Your Dreams" about how you can have happy--even wet--dreams as you
catch 40 winks. Then we did a piece on "Sexaholics Anonymous" as
a support group. These are all serious, well-researched pieces on
sexual topics.

Additionally, we have advice pieces that are related to sexuality.
For instance "How to Approach That Female Stranger You Desire";
and "A Single Girl Tells Ten Tips to Land Girls in Bed on the First
Date" and "How to Make the Man Shortage Work For You".

(3) We have a photo essay on an automotive topic every month. Recent
topics have been "Burnout", "Snowblasters" and "Dream Cars", which
are fantasy machines for the low budget.

(4) <u>Fiction</u>. Because our editorial budget has been so severely cut,
we have been recycling old illustrations and commissioning new
fiction pieces to go with them. Submitting fiction at this time
is not a good bet.

What we at Swank need most (besides a bigger staff and greater
editorial budget) are non-sex pieces and sex-related pieces. With
the non-sex piece, submit photos and a query. With a sex-related
piece, a good query (no photo) will get a quick response.

Thank you for your interest in Swank Magazine. We hope this memo
will help you determine our editorial needs.

Remember to send photos (samples only) that are chromes or transparencies...no "prints".

'TEEN

Dear Writer:

Thank you for expressing an interest in writing for 'TEEN Magazine.

At the present time, we are buying fiction and nonfiction on a limited basis only. We are looking for realistic, up-beat stories concerned with current teen interests and teen problems handled sensitively.

If you are interested in submitting <u>nonfiction</u>, please send query letters only in a quick summary or outline form along with a self-addressed, stamped envelope with sufficient postage. DO NOT SEND COMPLETED NONFICTION MANUSCRIPTS. Also send a resume and <u>copies</u> only of any recently published work that give evidence of your writing style.

Please keep in mind that rarely are the ideas themselves original. Rather, we are looking for an angle or approach to teen subjects that are fresh and innovative.

If we are interested, we will contact you to discuss rates, length and other pertinent information. Please be advised that we do not pay kill fees and that the agreed-upon purchase price is for all rights.

If you are interested in submitting <u>fiction manuscripts</u>, please keep these guidelines in mind:

1. Stories should have a teenage girl as the central character.
2. Length should be from 2,500-4,000 words (10-15 double-spaced, typewritten pages).
3. Subject matter and vocabulary should be appropriate for an average 16-year-old reader.
4. Payment is $100 upon acceptance for all rights.

You will hear from us within 10 weeks if your material is accompanied by a SASE. Material will not be returned without sufficient postage.

Thank you once again for thinking of 'TEEN. Best of luck.

Sincerely,

Roxanne Camron, editor

8490 SUNSET BOULEVARD • LOS ANGELES, CALIFORNIA 90069 • (213) 854-2950

THE THREEPENNY REVIEW

Wendy Lesser   *Editor and Publisher*

1. At present The Threepenny Review is paying $50 per story, poem, or article.

2. All manuscripts should be submitted with a stamped, self-addressed envelope.

3. All stories should be double-spaced, with at least one-inch margins. Short stories should generally be under 4000 words, though exceptions are possible.

4. Please do not submit more than two stories at a time; in general, we prefer to look at only one.

5. We will read xerox copies and dot-matrix-printed copies, though letter-quality printing is preferable. We will not read simultaneous submissions.

5. Response time for unsolicited manuscripts ranges from three weeks to two months.

6. Writers whose stories are accepted will be consulted if any editing is done on their pieces, and will have the opportunity to proofread galleys for typographical errors.

7. At this point we have rather a large backlog, so accepted material may have to wait up to a year to be published.

8. It is recommended that those submitting work for the first time to The Threepenny Review take a look at a sample copy beforehand. Individual copies are available from the publisher for $4.00 each (cover price plus $1.00 postage).

P.O. Box 9131
Berkeley, California 94709   (415) 849-4545

THE NATIONAL SOCIETY OF SUSPENSE
AND MAINSTREAM FICTION WRITER'S
P.O. BOX 922
SUMMERVILLE, S.C.   29484-0922

THRILLER

<u>WRITERS GUILDLINES FOR SUBMISSION</u>

We accept:

1) Fiction (Mainstream)
2) Interviews with Fiction/Suspense authors.
3) Book reviews on current Fiction/Suspense titles.
4) Short humorous comics.
5) Gag writing.

When submitting material for our consideration, please follow our simple guildlines:

1) Submit only categories listed above.
2) Use white typing paper only.
3) Double space.
4) Use wide margins.
5) Enclose adequate SASE if you want your manuscript returned.
6) Please enclose $2.50 for processing and handling fees.

We accept:

1) Short-short stories   500-2,000.
2) Short stories   2,000-4,500.
3) Long stories   4,500+

Reports in 2-3 weeks.

Payment rate varies.

We pay upon acceptance.

THRILLER Copies are available for $1.75

Thank you for considering our publication.

GOOD LUCK!

Sincerely,

-The Editors

Get a THRILL from THRILLER, Let the adventure begin...........

"CATCH THE THRILLER SPIRIT!"

TriQuarterly   Northwestern University
1735 Benson Avenue
Evanston, Illinois 60201

Thank you for inquiring about our interest in your work.

TriQuarterly publishes unsolicited short fiction, poetry, artwork and, occasionally, essays of a general and literary nature: memoirs, cultural criticism, unusually literate travel meditations, and so on. Work submitted should not include scholarly, critical or philosophical essays, or full-length novels. Nor does the magazine frequently publish excerpts from longer works. Less common forms such as the novella (on the short side), dramatic forms, long poems, and others, are welcome. Please query regarding essays, but poetry, fiction, and art work--send slides or photos--may be submitted at any time. All work submitted must be unpublished in the U.S. and elsewhere. This also applies to translations, for which translators must secure permission to publish.

All MSS should by typed, double-spaced, and accompanied by a stamped, self-addressed envelope. Please send originals or photocopies rather than carbon copies. We do not like to read MSS produced by dot-matrix printers. MSS submitted without return postage cannot be sent back to the author. We try to report on submissions within two months of receipt, but longer works may require more time.

Please study a past issue if you are unfamiliar with its format and general interests. Back issues may be ordered directly from **TriQuarterly.**

    ---the Editors

The Cincinnati Enquirer

617 VINE STREET
CINCINNATI, OHIO 45201

Tristate Magazine

Thank you for inquiring about our freelance needs. Below are guidelines that may be helpful.

WRITING: We use a considerable amount of free-lance copy. The only real limit on the material is to make it locally oriented (i.e. Cincinnati, Southern Ohio, Northern Kentucky, southeastern Indiana). Any article that is controversial must be balanced and fair, presenting both sides. All writers' allegations must be thoroughly substantiated and documented. Length: 500-1,500 words.

Fees range from $75 to $350 depending on length, quality of writing, amount of research. We accept manuscripts on speculation only, except in rare instances or when a specific story is assigned. Payment is made about the 10th of the month following month of publication. Depending on circumstances, we buy manuscripts on a first rights basis; occasionally on an exclusive "area rights" basis. Time lapse between acceptance and publication can run six months, but usually it is in a two-to-three month range.

FICTION: From time to time, we will publish short, short fiction, the kind of stories that can be completed on two facing pages. Limit, 1,000 words. Tri-State locales or story lines, please.

HUMOR: While most humor pieces are produced by staff, we will, on occasion, consider humorous essays or stories. They should not be esoteric pieces about one's family but rather appeal to the universal human condition which all readers share. Limit 700 words.

We also need short humor items for two columns, "Humor in the classroom" and "Wish I'd said that." Classroom humor anecdotes no more than 50 words, reflecting Tristate elementary through college incidents. Payment is $10 per anecdote. For short quotes published in our Tristate area, list date and source. Payment is $2.50 for each accepted item. No acknowledgments, no returns.

PHOTOS: We do not buy freelance work unless it accompanies a story.

ILLUSTRATIONS: We seldom use unassigned artwork, but welcome the opportunity to look at new portfolios by appointment. One panel cartoons that reflect Tri-State living or current situations are a possibility.

Alice Hornbaker, Editor

EDITORIAL GUIDELINES

INDIVIDUAL MAGAZINE NEEDS

MUCH OF THE MATERIAL USED IN ALL OF OUR MAGAZINES IS HEALTH-RELATED. THIS INCLUDES STORIES, POETRY, ARTICLES, AND ACTIVITIES.

TURTLE MAGAZINE FOR PRESCHOOL KIDS (ages 2 to 5)
HUMPTY DUMPTY'S MAGAZINE (ages 4 to 6)
CHILDREN'S PLAYMATE MAGAZINE (ages 5 to 7)

TURTLE uses bedtime or naptime stories (approximately 200 to 600 words) that can be read to the child. HUMPTY DUMPTY'S MAGAZINE and CHILDREN'S PLAYMATE use easy-to-read stories for the beginning reader. Fiction can be 500 to 800 words. All of these magazines use short, simple poems or stories in rhyme. Games and crafts should involve a minimum of adult guidance and have clear, brief instructions. Humorous stories and poems are especially needed. In HUMPTY DUMPTY and CHILDREN'S PLAYMATE, healthful recipes requiring little or no need for the stove are used.

JACK AND JILL (ages 6 to 8)
CHILD LIFE (ages 7 to 9)
CHILDREN'S DIGEST (ages 8 to 10)

Stories may run from 500 to 1800 words. Articles may run from 500 to 1200 words. When appropriate, articles should be accompanied by photographs or transparencies. Nonfiction material should list sources of information. We may use factual features dealing with nature, science, and sports—also some historical and biographical articles. Preferred fiction includes realistic stories, adventure, mysteries, and science fiction. Humorous stories are highly desirable. Also needed are healthful recipes (see page 2).

SAMPLE COPIES

We regret that we are unable to provide free sample copies of the magazines. Individual copies may be obtained for seventy-five cents each by writing to Children's Better Health Institute, P.O. Box 567, Indianapolis, IN 46206.

Children's Better Health Institute
Benjamin Franklin Literary & Medical Society, Inc.
1100 Waterway Boulevard
P.O. Box 567
Indianapolis, Indiana 46206

TURTLE MAGAZINE FOR PRESCHOOL KIDS

HUMPTY DUMPTY'S MAGAZINE

CHILDREN'S PLAYMATE MAGAZINE

JACK AND JILL • CHILD LIFE • CHILDREN'S DIGEST

Our goal at the Children's Better Health Institute is to provide children with good reading that not only entertains but also educates, primarily about good health. We have a constant need for high-quality stories, articles, and activities with an exercise, nutrition, safety, hygiene, or other health-related theme. Our emphasis is preventive medicine, and we are seeking material that will encourage young readers to practice better health habits.

Health information may be presented in a variety of formats. We are looking for fresh, creative ways to encourage children to develop and maintain good health. Fiction stories that deal with a health theme need not have health as the primary subject but should include it in some way in the course of events. Main characters in fiction stories should adhere to good health practices, unless failure to do so is necessary to a story's plot. Word and math puzzles, games, and other activities can also successfully convey health messages if they are enjoyable to youngsters and age-appropriate. We also use factual articles that teach scientific facts about the body or nutrition. Writers should avoid an encyclopedic or "preachy" approach. We try to present our health material in a positive manner, incorporating humor and a light approach wherever possible without minimizing the seriousness of what we are saying.

In all material, please avoid references to eating sugary foods, such as candy, cakes, cookies, and soft drinks. In recipes submitted for publication, ingredients should be healthful. Avoid sugar, salt, chocolate, red meat, and fats.

We are also interested in material with more general themes. We are especially in need of holiday material—stories, articles, and activities. Send seasonal material at least eight months in advance. Also remember that characters in realistic stories should be up-to-date. Many of our readers have working mothers and/or come from single-parent homes. We need more stories that reflect these changing times but at the same time communicate good, wholesome values.

GENERAL INFORMATION

MANUSCRIPT FORMAT

Manuscripts must be typewritten and double- or triple-spaced. The author's name, address, telephone number, Social Security number, and an approximate word count must appear on the first page of the manuscript. KEEP A COPY OF YOUR WORK. We'll handle your manuscript with care, but we cannot assume responsibility for its return. Please send the entire manuscript; queries are not necessary. The editors cannot criticize, offer suggestions, or enter into correspondence concerning unsolicited manuscripts that are not accepted, nor can they suggest other markets for material that is not published. MATERIAL CANNOT BE RETURNED unless it is accompanied by a self-addressed envelope and SUFFICIENT return postage.

PHOTOS

WE DO NOT PURCHASE SINGLE PHOTOGRAPHS. We do purchase short photo features (up to 6 or 8 pictures) or photos that accompany and help illustrate editorial matter. (Please include captions.)

REVIEW TIME REQUIRED

Time required to review manuscripts properly is about eight to ten weeks. Each manuscript is carefully considered for possible use in *all* the magazines, not only that one to which it was originally addressed; therefore, if a manuscript is returned, it should not be resubmitted to a different youth publication at this address.

RATES AND PAYMENT POLICIES

Fiction and articles: approximately six cents a word. Poetry: $7.00 and up. Photos: $7.00 minimum. Puzzles and games: no fixed rate. Payment is made upon publication. Each author will be sent two complimentary copies of the issue in which his or her material is published. Additional copies may be purchased for seventy-five cents each.

RIGHTS

We prefer to purchase all rights. Simultaneous submissions are not accepted.

CHILDREN'S CONTRIBUTIONS

Except for items that may be used in the children's columns that appear each month, the editors do not encourage submissions from children. Even highly talented young people are not usually experienced enough to compete on a professional level with adult authors.

2 AM PUBLICATIONS

PO Box 6754, Rockford, IL 61125-1754

EDITORIAL GUIDELINES

LENGTH: Each work of fiction imposes its own length on the writer. 2AM is looking for GREAT short stories. Make every word count and length will take care of itself. Most of the stories we publish are in the 500 to 5000 word range.

MANUSCRIPT FORMAT: Double-spaced, please. Indicate in a cover letter or directly on the submission if your manuscript is a disposable copy. Handwritten, single spaced, or poor quality dot-matrix manuscripts will be returned unread.

SLANT: The editors love dark fantasy/horror. Great SF & S&S stories are welcome. A GOOD ironic twist is appreciated, but each story will stand or fall on its own merit. We're looking for true wordsmiths -- magicians -- enchanters. Each story should cast a spell over the reader that unobtrusively suspends disbelief. If we can put the story down before we finish reading "END", we'll send it back to you. Fair enough?

POETRY: Hypnotic, enchanting, full of imagery. Any length. Pays $1.00 minimum per poem. No more than five poems per submission, please.

ARTWORK: Send photocopies first. Black and white line drawings preferred. Query for assignments. Cartoons and comic strips welcome.

NON-FICTION: We'll consider profiles of known and unknown writers, film-makers and intelligent commentaries on the world in general.

PAYMENT: Payment varies. Contributors will be offered an individual contract. Minimum payment is ½¢ per word for articles and fiction.

RIGHTS: 2AM buys one-time rights, first North American serial rights, the right to reprint in annual anthologies, and other rights which may be negotiated. Photocopies of previously published works will be considered for 2AM anthologies.

COPYRIGHT: 2AM is copyrighted. Contributors retain all rights unless specifically detailed in a written contract.

SASE: All submissions must contain a self-addressed stamped envelope. A #10 or larger is essential. Please make sure you add enough postage! We will not return submissions that do not have adequate postage. Nor will we pay to receive submissions sent to us without correct postage. Please do not send your submission registered or certified mail; if you want to be sure we received your submission, enclose a stamped self-addressed postcard.

REPLY (RESPONSE) TIME: We normally respond to all submissions within 6 to 10 weeks. If you haven't heard from us within 3 months, please query. We assume no responsibility for unsolicited materials, though we do our best while your manuscript is in our hands. We prefer a photocopy, as everyone has lost manuscripts in the mail at one time or another. We don't mind simultaneous submissions as long as you let us know.

COVER LETTERS: Tell us something about yourself, if you wish. Letters to the editor are also welcome. We reserve the right to publish letters, edited or unedited -- unless you state not for publication -- as space permits.

ADDRESS: All submissions should be addressed to Gretta M. Anderson, 2AM Publications, Box 6754, Rockford, IL 61125-1754.

(3/88)

VINTAGE '45

Writer's Guidelines

"Vintage '45" is a nationally distributed quarterly journal designed for active, introspective MIDLIFE women who continue to grow and redefine their lives. It is entirely freelance written.

Material appearing in "Vintage '45" falls into three basic categories:

1. Informative articles written by women actually working in various fields, such as: mental health, medicine, finance, law -- to name a few. These articles cover a specific topic, relating to the author's area of expertise, that would benefit "Vintage '45" readers. In depth treatment of the subject is required. Typical length: 1,000 words. The author must have direct experience in the field about which she is writing. No interviews, please. Query first with detailed description of topic and the way it will be treated.

2. "Coping" or "success" stories. These first person accounts describe a specific situation a woman has faced and reveal how she has adapted to it. The emphasis here is not on a detailed chronology of events, but rather on the personal, emotional aspects of confronting and tackling the situation. Topics might include, but are by no means limited to, divorce, husband's mid-life crisis, affliction of a parent, child or oneself, step-familyhood. Length: 1,000 to 1,500 words.

3. Creative writing. Poems, essays and short, short stories -- all relating in some clear way to midlife women -- are proper subjects for this section. Humor, where appropriate, can be a plus.

    Terms: "Vintage '45" offers a one-year subscription as payment for any work used. In addition, writers will be given not only a byline but also brief biographical space (up to 75 words) wherein they can mention other published works or professional affiliations. All rights revert to the author.

Always include SASE for reply and/or return of manuscripts.

THANK YOU FOR YOUR INTEREST!!

Sample copy: $2.50. Please address inquiries to:

Susan L. Aglietti, Editor/Publisher
Vintage '45
Post Office Box 266
Orinda, CA 94563-0266

SUBMISSIONS FROM WOMEN ONLY, PLEASE

Writers' Guidelines

William & Nancie Carmichael, Publishers
Becky Durost Fish, Editor
Denis Mortenson, Art Director

P.O. Box 850, Sisters, OR 97759
(503) 549-8261
Circulation 110,000
Standard length 1,000-1,500 words

Published 8 times per year
Query letter required
Pays on publication
Pays 10¢ per printed word
Buys first rights
Needs seasonal material 6 months in advance
Reports on manuscripts 6-8 weeks

VIRTUE is aimed primarily at Christian homemakers, and its purpose is to inspire women in every aspect of their lives. Each issue offers articles on creative home management, self-improvement, spiritual enrichment and family relationships. VIRTUE encourages the development of the whole woman, whether she is a full-time homemaker or employed outside the home either full- or part-time. Inspirational rather than doctrinal in focus, VIRTUE helps women to be informed and to incorporate the truths of the Bible into every facet of life.

The editors prefer that articles on all subjects be presented in a practical, non-judgmental style. Articles on spiritual subjects should be applicable to everyday life. Each issue features:

NON-FICTION: Interviews with Christian women who are actively living out their faith in interesting ways; information and insight for families—husband/wife relationships and the challenge of child-rearing; practical and innovative ideas for homemaking; fashion and beauty updates; food and entertainment tips; articles on individual spiritual growth, and current issues of interest to women. Each issue also contains one opinion piece in the "In My Opinion" column and one woman's testimony of how the Lord has worked in her life—"One Woman's Journal."

FICTION: One piece of fiction is included in each issue. Stories must be well-written and relevant. Maximum length: 2,000 words. No query letter required.

HOW TO BREAK IN: Queries are required for all articles except submissions to the "In My Opinion" and "One Woman's Journal" departments. The editors look for meaningful, well-researched pieces written in a lively and interesting style. No pat answers, please. Short, humorous articles relating to family life are welcome, as are more serious articles that challenge VIRTUE's readers. Articles that are too mystical or preachy will be rejected. Queries and manuscripts should be sent with a self-addressed envelope with proper return postage. We cannot be responsible for unreturned material if SASE is not provided. For a sample copy of the magazine, send $3 to cover postage and handling.

VIRTUE
THE CHRISTIAN MAGAZINE FOR WOMEN

STATEMENT OF FAITH

We believe the Bible to be the inspired and only infallible and authoritative Word of God. We believe that there is one God, eternally existent in three persons: God the Father, God the Son, and God the Holy Spirit. We believe in the deity of our Lord Jesus Christ, in His virgin birth, in His sinless life, in His miracles, in His vicarious and atoning death, in His bodily resurrection, in His ascension to the right hand of the Father, and in His personal future return to this earth in power and glory. We believe in the blessed Hope, which is the translation of the Church at Christ's coming. We believe that the only means of being cleansed from sin is through repentance and faith in the precious blood of Christ. We believe that regeneration by the Holy Spirit is essential for personal salvation. We believe in the resurrection of both the saved and the lost. . .the one to everlasting life and the other to everlasting damnation.

Notes to Washingtonian Writers

The Washingtonian

What Kind of Magazine Is This?

The Washingtonian is a city magazine—it focuses almost exclusively on the Washington metropolitan area. The magazine was started in October 1965, and its circulation in 1985 was over 135,000.

Our readers are concentrated in the District; Montgomery, Prince George's, and Anne Arundel counties in Maryland; and Arlington, Fairfax, and Prince William counties and the city of Alexandria in Virginia. Average household income of subscribers is over $84,000 a year; median age is 40; seven out of ten have finished college. It is an active, educated, affluent audience—our readers travel, dine out, go to plays, entertain, read, earn, and spend more than the average Washingtonian.

Thus, our readers are not a "mass" audience in the same sense as the *Washington Post's* 750,000 subscribers. The implication for the writer is that you do not have to write down to the proverbial "Kansas City milkman" or anyone else. You do have to write clearly, directly, and intelligently. Our readers recognize underreporting, overwriting, preaching, unclear thinking, and pseudo-sophistication when they see it.

What Kind of Writers Are We Looking For?

Freelancers come in all ages and types and backgrounds. Some make their living as writers; others are lawyers or housewives or professors or government officials.

More important than journalism experience is knowing a subject and being able to write clearly about it.

If you have something to say and can communicate your knowledge and interest to our readers, we want to hear from you.

What Kind of Articles Are We Looking For?

We are very open-minded—as long as the article idea is interesting and relates to the Washington area.

If we have not worked with you before, send us a written query about your article idea. Tell us who you are and what kind of article you propose to write. We'll try to let you know promptly if the idea has possibilities. If your article is already written, mail it to us or drop it off. We'll respond as soon as possible. If you want your article returned, include a stamped, self-addressed envelope.

The types of articles we publish include service pieces (How to Buy Antiques, Summer Pleasures, Guide to Fitness); profiles of people (Marion Barry, Sandra Day O'Connor, Willard Scott, William Webster); investigative articles (Air Florida Crash, Emergency Medical Care, Lie Detectors); rating pieces (Maryland vs. Virginia, Rating the Liberal Establishment, Ten Worst-Dressed Men); institutional profiles (Catholic Archdiocese, *Washington Times*, Marriott Corporation); first-person articles (What Am I Doing in Jail? Diary of a High School Senior); stories that cut across the grain of conventional thinking (Buildings We Should Blow Up; Are Lawyers Becoming Public Enemy Number One?); articles that tell the reader how Washington got to be the way it is; light or satirical pieces (send the completed manuscript, not the idea, because in this case execution is everything); and fiction that tells the reader how a part of Washington works or reveals something particular about the character or mood or people of Washington.

Subjects of articles include the federal government, local government, sports, business, education, medicine, fashion, environment, how to make money, how to spend money, real estate, performing arts, visual arts, travel, health, nightlife, hobbies, self-improvement, places to go, things to do, and more. Again, we are interested in almost anything as long as it relates to Washington.

We don't like "puff" pieces or what are called "isn't-it-interesting" pieces. There should be an idea behind the story. We don't run articles on people, places, or businesses just because they're there.

In general, we try to help our readers understand Washington better, to help our readers live better, and to make Washington a better place to live.

What Makes a Good Washingtonian Article?

A magazine article is different from a newspaper story. Newspaper stories start with the most important facts, are written in short paragraphs with a lot of transitions, and usually can be cut from the bottom up. A magazine article should have more shape—it usually is divided into sections that are like the chapters of a short book.

The introductory section is very important—it captures the reader's interest and sets the tone for the article. Anecdotes are often used to draw the reader into the subject matter, the writer starts with specific descriptions and then moves into a general explanation. The introductory section should foreshadow what the article is about without trying to summarize it—you want to make the reader curious. Each succeeding section develops the subject. Evaluations, recommendations, and conclusions come in the closing section.

We think there are three qualities to a good magazine article: Most basic are thorough research and reporting, and a writing style that is appropriate to the material. But what separates the very good from the adequate is the writer's ability to fit his material together and to give it meaning and focus. Newspaper reporters ask who, what, when, where, and why?

The most important question a magazine writer asks is, "What does it all mean?"

Also remember that a magazine writer is usually more subjective than a newspaper reporter; try to relate directly to the reader.

And because *The Washingtonian* is a monthly and has a six-week lead time, keep in mind that our articles should have a long-term perspective that makes them as readable several months from now as they are today.

Deadlines and Other Specifics

The magazine is published about the 28th of each month. The October issue, for example, is on the newsstands and reaches subscribers about September 28. We need completed manuscripts six weeks before publication. Thus, an article for the October issue should be submitted by August 10.

Include your name, address, and telephone number on the first page of the manuscript. We prefer 8½- by 11-inch paper, with copy typed and double-spaced, and with a margin of at least an inch. Copy does not have to be perfectly typed, but it should be easily readable.

The length of articles varies. We don't like to specify a length—we'd like each piece to run at its optimum length. Capital Comments range from 50 to 600 words. Most front- and back-of-the-book pieces run 1,500 to 3,000 words. Center-of-the-book pieces are usually 2,000 to 7,000 words, but some run as long as 20,000 words. When in doubt, ask us about it.

Our regular payment is 20 to 40 cents a word, depending on the length of the article, the amount of research, the number of interviews, and how much work we have to do on it. We pay one-third upon acceptance of the manuscript and the remaining two-thirds on publication. Again, if you have doubts or questions, talk to us. We normally don't pay expenses, but sometimes do when an unusual amount of travel or luncheon interviews or long-distance calls are involved: Talk to us first.

Basically, we buy first North American rights. After the article is published, the author is free to sell it to any other publication; in such cases, we will arrange for a transfer of copyright. The Los Angeles Times Syndicate sells second rights to our articles to other publications—usually to large newspapers. When that happens, we share 50-50 the second-rights payment with the author.

Some Generalities

First, we hope our writers are readers of the magazine. It is the best way to get a feel for what we are trying to do and how your article might fit in.

Before you start an article for us, we'll want to talk with you about your research, your interviews, the kinds of questions you are going to try to answer, the way the article will be organized. We may have suggestions on where to find background information and appropriate people to talk with.

For major articles, you probably will want to check the *Reader's Guide to Periodical Literature* to see what already has been written on the subject. You may want to look at clips in the Washingtoniana room of the Martin Luther King Library or at the National Geographic library. The Library of Congress is a very good resource.

As your research and interviews continue, don't hesitate to call us if there is some question about the direction you are taking. After you have finished gathering material, it's usually a good idea to talk to us before you start writing. Many writers find it best to organize their material into a rough outline and to go over it with us before they start writing.

Suggestions on Style

We have no rules on writing style. The style should come naturally from the writer and the material. In *The Elements of Style*, William Strunk made these suggestions:

1) Be specific, concrete, definite.
2) Use the active rather than the passive voice.
3) Put the statements in positive form.
4) Write with nouns and verbs.
5) Don't overstate.
6) Avoid the use of qualifiers.
7) Don't explain too much.
8) Avoid fancy words.
9) Be clear.

In his essay "Politics and the English Language," George Orwell pointed to these sins of bad writing: "Staleness of imagery . . . lack of precision . . . the concrete melts into the abstract . . . a lack of simple verbs." Some of Orwell's suggestions:

1) Never use a metaphor, simile, or other figure of speech that you are used to seeing in print.
2) Never use a long word where a short one will do.
3) If it is possible to cut a word out, always cut it out.

4) Never use the passive where you can use the active.
5) Never use a foreign phrase, a scientific word, or jargon word if you can think of an everyday English equivalent.
6) Break any of these rules sooner than say anything outright barbarous.

One last word: Speak to the reader as an intelligent friend. The best style is clear, honest, and direct. We like sophisticated ideas and simple language, not the reverse. And don't forget the favorite question of the late *New Yorker* editor Harold Ross: "What the hell do you mean?"

—JACK LIMPERT

WASHINGTONIAN
1828 L Street, NW, Washington, DC 20036 202-296-3600

Guidelines for <u>Wee</u> <u>Wisdom</u>'s Authors:

<u>Wee Wisdom</u> was printed for the first time in August of 1893. In the words of the founder, Myrtle Fillmore, "The mission of <u>Wee</u> <u>Wisdom</u> is not to entertain children, but to call them out." Although we have no objection to accepting material that is entertaining and/or amusing, our first objective is still to "call out" the best in children. Our magazines are used often in schools, and we wish also to be exemplary in style and good composition.

Capsulized rules and enlargement on our needs follow:

1. <u>Promote positive, happy thinking in the readers</u>. Write interesting stories containing seed ideas to help children develop true values and standards that will help them achieve their higher potential. Use realistic situations, even when you write fantasies. Children must identify with them.

2. <u>Do not talk down to the younger children</u>. Visualize real children as you write. Even animals that are personalized must possess human characteristics. Listen with a child's ear to the dialog that is used to carry the story and to develop its characters and personalities. Neither should it sound unduly slangy.

3. <u>In writing for the older children (10-12 or so), do not assume that the children are just small adults</u>. Today's children often give the appearance of being sophisticated. However, sophistication can be purely surface, leaving the children with the same need for understanding and wisdom that we experienced when we were their age.

4. <u>Write your stories with good racial balance</u>. We have a very diverse readership, and we wish to satisfy the needs of all of them, as nearly as possible.

5. <u>Follow the accepted rules of good composition</u>. Simplicity, orderliness, and clarity are desired.

6. <u>The length should not exceed 800 words</u>.

    (a) <u>The writer should resist overusing adverbs and adjectives</u>. Marvelous, wonderful, terrible, descriptive words tend to muddy the story, as do those words that tell you that a child reacts excitedly, angrily, hastily, eagerly, anxiously, sweetly, et al. Better the use of verbs to stimulate the reader's imagination. Development of the story should create the mood. Paring unnecessary words that writers savor could benefit the final product enough to interest a copy reader.

    (b) <u>Suggestion and understatement are more effective</u> in making a story interesting to a child than exaggeration. The child's imagination will supply the exaggeration that a good story may spark.

(over)

Guidelines continued: Page 2

7. Avoid the Sunday school image. Wee Wisdom is a character-building, non-denominational magazine.

8. Puzzles must be fun and have a positive tone. They can also be
interesting and educational; or give a child an opportunity to use
and develop skills of observation, deduction, logic, etc.

9. Submit seasonal material 10 to 12 months ahead of the holiday
or season.

10. The appearance of the manuscript is important: It must be
double-spaced, in clearly readable type. Margins should be ample.
Each page must be labeled with author's name, story title, and page
number at the top. Manuscripts should not be stapled. SASE must
be included.

11. Query letters are not desired.

A rejection slip from us does not automatically mean that we did
not like your submission. Perhaps it will find a home elsewhere.
We receive about 175 to 225 manuscripts each month and can print
only 5 or 6 stories, an occasional poem, and 4 or so puzzles in
each issue. Keep trying!

WEIRDBOOK (EERIE COUNTRY, too) is so overstocked that I HAVE TO STOP READING UNSOLICITED MANUSCRIPTS. ALL MANUSCRIPTS WILL BE RETURNED UNREAD. In the case of artwork: I will probably look at it and give a brief opinion.

This condition will continue until at least January 1, 1989. Maybe longer. Sorry, but I have to get the material already on hand into print.

To find out when WEIRDBOOK will again be an open market, try subscribing to some of the magazines for writers. In particular, I recommend very highly SMALL PRESS WRITERS & ARTISTS ORGANIZATION dues are $10 the first year, $7.50 for associate membership if you are not a published writer or artist: write Audrey Parente, Secretary/Treasurer, SPWAO, 411 Main Trail, Ormond Beach, FL 32074. If their flyer is available, I have enclosed it. Also highly recommended: SCAVENGERS NEWSLETTER (60¢ sample, $7 per year) from Janet Fox, 519 Ellinwood, Osage City, KS 66523.

GUIDELINES FOR WRITERS AND ARTISTS

The worst mistakes by a beginner: not putting name & address on manuscript (occasionally it's not anywhere). Artists not doing ditto on back of drawings. Poor manuscript: handwritten (a no-no), or typed single spaced, or typed with an unreadable typeface (like script). Read THE WRITERS MARKET or WRITERS HANDBOOK (available in most libraries) on how to prepare a manuscript. You MUST enclose a stamped self addressed envelope for return of the manuscript, and it MUST be (1) large enough and (2) provided with enough postage. If you don't want it back, say so, and enclose a SSAE for the rejection slip. Many editors will THROW OUT a manuscript if there is no SSAE enclosed with it. (And they will not even read it first! Those who have mastered the basics often forget another important rule: KNOW YOUR MARKET! Be sure that your manuscript is the kind of thing an editor is looking for. Don't send science fiction to WEIRDBOOK or pornographic novels to Harlequin Books!!

I WANT: stories with action, suspense, a clearly defined plot, a fantasy or supernatural element, an effective ending (but not necessarily a "surprise" ending), and strong characterization. I do not usually publish beginners.

I DO NOT WANT: sex (in art, no nudes); science fiction of any kind; re-writes or follow-ups on traditional or media material or famous best-sellers like FRANKENSTEIN, DRACULA, ROSEMARY'S BABY, THE WOLF-MAN, FANTASY ISLAND, etc etc. I DO NOT WANT: stories without a fantasy element: please, no psychological stories, no mystery or detective stories, no pure thrillers, and please limit sadism & blood). No pure adventure lacking a fantasy element. Certain plots are done over and over again by beginners (I get several of each type every year). DO NOT SEND ME any of these. Examples: ordinary ghost stories where the protagonist meets somebody and later finds out it was a ghost; stories in which the lead characters turn out to be Adam and Eve; stories where the main character turns out to be [surprise] dead; stories about cannibals; stories in which the protagonist, mysteriously imprisoned, turns out to be a baby about to be born ["and the doctor patted him on... THE END"]; stories about bad guys who die and go to HELL; stories about writers (they deal with the devil, discover a magic typewriter, etc etc.); stories in which "it was all a dream." These ideas are so ancient that they will not carry a story by themselves (or else they're my pet peeves).

All material is accepted by me and is at my disposal to be used in WEIRDBOOK, WEIRDBOOK SAMPLER (formerly EERIE COUNTRY), etc. If possible, they will be used in WEIRDBOOK. Rights purchased are 1st N.A. serial rights, and right to reprint as part of the entire issue.

PAYMENT SCHEDULE: minimum rates. FICTION ½¢ - 1¢ a word (WEIRDBOOK), ¼¢-½¢ (WEIRDBOOK SAMPLER). ART: front cover, $20 (WB), $15 (WBS), $10 (FANTASY MONGERS). Interiors, somewhat less. POETRY: no payment. All contributors get 1 complimentary copy.

Art should be black & white only, size to conform with size of magazine. Good copy acceptable.

Fiction: 25,000 words or less; prefer 3000-12,000 words. Heavy manuscripts may be sent special fourth class rate (marked "return postage guaranteed"). FANTASY MONGERS uses articles but there is no payment; study this magazine before submitting to it. (A FREE copy may be had for a 2½¢ stamp).
W. PAUL GANLEY: PUBLISHER, P O Box 149, Amherst Branch, Buffalo, NY 14226.   July, 1985

west coast review a quarterly magazine of the arts

June 1987

GUIDELINES FOR CONTRIBUTORS:

* All mss. must be in English.

* No restrictions as to style, theme, subject matter, etc., but prose mss. should not exceed 10,000 words and poetry mss. should not contain more than 6-8 poems.

* Mss. will be returned only if accompanied by SASE and sufficient Canadian postage or IRC.

* Replies within 8-10 weeks.

* Payment upon publication at a rate of approximately $5-10 (Canadian) per published page.

* West Coast Review purchases first North American serial rights only.

* No previously published work will be considered.

* No simultaneous submissions.

simon fraser university
burnaby (vancouver) b.c.
canada V5A 1S6
(telephone : 604-291-4287)

WESTERN LIVING

FREELANCE GUIDELINES

Western Living magazine is a monthly publication of general interest to western Canadians, with a special emphasis on home design. It seeks to provide the reader with authoritative coverage of its subject areas, which include cuisine, fashion, recreation, the arts, foreign and local travel, architecture and interior design. We want only the best writing, photography and illustration available. The magazine is distributed free to upper-income homes in Victoria, Vancouver, Calgary, Edmonton, Saskatoon, Regina and Winnipeg, and the editorial is geared to the interests of homeowners with disposable income. We want to be a showcase of all the good things in the West. Stories should have a stimulating or off-beat angle that will capture the attention of educated readers, both male and female. Whenever possible, we want a regional, Western angle. We are more likely to be interested in a story idea that will appeal to readers right across western Canada than one that will appeal only to readers in, say, Victoria or Regina. Western Living is a signatory to the code of ethics and standard contract of the Periodical Writers Association of Canada.

Note: This is a general guide only. Study back issues for indications of recent trends in our style and content.

EDITORIAL AREAS

1. Homes and gardens. Unusual or beautiful design; a clever solution to a common home design problem; advances in home furnishings or appliances; renovation ideas; profiles of architects or interior designers; collectibles; history of design.

2. Food and cooking. Specialty foods; ethnic cuisines; profiles of cooking personalities; advances in cookware or cooking utensils; humorous or historical pieces related to cooking, food or drink.

3. Local travel. Out-of-the-way places in the West; familiar places given an unusual angle; places with interesting social or natural histories.

4. Foreign travel. As with local travel, we're interested in any place that is written about in a clever way. Most people in our readership have travelled to a foreign country, and expect more from a a foreign travel piece than a recounting of the sights. Again, we're looking for angles.

5. Recreation. Unusual sports, hobbies.

6. The arts. Outstanding local artists or events, craftsmen at work; unusual collections or techniques.

7. Fashion. Trends, history, sociological and psychological aspects of fashion, profiles of designers.

8. Profiles. Especially of designers, artists and writers, but we will consider any profile proposal if it seems right for the magazine.

9. History. Entertaining, well-written features on overlooked aspects of western Canadian history.

10. Fiction and poetry. We occasionally take short stories and poetry collections from well-known western Canadian writers.

11. Marketplace. Concise, well-researched consumer guides to products and services of interest to western Canadians.

MANUSCRIPTS

No responsibility assumed for unsolicited manuscripts. Manuscripts must be typed (double-spaced) and include a stamped, self-addressed envelope. Be sure to keep a copy. Language should be simple, clean English unless there is a good reason for a different style. We prefer writers to query us first with a typed, single-page outline. Address all queries to the Editor. Be specific with all story proposals and demonstrate that you know your topic. We don't like vague phone queries. For those with word processors, we prefer letter-quality copy. Contact us about possible modem transfer of copy or submission of Xerox-format disk. Our house style is based on Canadian Press and Oxford. We are metric. Spelling, facts and names should be carefully checked before a manuscript is submitted. The writer must supply a list (with phone numbers) of every person interviewed for a story.

LENGTH

Usually 2,000 to 3,000 words. Occasionally longer.

RIGHTS

Unless otherwise agreed, we buy only first, western Canadian serial reproduction rights. We reserve the right to publish any article in all seven of our regional editions, even if this takes place over the course of several months. No other media can carry the story before we do. We do not buy reprints.

DEADLINES

Manuscripts must be submitted three months prior to anticipated publication date. Queries must be received four to six months before anticipated publication date.

PAYMENT

Full payment will be made within 30 days of acceptance of a story and averages 30 cents a word depending on research time and complexity of the story in question. Photos: $25 to $200 each, depending on published size and number used.

PHOTOGRAPHY

All pictures must be accompanied by appropriate captions. Black and white: prefer 8x10 glossies of medium contrast. Color: positive transparencies required; prints used only in unusual circumstances. Transparencies may be of any size but we prefer 2¼ or 4x5. Prefer Ektachromes and Kodachromes of medium density and brightness. 35mm slides may be returned with sprocket holes cut off but mounted for projection in quality mounts. We don't publish "pretty pictures" by themselves. All pictures must be related to a magazine story.

For further information, call the editorial department at (604) 669-7525 or write 504 Davie Street, Vancouver, B.C. V6B 2G4. Editor: Andrew Scott. Associate editors: Carolann Rule (Homes & Gardens), Audrey Grescoe.

WOMEN'S SPORTS & FITNESS

501 Second Street
Suite 400
San Francisco, CA
94107
(415) 442-0220

WRITER'S GUIDELINES

Women's Sports & Fitness is a monthly national magazine for women who are vitally interested in sports, fitness, and health. The average reader is 28 years old and participates in two or more sports. Circulation is currently 350,000 and growing. We buy material from free-lancers for the following:

DEPARTMENTS

Fast Breaks: This section contains 100- to 500-word sports-related news items and short profiles of collegiate and high school athletes, as well as women of any age who show promise in the sports world. Payment is $50-$125. Send queries or manuscripts to Fast Breaks Editor.

Personal Best: This is our lifestyle section. It contains short (500 words or less), informative, lively pieces concerning developments in sports medicine, research, and training techniques, as well as sports travel stories and sports-related beauty tips. Payment is $75-$125. Send queries to Personal Best Editor.

COLUMNS

Aerobics: News and developments in aerobic dance. Pieces should be well-focused and contain fresh information. 750 words, $200. Send queries to Aerobics Editor.

Cycling: Aerodynamic equipment, how to enter a race, why sponsorship is waning, and profiles of a mountain biker are some of the recent topics covered in this column. 750 words, $200. Send queries to Cycling Editor.

Eating Right: Sports nutrition information our readers will not have read elsewhere. (NO weight-loss pieces.) Each article should focus on a single subject. 750 words, $200. Send queries to Eating Right Editor.

Running: News, opinions, or controversies in the world of competitive or recreational running. Recent examples: new perspectives on altitude training, profile of an ultramarathoner, the pacing controversy. 750 words, $200. Send queries to Running Editor.

Finish Line: This is our opinion column. It can be political, personal, humorous, or controversial, but it must be specific, well-focused, and substantial. 750 words, $200 and up. Send queries to Finish Line Editor.

FEATURES

Personality profiles: We're looking for in-depth portraits of women who have achieved extraordinary results in their field, as well as of lesser-known women who would be an inspiration to our readers because of unusual accomplishments or experience.

General sports-oriented stories: Profiles of teams, issues and controversies, concepts, how-tos, analyses, etc.

Recreational and off-beat sports and adventure: Stories that inform and encourage involvement in active living (e.g., backpacking, kayaking, windsurfing).

Non-sports authoritative articles: Stories on fitness, nutrition, and sports-related health issues. Subjects we've covered in the past include osteoporosis, vegetarianism, steroids, and the effects of sleep on performance.

Strong personal reminiscences will be considered, as will **sports-related fiction,** (although we do not publish much fiction).

Coverage of sporting events: Most of this text is staff-written because of fast closing, but we will look at materials on spec.

It is a good idea to query the Features Editor first. Features range in length from 1,500 to 3,000 words. We pay approximately $300-$750 upon publication.

QUERIES

Queries should be in writing, and about one page in length. In addition to describing what will be included in the story, let us know why our readers will sit up and take notice. Articles must have a broad appeal so that they can be enjoyed by readers without a special knowledge of the subject or personality. Describe the availability of photographs for your article. Photography may help sell your idea, but *DO NOT* send unsolicited art. Please send copies of previously published stories with your query. **Read a few recent issues of our magazine to determine our focus before you send manuscripts or queries.** Back copies can be purchased for $2; one-year subscriptions are $14.95.

Address all queries and manuscripts to the appropriate editor at the above address. Be sure to include a self-addressed, stamped envelope, or work will not be returned. Response time is generally six to eight weeks.

177 NORTH DEAN STREET
ENGLEWOOD, N.J. 07631
(201) 569-0006

FICTION GUIDELINES

SHORT STORY

Our feature fiction each week is a short story with a light romantic theme, at a length of approximately 4,500 words. The stories can be written from either a female or male point of view.
Women characters may be single, married, divorced or widowed. I like to see strong, interesting characters. Plots must be fast-moving, emphasizing vivid dialogue and plenty of action. The problems and dilemmas should be contemporary and realistic, handled with warmth and a sense of humor. The stories must have a positive resolution.

We are not interested in science fiction, fantasy, historical romance or foreign locales. We do not want explicit sex (although a strong attraction between the main characters should be apparent early on), graphic language or seamy settings. Stories slanted for a particular holiday should be sent at least 6 months ahead.

We purchase North American rights for 6 months at a standard rate of $1,000, paid on acceptance.

MINI MYSTERY

The mini mysteries, at a length of 1,600 words, may feature either a "whodunnit" or "howdunnit" theme. The mystery may revolve around anything from a theft to a murder. However, we are not interested in sordid or grotesque crimes. Emphasis should be on the intricacies of plot rather than gratuitous violence. We don't print horror or ghost stories, science fiction, fantasy or foreign settings. Stories slanted for a particular holiday should be sent at least 6 months ahead.

We purchase North American rights for 6 months at a standard rate of $500, paid on acceptance.

Send fiction manuscripts to: Elinor Nauen, Fiction Editor
Woman's World
Box 6700
Englewood, NJ 07631

Sorry, no manuscripts returned without SASE (or International Postal Coupons).

I strongly encourage you to examine a sample copy (available for $1) before sumitting your manuscript.

HEINRICH BAUER NORTH AMERICA INC.
177 NORTH DEAN STREET • P.O. BOX 671 • ENGLEWOOD, N.J. 07631 • (201) 569-0006 • TELEX 642802

Wonder Time

A PUBLICATION OF THE

CHILDREN'S

MINISTRIES DEPARTMENT

CHURCH OF THE NAZARENE

TO OUR CONTRIBUTORS

Your interest in submitting material to *Wonder Time* is appreciated. We are glad to give consideration to any material which conforms to the standards outlined in this pamphlet.

SUBMISSION OF MANUSCRIPT

Ten to twelve weeks should be allowed for the editor to read and report on material. *Wonder Time* is prepared twelve months ahead of the circulation date of the periodical.

Direct all manuscripts to *Wonder Time* at the address shown on the back of this pamphlet.

COPYRIGHT REGULATIONS

Wonder Time is copyrighted. This is done basically for the protection of the author, therefore, materials submitted must comply with copyright regulations. *Wonder Time* purchases first or second rights. We retain the right to reprint any material purchased.

RETURN ENVELOPE

A self-addressed, stamped envelope must accompany manuscripts to ensure return of those not accepted.

PAYMENT

Payment is made on acceptance, and complimentary copies of the periodical are mailed to the contributors on publication. The rate of payment is as follows: Prose 3.5¢ a word for first rights, 2¢ a word for reprints; Verse 25¢ per line, $2.50 minimum; Photographs 5 x 7 or larger, accompanying manuscripts, are payed according to quality and use.

Editor: *Evelyn J. Beals*

Editorial Assistant:

Patty L. Hall

Executive Director: *Miriam J. Hall*

Editorial Director:

Robert D. Troutman

Editorial Office:

Wonder Time
Dept. of Children's Ministries
6401 The Paseo
Kansas City, MO 64131

Publisher:

Nazarene Publishing House
PO Box 527
Kansas City, Mo 64141

Wonder Time is a leisure reading piece for first and second graders. It is published weekly by the Department of Children's Ministries of the Church of the Nazarene.

The major purposes of *Wonder Time* are to:

...provide a leisure reading piece which will build Christian behavior and values.

...provide reinforcement for Biblical concepts taught in the Sunday School curriculum. The focus being life related.

Wonder Time's target audience is children ages six to eight in grades one and two. The readability goal is to encourage beginning readers to read for themselves.

EDITORIAL NEEDS

1. FICTION: Stories should vividly portray definite Christian emphasis or character-building values, without being preachy. The setting, plot, and action should be realistic. 400 to 550 words.

2. POETRY: Verse should be four to eight lines. It should not deal with much symbolism.

3. CARTOONS: Humor should be directed to children and involve children. It should not be simply child-related from an adult viewpoint.

4. CRAFTS AND PUZZLES: Should be simple and within the ability of young readers.

BASIC THEMES

Wonder Time is committed to reinforcement of the Biblical concepts taught in the Sunday School curriculum. Because of this, the themes needed are mainly as follows:

Faith in God
Putting God first
Choosing to please God
Understanding Jesus is God's Son and our Savior
Choosing to do right
Asking forgiveness
Trusting God in hard times
Prayer: trusting God to answer
Appreciation of Bible as God's Word to man
Importance of Bible memorization
Understanding both meanings of church:
 a place where we worship God
 a fellowship of God's people working together
Understanding each person's value to God and to others
Showing love and kindness to others

BASIS FOR SELECTION

1. Adapted to age level in interest and readability

2. A vital Christian message

3. Human interest and lifelike characterizations

4. Follow story from--short catchy beginning, plot with a climax and a satisfying conclusion

5. Problem solving or surprise element

6. Dialogue and action

7. Freshness and originality

8. Correct grammar and punctuation

9. Neatness, careful preparation--typewritten, double-spaced, on one side of the sheet

POINTS CONSIDERED IMPORTANT

1. Definite Christian experience

2. Proper Sabbath observance, church loyalty

3. Clean living, high ideals, and temperance

4. Wholesome social relationships and activities

5. Disapprove: liquor, tobacco, drugs, movies, dancing, gambling, profanity, and slang.

230 PARK AVENUE, NEW YORK, NY 10169

WRITERS' GUIDELINES

Thank you for your interest in WORKING MOTHER. The magazine is looking for
articles (About 1,500 to 2,000 words in length) that help women in their
task of juggling job, home and family. We like humorous pieces and
articles which sensibly solve or illuminate a problem unique to our
readers. Topics that particularly interest us include: time, home and
money management, health, family relationships, single parenthood and
job-related issues. Pieces dealing with food, beauty, and fashion are
usually staff-written.

If you submit a manuscript, it should be typewritten, double-spaced and
accompanied by a self-addressed, stamped envelope large enough to contain
the manuscript. Manuscripts must be submitted on speculation at the
author's risk. (We will not be responsible for lost material.) We prefer
receiving proposals for pieces, rather than completed work. Then, if we
find the subject suitable, we can discuss the best way to handle the
material.

We occasionally publish short stories (about 750 to 3,000 words in length)
which are entertaining or enlightening and whose characters have
experiences similar to those our readers might have. We prefer receiving
manuscripts rather than proposals for fiction and humor pieces.

All manuscripts and queries should be addressed to the Editorial
Department, WORKING MOTHER MAGAZINE, 230 Park Avenue, New York, NY 10169.

The Editors

WRITERS' FORUM

University of Colorado, Colorado Springs
Colorado 80933-7150

Writer's Guidelines

Writers' Forum, edited by Alex Blackburn, Victoria McCabe (poetry), Craig Lesley (fiction), Bret Lott (fiction), University of Colorado at Colorado Springs, Colorado Springs, CO 80933-7150, (303)599-4023. Book, avg. 200 pages, published once a year in Fall since 1974. Per vol. fiction, 12-15 stories, novel-excerpts, and novelle up to 15,000 words; per vol. poetry, 25-40 poems. Will consider: up to 5 poems by one author; long poems; translations of living authors; Hispanic-American poetry. Circ. 1,000. Subscription price: $8.95 (discounted for libraries). Latest vol. sample: $8.95. Previous vol. sample: $5.00. Check or money order payable to "Writers' Forum." Reporting time: 3-6 weeks. Payment: free copies only. Copyrighted, rights revert to author.

We publish the best in contemporary American literature and especially encourage Western American literature.

We want solidly crafted imaginative work, verbally interesting with strong voice. Fiction: structure, style, characterization and theme must work together. Poetry: feeling and form must work together, with diction articulated beyond prosiness.

Send complete typed manuscript and include stamped self-addressed envelope of appropriate size and with correct postage (mss. without SASE may not be returned). We welcome a personal cover letter giving relevant biographical and career information. No submissions between 15 May and 15 October, please.

Editorial Comment

TROUVERE COMPANY

RT. 2, BOX 290
ECLECTIC, ALABAMA 36024

NEW GUIDELINES for the

WRITERS GAZETTE

A copyrighted publication for writers, by writers, about writing.

As of May 1987 Trouvere Company has chose to combine Trouvere's Laureate, Short Story Review and Just A Little Poem with WRITERS GAZETTE. Please read the following guidelines carefully and note the new changes involved.

Publication Dates: Spring - Summer - Fall - Winter   Quarterly publication
Sample copy: $4.00   random selected   Subscription: $18.00 year
Editor: Brenda Williamson

Small publications often have a difficult time in staying afloat from year to year, for this reason payment will vary in accordance with our present budget. Most often payment will be in form of a contributors copy or subscription, cash will be a scarcity. Our aim is to publish new writer's works and that of established writers that are willing to help support these beginners. If money is all you're looking for, then you should stick to large publications, we are only looking for the writer that writes out of joy, inspiration, need and to lend a helping hand to those that have not yet aquired the full skills of a professional writer.

If you found that this is a publication that you would like to contribute to, please continue reading, and by the way, **WELCOME** to WRITERS GAZETTE.

GUIDELINES

POETRY .... Any style or topic. Maximun 100 lines. Uses 50-150 yearly.(Editors notes: I prefer to see poems of 12-36 lines, but I enjoy all types and lengths and I'm very objective when picking poems. Though I do not like to restrict the thoughts and crativeness of the poems I consider, I love poems that rhyme and have surprise endings, but please don't everyone send just that type of poem, I do like variety.)

ARTICLES..................... Articles should be writing related. Though through the years this field has expanded to include photography, illustrating, cartoons, Using word processors and computers.Maximum 1500 words. Uses 15-30 yearly. (Editor notes: I prefer articles to be compact and direct. I like to use more shorter articles of 300-700 words, than only a couple of long ones. Skip the "...rejection slip blues..." I see far too many of these and everyone has their story of how rotten it is of the editor to reject a manuscript that took a great deal of time(in some instances) to prepare. To keep publishing these only depresses readers as well as myself,Like always, don't let that stop you from sending one if you feel it is of special merit.)

SHORT STORY FIRST FEATURE....... Announced theme.Maximum 2500 words. Uses 8-12 yearly.(Editor notes:
        SECOND FEATURE   Deciding on the announced theme method was hard. I try not to restrict
        THIRD FEATURE   too much, but I felt this would give writers a more incentive in trying to write something specific on a deadline type schedule, but fear not for those that have their own ideas we have left one issue a year for

for variety. We have a 2500 word limit, but I will sometimes except
longer if excellent. I prefer stories to be under 1500 words.)

THEMES

for **1987**	for **1988**
Summer...... Any subject	Spring....... Detective mystery
Fall ...... Horror	Summer ...... Any subject
Winter ..... Christmas	Fall .... Espionage
	Winter ...... Gothic/Romance

POET LAUREATE FEATURE .... This is one page of poetry by one writer. Submit minmum of 10 poems, bio
and photograph (if available)

JUST A LITTLE POEM CONTEST ..... Any suject, titled, 2-12 line limit. 5 entries per month max. FREE entry
to subscribers, $1.00 per poem entry fee to non-subscribers. Put name
and address on each poem and month the poem is entered for. We must
receive entries 3 months prior to publication.Entries will not be returned.

> Nov. for   March,April,May (Spring Issue)
> Feb. for   June,July, Aug. (Summer Issue)
> May for   Sept.,Oct.,Nov. (Fall Issue)
> Aug. for   Dec.,Jan.,Feb. (Winter Issue)

PRIZES: 1st place- 1 yr.sub. + $20.00 , 2nd place-$10., 3rd place-$5.
entries can be resubmitted if non winners.
Winners will be published plus random entries as space permits.

SHORT STORY REVIEW .... Each subscriber will be entitled to have at least one short story per
year published in this section of Writers Gazette, but the guidelines must
be followed exactly. Your story can be on any subject. 3 page max.
> 1. Type **SINGLE** space.
> 2. Leave only a 1/2 - 1 inch margin around page.
>   We will be copying your original for publication,so be neat.
> 3. Put title at the top of the first page and your name below the
>   title. (if you wish to remain anonymous leave your name off.
> 4. Use the smallest type you have available.
> 5. Put address on back of manuscript. With your subscriber number
>   (this number can be found on your mailing label) If you have
>   lost your number or it is not on your label, be sure to write
>   on the back of the manuscript that you are a subscriber.
> 6. Address your envelope to Trouvere Co. Dept. SSR.
An award of $10. will be given to best short story for this section.

COLUMNS....... The Book Report - Submit a review copy of your book with ordering information for a review
in an issue of Writers Gazette.
Chatty Patty Notes & News - This section gives updates in the publishing world, from markets
to personal items about WG readers being published. Send us your news.
Illustrations, Cartoons, Photographs, Quizzes, Puzzles, etc... from time to time we will
include these items also.

Include a SASE with ample postage when ever you write or submit manuscripts, entries etc. If none is
supplied we can not respond.

Subscribe to small press publications, you're
their only support in most cases.

Donations are always a welcomed from our readers. We appreciate your support in what ever way
is possible for you, through your subscriptions, donations, and contributing manuscripts.

WYOMING RURAL ELECTRIC ASSOCIATION

SUITE 101
WREA BUILDING
340 WEST "B" ST.
CASPER, WYOMING 82601
(307) 234-6152

WYOMING RURAL ELECTRIC NEWS

WRITERS' GUIDELINES

All submissions and queries should be sent to:

Gale A. Eisenhauer
Wyoming Rural Electric News

TOPICS

WREN is interested in topics related to Wyoming, its history, people, natural phenomena, wildlife and geography. Standing columns, for which freelance materials will be considered, include energy, finances and recipes, and poetry.

SPECIFICATIONS

All articles should be double spaced, typewritten on white paper. Clean photocopies are acceptable. Dot-matrix, daisy wheel or standard typewriter characters are acceptable.

Send clear, clean articles, do not hypehnate words. Do not force-justify computer generated copy. Where possible, break pages at paragraphs.

The AP Stylebook should be followed.

PAYMENT

WYOMING RURAL ELECTRIC NEWS pays upon publication. The rate varies, at the editor's discretion, from a minimum of $25 to a maximum of $75. Around 1,200 words is the prefered length for feature stories.

WYOMING RURAL ELECTRIC NEWS will consider previously-published materials, depending upon the prior audience and article content. Inquire regarding rates. Please be prepared to provide proof that you retain rights to previously-published materials.

BY-LINES

Authors will receive by-lines. Please make special note if material is copyrighted.

PHOTOGRAPHS

Accompanying photographs add to a story and are encouraged. The rate is $5 per black and white photo used with the article. WREN reserves the right to use other photographs and/or artwork it considers suitable.

MATERIAL REVIEW AND PUBLICATION DATES

Every effort will be made to review materials within six weeks. A SASE should be enclosed for prompt return of materials. Manuscripts and photographs will be treated with care; however, WREN assumes no responsibility for damaged or lost materials. WREN reserves the right to change publication dates as necessary.

YANKEE PUBLISHING INCORPORATED

GUIDE TO FICTION WRITER FOR *YANKEE* MAGAZINE

Because *Yankee* is a regional magazine, the fiction we publish is either located in New England specifically or in some way ties in with New England. There's no need to insert New England references just as long as the story could have happened here. We avoid stories that use New England dialect like "ayuh," except in very rare cases where the use of such dialect works.

Well-written fiction avoids stereotypes in any case; the emphasis should be on character development rather than plot; however, something has to happen, some change must take place, even though it may be as subtle as a change in perception.

That *Yankee* fiction be realistic is also important. We don't want stories that paint life the way we wish it were — with happily-ever-after solutions and all the ends tied up; rather stories that reflect life as it is — complexities and ambiguities inherent.

We have no formula for fiction and publish all kinds of stories — love stories, stories about death, murder — though not stories with explicit sex or offensive language.

We prefer stories to be about 4,000 words maximum (absolutely no novels or novellas), typewritten and double-spaced, with a stamped return envelope (large enough to hold the ms.) included. You should hear from us within 2 to 6 weeks. *Yankee* pays $1000 for fiction, and we award an additional $600 as an annual prize to the best of the 12 stories we publish each year.

Send fiction mss. to: Fiction Editor, *Yankee* Magazine, Dublin, NH 03444.

Main Street, Dublin, New Hampshire 03444 • (603) 563-8111

Publishers of: *Yankee* Magazine, est. 1935: *The Old Farmer's Almanac(k)*, est. 1792; *New England Business* Magazine, est. 1953; *Yankee Magazine's Travel Guide to New England*, est. 1971; *Yankee Homes*, est. 1985; *ALASKA®* **Magazine**, est. 1935.

Young American

P.O. BOX 12409 • PORTLAND, OREGON • 97212 • (503) 230-1895 • AMERICA'S NEWSMAGAZINE FOR KIDS

WRITERS GUIDELINES

<u>Young American</u> is a 16-24 page, tabloid-size newspaper for kids, ages 5-15. It is a supplement to suburban newspapers and is also distributed into schools. It is currently published twice monthly with a circulation of 140,000. Beginning in the fall of 1987, <u>Young American</u>'s circulation will be more than 1,000,000 in Oregon, Washington and California.

<u>Young American</u>'s focus is on children--and they are taken seriously. Articles are intended to inform, entertain, stimulate and enlighten. They give children a sense of being a part of today's important events and a recognition which is often denied them because of age.

Articles are written in a clear and concise style. The material is timely and pertinent.

Kids tell us they want to read about other kids around the country. <u>Young American</u> publishes the good news about today's active and sophisticated kids. Your stories about newsworthy kids will be considered for publication before any other articles. High quality photographs enhance your article.

Articles of 50-300 words in the following areas are also welcome:

Current events: featuring kids or news that relates to their lives.

Sports: kids involved in sports, fitness tips and new trends in sports.

Science: recent discoveries, nature, astronomy, health, nutrition, etc.

Computers: computer news, new uses for computers, games, etc.

Entertainment: book, film, theatre, television and record reviews. Interviews with famous television, movie or rock stars.

Other areas of interest:

Fiction: 750-1000 words. Humor, suspense and fantasy. Published with original art by our staff.

Comic Strips: Humor geared to children of all ages. Submit 10 strips for consideration as a regular feature.

Poetry: Rhyme or verse, serious or nonsensical.

Children's submissions: <u>Young American</u> is very interested in publishing children's work. Please state age with each submission.

Sample copy: THE BEST WAY TO REALIZE WHAT <u>YOUNG AMERICAN</u> PUBLISHES--available for $1.50.

Submitted material must be neatly typed, double-spaced, scrupulously fact-checked, identified with name and address and accompanied with SASE.

No simultaneous submissions or queries.

Payment: <u>Young American</u> buys first North American rights. Payment is $ .07 per word on publication.

Photographs greatly enhance articles. If published with story, payment is $5.00.

Please address submissions to: Editor
                                   <u>Young American</u>
                                   P.O. Box 12409
                                   Portland, Oregon 97212

You may expect a response within two months. Thank you for your interest and good luck.

YOUNG JUDAEAN MAGAZINE

50 West 58 St., New York, N.Y. 10019 (212)-355-7900 Ext. 452
Mordecai Newman, Editor

WRITERS GUIDELINES

YOUNG JUDAEAN
50 West 58th Street
New York, NY 10019
Tel: 355-7900 Ext. 452
Editor: Mordecai Newman
Frequency: 7 issues a year between September and June
Circulation: 4,000

Publication of the Young Judaean Zionist youth movement. Geared to 9-12 year-olds, especially movement members. Contains material of Jewish interest only, emphasizing Israel, Jewish life and culture, holidays, religious tradition, Young Judaea news and events, etc. We buy nonfiction, fiction, photos, and fillers.

Nonfiction: Informational (300-1000 words); how-to (300-500 words); personal experiences, interviews and personality profiles, historical pieces, opinion, travel (500-1500 words); also, reviews of books, movies, and Israeli records (300-800 words). We pay $20 - $40 per article, plus contributors copies. Articles must be lively, preferrably anecdotal, and appeal to a child's interests and point of view.

Fiction: Stories of Jewish interest for children accepted in all genres (500-1500 words). We pay $20 - $40 per story, plus contributors copies.

Photos: Photos purchased with accompanying manuscripts. Captions requested. 5" x 7" maximum. Payment included in fee for article.

Poetry and fillers: All forms of poetry accepted. Poems must pertain to the Jewish and Zionist emphasis of the magazine. Puzzles, riddles, jokes, short humor -- all with a Jewish slant -- welcomed for fillers. We pay $5 - $10 per poem, $5 a piece for fillers, plus contributors copies.

Interested writers may obtain a sample copy for $.75.

MN:sg

WRITER'S GUIDELINES FOR FICTION

Thank you for your interest in YM.

We publish stories about teens -- their attitudes, problems, relationships, and concerns.

Our most successful stories combine a good and logical plot with narrative and dialogue. We like all kinds of stories -- humor, romance, family drama, and mysteries. There are very few issues we are not willing to consider, but please refrain from graphic sex, violence or excessively bad language.

Most of our fiction runs about 3,500 words. Please do not send us anything longer than that. We accept fiction by teens, and we do not accept poetry by writers over nineteen years old.

Submissions must be accompanied by a stamped, self-addressed envelope. We request that you do not send queries. <u>We read all manuscripts, but unfortunately we cannot reply personally to each writer or offer criticism</u>. Stories are considered on speculation, and we pay upon acceptance of a manuscript.

If you would like to familiarize yourself with YM fiction before submitting your manuscript, check your library for back issues, or send $2.00 plus a stamped, self-addressed envelope and we'll send you a current issue.

                    Best wishes,

                    T H E   E D I T O R S

685 THIRD AVENUE, NEW YORK, NY 10017
(212) 878-8700

Magazines That Accept Freelance Contributions But Have No Writer's Guidelines

ALTERNATIVE fiction & poetry
7783 Kensington Lane
Hanover Park, Illinois 60103

Philip Athans, Editor/Publishers: "I don't use formal guidelines anymore as I found them to be continuously misunderstood in one way or another and limiting in many ways.

"I'm always looking for material, however, and would like to be included in *Fiction Writers Guidelines*. *All* of the material I use is from "unsolicited" submissions by freelance writers. In fact, it's one of my strictest editorial policies never to accept any material submitted by agents or other representatives; I prefer to deal with the artists themselves.

"What I'm looking for is serious short fiction of any length (though very long pieces are rarely picked up). Subject matter must focus on some issue, be it political, social, emotional, etc.—as long as I can tell how it *feels*. Very experimental or "avant-garde" material is most welcome, though I do try to let each individual define his or her own "alternative." I'm not interested in the new Hemingway, or the new anybody for that matter, and academic forms are pretty much frowned upon. I do not accept science fiction, horror, sword and sorcery or religious material ever.

"Please do not send original mss.—add a SASE of some description and be a little patient. My response time has slipped to about 4 or 5 weeks, though I am trying to pick up that pace. I always respond personally to every submission—you will *never* see a form-rejection from me. Payment is in (2) copies, on publication.

"It's always a good idea to see a sample copy first. They're available for $3.00 (1 year, 4-issue subs: $10. Overseas air mail: $4/$14). Check or money order payable to *ALTERNATIVE fiction & poetry*. All correspondence can be addressed to me directly. . . . *Af&p* is issued quarterly—the fifteenth of January, April, July and October.

"Oh yeah—PLEASE send *one* short story at a time! I do not print anything that has appeared in print anywhere before—ever."

The Atlantic
8 Arlington Street
Boston, Massachusetts 02116

C. Michael Curtis, Senior Editor: "*The Atlantic* has no fiction guidelines, per se, but prefers manuscripts in the 2,000 to 6,000 words range. We like a sense of "event," narrative movement, plausible characters and dialogue—but we're open to any work we think artful and imaginative."

The B'nai B'rith International Jewish Monthly
1640 Rhode Island Avenue, NW
Washington, D.C. 20036

Marc Silver, Editor: "We accept fiction on occasion but have no formal guidelines. We are *not* interested in fictionalized holocaust accounts or immigrant memoirs. We are interested in thoughtful, original fiction that considers some aspect of the Jewish experience."

Croton Review
P.O. Box 277
Croton on Hudson, New York 10520

Ruth Lisa Schecter, Executive Editor: "Queries welcome with SASE for 1988 Issue #11: SPECIAL AWARDS/ANTHOLOGY ISSUE & 'A TRIBUTE TO ANNE SEXTON' American Pulitzer Prize winner. *Before submitting your work*, send for Guidelines to: Linda Ashear, Two Harrimans Keep, Irvington, New York 10533. Cash Awards in short fiction and essay from August to December 15, 1987 deadline. Page limit: 10 pages, double spaces.

"TENTH ANNIVERSARY ISSUE available June 1987 with $4.75 postage and handling to *Croton Review*, P.O. Box 277, Croton-on-Hudson, New York 10520."

Gargoyle
Box 3567
Washington, D.C. 20007

Richard Peabody, Editor: "I don't believe in writer's guidelines. I think they're for amateurs. If a writer has a specific question I'm always open to answering whatever they ask. I read 8,000 stories in a six-month period in order to take 26 for F/86. Easily 4,000 of those stories would never have been sent my way if the writers had bothered to pick up a copy of *Gargoyle*. That's the real problem . . . know the marketplace and you won't need guidelines."

Harper's
666 Broadway
New York, New York 10012

The Editors: Harper's accepts fiction submissions from agents only and does not accept any original poetry.

Jewish Currents
22 East 17th Street
New York, New York 10002

Morris U. Schappes, Editor: "We have no formal guidelines, but we do accept freelance submissions (although we cannot afford to pay our contributors outside of a year's free subscription to the magazine and six copies of the issue in which they appear). Submissions should be typed, double-spaced, accompanied by a SASE, and should not exceed 5,000 words. Material should also have Jewish content. Our point of view is secular rather than religious, dedicated to the cultural, ethical and historical aspects of the Jewish tradition rather than the theological, and our stance is politically progressive. Submissions should ideally align with this perspective."

The Mickle Street Review
328 Mickle Street
Camden, New Jersey 08103
    Geoffrey Sill, Editor: *"The Mickle Street Review* is a journal devoted to work about Walt Whitman—primarily poetry in the Whitman tradition and nonfiction essays. We will look at *some* fiction that has a Whitman theme, but we publish very little."

New Blood Magazine
540 W. Foothill Blvd. Suite #3730
Glendora, California 91740
    Chris Lacher, Editor: "I do not have a formal guideline sheet that I pass out to contributors. Only three issues of *NB* have been published in our first year, yet we are about as successful as *The Horror Show;* circulation for *NB* is near 5,000 and a national distribution is pending. I believe the reason we are so successful after such a short time is due to the fact that I answer all queries, requests for guidelines, orders and submissions with a personal response... I don't have a formal guidelines sheet because queries and requests for guidelines are answered with a personal letter."

The Old Red Kimono
Box 1864
Rome, Georgia 30163
    Jo Anne Starnes, Editor: "Published once a year—in May. We consider fiction (1500 words or less) and poetry. Submissions should be accompanied by SASE. Payment: 2 copies. Sample copy: $2 each."

The Society of Promethean Writers Newsletter
Route 2, Box 290
Eclectic, Alabama 36024
    Brenda Williamson, Editor: "Bi-monthly publication for members. Membership: $8.00 year. Will accept manuscripts from non-members but members have priority. Besides work from writers, also included is contest and market information. Payments are in copies. Sample $1.00. No SASE needed. Need: Articles about writing, under 600 words. Short-Short Stories under 1000. Poetry under 50 lines, any style or subject."

The Spirit That Moves Us
P.O. Box 1585-GL
Iowa City, Iowa 52244
    Morty Sklar, Editor/Publisher: "Please query first, with a SASE, for current needs and time-frames.
    "We publish work based on the work itself, not on reputation of the writer, so that in the same issue we'll have a previously unpublished writer as well as a nationally or internationally well-known one. We prefer work which is expressive of feelings, as well as skillfully put together.
    "An excellent sampling of our tastes is *The Spirit That Moves Us Reader,* which contains reprints from the first seven years, as well as reproductions of the covers. It is offered at a special price of $5.00 postage-paid, as a sample.
    "Some (few) issues are single-author ones, and one of those, *The Casting of Bells,* by Jaroslav Seifert, was published in 1983, a year before the author won the Nobel Prize for literature."

StoryQuarterly
P.O. Box 1416
Northbrook, Illinois 60065
    Ann Brashler, Editor: *"StoryQuarterly* (one word) is published twice yearly. Single Issue—$4.00. Please note updated zip code. Current managing editors: Anne Brashler and Diane Williams."

The Texas Review
Division of English, Foreign Languages, and Journalism
Sam Houston State University
Huntsville, Texas 77341
    Paul Ruffin, Editor: "We seek the very best fiction available. We prefer stories running no more than 10,000 words. Due to the heavy flow of manuscripts we stay backlogged, and, frankly, we rarely publish new talent. In assessing manuscripts, I look for strong beginnings and conclusions, sharp imagery, thorough characterization, etc.—all the 'things' one should expect in a good piece of fiction."

The Virginia Quarterly Review
A National Journal of Literature & Discussion
One West Range
Charlottesville, Virginia 22903
    Staige D. Blackford, Editor: *"The Virginia Quarterly Review* has no specific fiction writers guidelines.... We merely require that our stories be of reasonable length and that the grammar and spelling be acceptable."

Index